ATTACK & SINK

The Battle of the Atlantic
Summer 1941

Bernard Edwards

Also by Bernard Edwards,

Masters Next to God
They Sank the Red Dragon
The Fighting Tramps
The Grey Widow Maker
Salvo!
SOS, Men Against the Sea
Return of the Coffin Ships
Blood & Bushido
Dönitz and the Wolf Packs
Beware Raiders!

ATTACK & SINK

The Battle of the Atlantic
Summer 1941

Bernard Edwards

Brick Tower Press
New York

Brick Tower Press, 1998

© Bernard Edwards, 1998

Edwards, Bernard
Attack & Sink–The Battle of the Atlantic, Summer 1941
Includes Bibliography and Index

ISBN 1-899694-40-4 Trade Paper, 2nd Ed., January 2002
ISBN 1-883283-34-5 Hardcover, First Edition, January 2002

Library of Congress
          Control Number: 98-73939, Trade Paper
          Control Number: 2001132549, Hardcover

Contents

ATTACK & SINK

PREFACE

"This convoy must not get through—
U-boats pursue, attack and sink."
−Admiral Dönitz to all commanders *Markgraf*
group, 9 September 1941

On 30 August 1941, convoy SC42, consisting of 67 ships carrying half a million tons of cargo, sailed from Canadian waters, for the United Kingdom. The merchant ships, moving in 12 columns abreast and covering an area of 25 square miles of sea, were predominantly British; many were old and dilapidated, all were slow and heavy-laden. SC42's ocean escort was made up of a destroyer and three corvettes of the Royal Canadian Navy, all untried in combat.

For the first week at sea, the convoy encountered dense fog, icebergs and fierce easterly gales, so that for much of the time its speed was down to about 3 knots, no more than a moderate walking pace. The difficulties encountered in keeping this great mass of unwieldy ships together were enormous.

SC42 was routed north to within sight of Cape Farewell, the southernmost point of Greenland, before turning east across the Atlantic, the reasoning behind this being that German U-boats were unlikely to venture so far north. However, Admiral Dönitz had received word of the convoy's sailing, and ordered the 21 boats of the *Markgraf* wolf-pack to "pursue, attack and sink!"

The attack commenced on the morning of 9 September, in sight of the coast of Greenland, and a running battle ensued that lasted for seven days, and covered 1,200 miles of ocean. The Canadian escorts were hopelessly outnumbered and outclassed, but fought valiantly, as did the merchantmen. It was fortunate that the majority of the U-boats were also in action for the first time; as it was, 18 merchant ships were sunk, for the loss of two U-boats. Only the arrival of Royal Navy destroyers from Iceland and the onset of dense fog saved SC42 from almost certain annihilation.

INTRODUCTION

On the last day of September 1938, Britain's prime minister, Neville Chamberlain, returned from his meeting with the German chancellor, Adolf Hitler, confident that he had secured lasting peace in Europe. History has never clearly decided whether Chamberlain was incredibly naive, or a shrewd diplomat scheming to buy time for his country to rearm for a conflict lie knew to be inevitable. One thing seems certain, however–that when he acted out the ridiculous "peace in our time" charade in Hitler's Munich flat Chamberlain was not remotely aware of happenings at sea. Even as the two men faced each other across the table, Admiral Karl Dönitz, the Führer's commander-in-chief U-boats, was at work throwing a secret cordon around the British Isles.

It was all done behind a curtain of legality, it having been widely announced a day or two earlier that the German Navy would be carrying out exercises in the North Sea and Baltic. There was nothing unusual in this–the Royal Navy did the same thing from time to time. Consequently, no eyebrows were raised when, under the cover of darkness on the night of 29 September, a force of 25 U-boats entered the North Sea from Kiel and Wilhelmshaven. By the time Chamberlain left Munich clutching his worthless piece of paper, all the approaches to Britain, her vital trade routes, were covered by U-boats, armed and at full battle stations. Dönitz withdrew his wolves 72 hours later with the British public unaware that the pistol had been at its head and ready to fire.

During the First World War, German U-boats sank 2,099 British merchant ships, totalling over 6.5 million tons gross, with the loss of 12,723 lives. For an island nation dependent on its imports for survival and on its sea trade for economic prosperity, this was a catastrophic blood-letting that all but brought her to her knees. And yet, although lessons were learned, they were quickly forgotten. When Britain, 12 months after Munich, with no other cheek to turn, went to war with Germany, she was neither awake to the threat posed by the U-boats nor prepared to meet that threat.

Once again, the wily Dönitz pre-empted the politicians. He

then had at his disposal a total of 56 U-boats, 40 of which were operational, and on 19 August 1939, two weeks before the outbreak of war, he sent these to sea. When hostilities began, 29 U-boats were at their battle stations around the British Isles. Ten hours later, U-30, commanded by Oberleutnant-zur-See Fritz-Julius Lemp, sank without warning the 13,581-ton Donaldson liner *Athenia* 250 miles north-west of Ireland. The *Athenia* was on her way to the United States carrying women and children, many of whom died when the ship went down. Outrage was expressed, and Lemp was duly reprimanded by Dönitz, but this amounted to no more than a private wrist-slapping. The Oberleutnant's action was, after all, only the revival of a particularly dirty form of warfare held in abeyance since the armistice of 1918. The British Admiralty should have known this would happen, yet it sent the *Athenia* to sea unarmed and unescorted. The war in the North Atlantic was quickly off the mark, and seemed about to follow a familiar pattern.

In direct contrast, the war on land was slow to get under way, the weather being to some extent responsible. The winter of 1939 in Western Europe was one of the worst on record, with torrential rains, followed by snow and ice, making life a misery for the great armies facing each other across the barbed wire. It was as if nature was reluctant to tolerate a repeat of the senseless slaughter of an earlier generation.

For more than six months after the fall of Poland there was almost total inactivity; then on 10 May 1940 the German Panzers rolled forward into the Low Countries. Holland surrendered four days later, Belgium lasted another fortnight, and the disaster no one had yet dared contemplate followed. The French Army, with 86 divisions in the field, lost heart and crumbled before the German advance. On 25 June, France sued for peace, and it was all over on the Western Front.

Britain had, by the miracle of Dunkirk, managed to extricate some 300,000 of her expeditionary force, minus arms and equipment, and she now stood alone. She had a population of 45 million to feed, an army to re-equip and a huge war machine to mobilise; much of this was dependent on supplies brought in by ship from overseas. She was fortunate in that she had the world's largest merchant fleet, over 4,000 ocean-going ships, but her needs were great. A minimum of 3.5 million tons of food and raw materials were needed every month to ensure survival, much of which must cross the broad reaches of the North Atlantic, where the weather was foul and the U-boats roamed free.

Although the British and Commonwealth navies were formidable, comprising 12 battleships, 7 aircraft carriers, 41 cruisers, 116 destroyers and 57 submarines, they were charged with defending an empire covering one third of the world's surface, populated by 450 million people. Germany, on the other hand, although possessing a much smaller surface fleet, had no overseas territories to defend. Her Navy, Konter-Admiral Dönitz's U-boats in particular, was free to concentrate on cutting Britain's vital supply lines. The effect was immediate and calamitous.

In the first eight months of the war, up to the end of April 1940, no fewer than 172 British, Allied and Neutral merchant ships of 743,000 tons were lost through enemy action. This was bad enough, but after the collapse of France, which gave the U-boats untroubled access to the North Atlantic, the losses rocketed to an average of 90 ships of 400,000 tons a month. By the end of June 1941, British, Allied and Neutral merchant shipping losses stood at 1,984 ships, totalling 7,592,826 tons. More than 100 ships a month were going down, most of these sunk by U-boats in the North Atlantic. This was five times the rate at which the shipyards were able to turn out replacements, and unless something was done to stop this dreadful haemorrhage Britain could not hope to survive another year unless the convoys continued to get through. This book charts the progress of one such convoy, SC42, which sailed from Nova Scotia to cross the Atlantic in the autumn of 1941.

ACKNOWLEDGEMENTS

The author wishes to acknowledge the assistance of the following in writing this book: Horst Bredow, of the U-boat Archives, Cuxhaven/Altenbruch, who kindly gave unlimited access to his comprehensive files; Ian A. Millar, of the Trident Archives, Kernersville, North Carolina, for his patience and co-operation in answering many enquiries; the Public Record Office, Kew, the National Archives, Washington D.C., and the Registry of Shipping and Seamen, Cardiff.

Those who were with SC42 and related their experiences are: John Buckingham, HMCS *Skeena;* Herbert J. Dow, HMCS *Kenogami;* John A. Mitchell, HMCS *Skeena;* W. H. Wilson, HMCS *Skeena;* James Corcoran, SS *Berury;* John Dewar, SS *Baron Pentland;* Brian Greenaway, SS *Everleigh;* Dan Hortop, MV *Jedmoor;* Bernard Liley, SS *Thistleglen;* Robert C. Smith, SS *Yearby;* Douglas White, SS *Trefusis;* Sverre E. Karlsen, SS *Vestland.*

Others who offered their help and advice are: Donald B. Ferguson, John H. Harland, W. A. Macquarrie and Joe Marston in Canada; J. Kinross Kennedy in the United States; and Ralph Erskine, John Guthrie, Fred Hortop, Len Matthews, Andrew Milne, A. Moffett and Frank J. Purcell in the UK.

1

U-501 Enters the Arena

February is a dismal month on Germany's North Sea coast. Even with the sun at its zenith the sky remains a dark, glowering canopy, drawn tightly from horizon to horizon, merging with the banks of cheerless drizzle drifting endlessly in from a grey, soulless sea. Yet, each February without fail, the port of Wilhelmshaven, huddled miserably on the western side of Jade Bay, phlegmatically endures these last tantrums of a dying winter, sure in the knowledge that the arrival of spring will soon be a reality.

In February 1945, however, it seemed that spring would never again return to Germany. The glorious Third Reich, born of a Wagnerian delusion, and predicted to last 1,000 years, tottered on the brink of catastrophe.

In the east, Soviet T-34s, backed by a People's Army 7 million strong, raced across the plains of Poland, hell-bent on a terrible revenge. The Oder had been crossed, and Berlin lay only 36 miles behind the advancing front, helplessly awaiting a fate too awful to contemplate. To the west, 85 divisions of American and British troops rolled confidently towards the Rhine, pushing before them the remnants of a German army summarily and bloodily ousted from its once-impregnable Western Wall fronting the Channel. Within the shrinking perimeter that was Germany all hope had gone, for every single day 20,000 tons of Allied bombs rained down on a cowering civilian population with nowhere left to hide. All the while, 50 feet below the ruins of the New Reich Chancellery in the doomed capital, Adolf Hitler, the architect of this dreadful cataclysm, sat brooding beneath the portrait of his revered hero Frederick the Great. The day of reckoning for a nation that foolishly dreamt of world conquest drew ever nearer.

Over Wilhelmshaven, the cold February drizzle mingled with a column of smoke rising from the shattered remains of a port that had so often in the past resounded to the thump of military bands and the jingle of Iron Crosses as the men of Admiral Karl Dönitz's U-boat Arm sailed in to taste the sweet fruits of victory. Now bereft of all its former glory and deserted by a beaten Kreigsmarine, Wilhelmshaven, like Hitler, also brooded, awaiting what cruel penance the victorious enemy might exact. It was here, on the 27th of the month, that 39-year-old Hugo Förster, unable to endure yet another gross humiliation, put a gun to his head and shot himself. So died ignominiously the last victim of the battle of convoy SC42.

When, in early August 1941, U-501, commanded by Korvettenkapitän Hugo Förster, sailed on her first patrol, Germany was riding on the crest of a breathtaking wave of triumphal conquest. Much of Europe, from Norway's North Cape to the Mediterranean island of Crete, and from Biscay to the Carpathians, was in Axis hands. In a lightning campaign opening on 22 June, German Panzers had struck deep into the heart of the Soviet Union, and it seemed that Moscow must also fall before the onset of winter. Only Britain, beleaguered and staggering under the hammer blows of the Luftwaffe's blitzkrieg, refused to yield.

At sea, in the long-running action Winston Churchill christened the "Battle of the Atlantic," the U-boats reigned supreme. Much of their success was due to the fall of France, which handed over to Dönitz the Biscay ports of Brest, Lorient, La Pallice and St-Nazaire, deep-watered and easy to defend, from which his submarines sallied forth into the shipping lanes of the Atlantic unmolested. In response, the Admiralty laid a huge minefield across the Western Approaches, sealing off the Channel and the Irish Sea from the Atlantic. From then on, all shipping to and from British ports was routed via the Northern Approaches, ships for London and the East Coast ports being condemned to the long haul around Cape Wrath.

The effect of this was to shift the front line of the Battle of the Atlantic further north, but it did nothing to reduce the sinkings. In fact, the total of ships lost by enemy action went on climbing at an alarming rate. Britain, wholly dependent on her merchant fleet for raw materials, food and oil, was in imminent danger of being blockaded into surrender. Convoys were routed far to the north of the normal transatlantic lanes in order to take advantage of air cover from newly appropriated bases in Iceland, and President Roosevelt, alarmed by the worsening crisis, agreed to provide surface escorts for Allied ships within 500 miles of the American coast. Nevertheless, with the United States still officially neutral, her Navy was reluctant to take all-out offensive action against the U-boats. Then there was the unbridgeable air gap, appropriately named the "Black Pit" by those obliged to cross it. This 600-mile-wide ocean corridor off southern Greenland was beyond the reach of British and Canadian long-range aircraft, and it was here in the summer of 1941 that the U-boats were reaping the bulk of their bloody harvest.

U-501 was well suited to enter this arena. Built on the River Elbe at the renowned Deutsche Shipyard at Finkenwerder, she was a Type IXC, a marked improvement on the Type VIIC in which the much-lamented aces Kretschmer, Prien and Schepke had wreaked such terrible havoc, before they were brought to book by the Royal Navy. At 1,120 tons' displacement, and with an overall length of 252 feet, the IXC was heavier and longer than the VIIC by 350 tons and 52 feet respectively, although, owing to her size, she took a crucial 10 seconds longer to dive. However, with her two 6-cylinder diesels producing 4,400 horsepower, and her electric motors rated at 1,000 horsepower, she was capable of a top speed on the surface of 18.3 knots and a submerged speed of 7.3 knots. In contrast, the British "Flower" Class corvette, which did much of the convoy escort work in the North Atlantic, could barely muster 16 knots, and that only when hard-pressed. The IXC's armament consisted of four bow and two stern torpedo tubes, one 105-mm deck gun and four 20-mm anti-aircraft cannon. Perhaps her greatest asset, however, was her cruising range of 14,000 miles. This would enable her to carry the war to the Caribbean, and even to the Indian Ocean, and it was for this extended role that the Type IXC was primarily built.

After commissioning, on 30 April 1941, U-501 moved to the Baltic, and later to southern Norway for extensive trials and training exercises. Over the months that followed, the submarine's deficiencies were righted and her idiosyncrasies learned. At the same time, Hugo Förster turned his new and mostly untried crew into an efficient fighting unit.

U-501 carried a total crew of 45, including four watch-keeping officers, two midshipmen, and an engineer officer. Förster, a quiet, mild-mannered Berliner, did not see eye to eye with his senior watchofficer, Oberleutnant-zur-See Werner Albring, a somewhat dogmatic Rhinelander with political leanings. However, Förster's strong personality prevailed, and when she finally completed working-up U-501 was not only an efficient boat but also a happy one. This was just as well for the men who were to live in such cramped conditions for months on end, facing fearful dangers from the sea and their formidable enemies. Their future, to say the very least, was uncertain. Eight out of ten of them would die violently, and many of those who survived could expect to fall prey to the common U-boat afflictions of rheumatism, gout, kidney disease and rotten teeth.

It was a condition laid down by Admiral Dönitz that each Type IXC must carry out one North Atlantic patrol before venturing into more distant waters. This was by way of a proving voyage for both men and ship; Dönitz reasoned that, if they survived this, the most hazardous battlefield, they would be well fitted to move further afield. So, when U-501 sailed from Trondheim on 7 August, she headed out into the Atlantic to join a group of U-boats forming up to the south of Iceland. As was usual at the start of a patrol, every cubic centimetre of the submarine's hull not occupied by machinery, spares and ammunition was packed with food for the voyage. It would be some days before the healthy appetites of the men had cleared enough space for them to move around freely in the boat.

Admiral Karl Dönitz
(Photo: Süddeutscher Verlag, Munich)

Once clear of the Norwegian coast, Förster remained on the surface, pushing north-westwards at a comfortable and economical 10 knots. It was unlikely that enemy ships or aircraft would be met in this area, but there was no relaxing of vigilance. The conning tower watch, which was changed every two hours and consisted of an officer, a petty officer and two ratings, all armed with powerful Zeiss binoculars, left no quarter of the sea and sky unguarded. The weather was fine, with light south-south-easterly winds and a smooth sea–something of a mixed blessing. In the crisp, cold air, watchkeeping on deck was a pleasure, but on the flat, empty ocean U-501 stood out like a half-tide rock in a lagoon. Förster took more than a little comfort from the fact that the barometer was falling steadily.

Forty-eight hours later, on the morning of the 9th, U-501 was in latitude 65° north and 200 miles to the east of Iceland. It was Förster's intention soon to steer south-westwards to pass midway between Iceland and the Faeroes, traversing the area covered by the Royal Navy's Northern Patrol at night and at full speed. The deadly chill of the Arctic Circle was in the air, but the wind remained light and the sea relatively calm, even though the glass continued to fall. Förster took the opportunity to bring his men up on deck in relays for fresh air and exercise. For each man this amounted to only a very brief stroll on the casings, a cigarette and a few deep breaths of the ozone-laden air, before returning to the stench of diesel and unwashed bodies below decks, but a little was better than nothing. With bad weather and the enemy in the offing, this might be their last chance to savour the outside world for weeks to come. There were no grumbles, for every man was a volunteer. There were compensations to look forward to, of course. When—and it was always *when*, not if—they returned to base, there would be hot baths, fresh strawberries and rosy-cheeked nurses in plenty. First, however, there was serious work to be done.

Later that day, the first indication of impending action was received from Lorient, where Admiral Dönitz, as BdU (Befehlshaber der Untersee-boote or C-in-C Submarines), had set up his head-quarters. An urgent signal ordered Förster to join the *Markgraf* group, assembling off south-west Iceland to intercept a westbound Allied convoy. When at strength, *Markgraf* was to consist of no fewer than 21 U-boats. The rendezvous given was 650 miles to the southwest of U-501's position and it was unlikely that she would arrive in time to participate in the proposed interception. However, the unusual size of the wolf-pack indicated that Dönitz was casting an impenetrable net across the British northern convoy route. There would be time enough, and chance enough, for U-501 to prove her worth.

That night, in the three hours or so of comparative darkness available in these high latitudes in summer, U-501, her throbbing diesels driving her at 18 knots, slipped across the track of the Northern Patrol. So stretched was this thin line of British armed merchant cruisers and trawlers keeping a lonely vigil in these grey waters that there was little risk of a submarine being detected. With the coming of full daylight, Förster reduced once again to an economical speed, considering it pointless to waste precious fuel in rushing to join the *Markgraf* group.

The decision was well made, for as the new day wore on so the weather deteriorated. By early evening, when course was altered to pass south of Iceland, the wind was blowing strongly from the north-northeast and angry white horses galloped in to break over the casings and give the boat an uncomfortable roll. Now there was no more thought of exercise on deck, and those unfortunate to be keeping watch in the conning tower were grateful for the protection of their heavy oilskins.

For the next three and a half days U-501 motored westwards on the surface, maintaining an average speed of 7 knots.

There was no improvement in the weather, and from time to time the monotony of the passage was relieved by prowling Hudsons of RAF Coastal Command sweeping low over the water. These aircraft were based on Iceland and would be with them for some time to come.

Soon after the outbreak of war, it became obvious that whoever held Iceland would be in a position to exercise a great deal of control over the North Atlantic shipping routes. Germany had early plans to take control of the island, but she was too heavily occupied elsewhere, and British troops landed soon after Denmark surrendered in the spring of 1940. The Icelanders did not welcome the British occupation, at times actively opposing it, but this was not time for false diplomacy. The British Army stayed, and bases were established for the Royal Navy's escort ships and Coastal Command aircraft. These significantly extended the range of cover for the convoys and created major hazards for the U-boats.

In May 1941, the threat to the U-boats from Iceland was made worse when U-69 sank the US merchantman *Robin Moor* while on a voyage from New York to Cape Town. America was not yet in the war, but when the *Robin Moor* was stopped and searched by U-69 she was found to be carrying war supplies for Britain. Under International Law, her sinking was therefore justified, but the US Government did not agree. Branding the incident as an act of piracy, it froze all Germany's assets in the United States, closed down her consulates, and, much to the delight of the British, offered to take over the defence of Iceland. US troops landed on the island on 7 July. The Icelanders, now fearful of German reprisals, greeted the arrival of the Americans with even less enthusiasm than they had accorded the British. For the moment, however, their fears were groundless. Hitler was furious when he heard the news, but he was far too busy with the invasion of the Soviet Union to worry about an American takeover of a remote island on the edge of the Arctic Circle. Thereafter US convoys, escorted by the US Navy, ran regularly to the island with supplies for the garrison. Although the significance of this may not have been apparent to Hitler, Dönitz was troubled. Although the US warships were still neutral, their mere presence in the area added yet another danger to those already faced by the U-boats.

On this occasion, U-501 was neither attacked nor, it would seem, sighted from the air, but Förster was wise enough to take no risks. Each time an enemy aircraft appeared, he took the submarine under in a crash dive. In this way his men were kept on their toes, learning the essential lesson of self-preservation the hard way.

By the night of the 14th, Förster had reached a position midway across the southern entrance to the Denmark Strait and was ordered by BdU to heave-to and await developments. No other boats were in sight, but their radio transmissions could be heard. The *Mark*graf group was in place, with 5 miles between each submarine, and strung out in a long north-south line facing the coast of Greenland and directly across the route taken by Allied eastbound convoys. It only remained to wait, to watch, and to listen.

Excitement mounted when, in the early hours of the 18th, U-38, commanded by Korvettenkapitän Heinrich Schuch, and in position 60 miles south of U-501, reported sinking a 1,700-ton steamer. Unfortunately, the victim turned out to be the Panama-flag *Longtaker*, a lone neutral which was optimistically challenging the blockade. There appeared to be a sudden dearth of convoys.

BdU now issued orders for the Markgraf group to retreat to the east, presumably in search of a convoy that had already slipped through the net. This move proved equally futile, for the weather was on the change, with a falling wind bringing calm seas and restricted visibility. When, by the morning of the 21st, nothing had been sighted, Dönitz sought to ease his frustration by moving the Group closer to Iceland.

Early on the 23rd, having survived the attentions of several inquisitive Sunderlands, U-501 was on station 70 miles south of Reykjavik. A confident BdU predicted that both an eastbound and a westbound convoy would pass through the area in the following 48 hours. However, Förster saw no ships either that day or during the night, the only thing of note being a plunging barometer. By daybreak on 24 August, it was blowing Force 7 from the east, with a very rough sea making the boat difficult to handle, and life below decks almost unbearable.

It might have eased the agonies of the storm for Förster and his men had they but known that, just over the horizon, one of their number was in even worse trouble. U-452, caught on the surface by a Catalina of RAF 209 Squadron, had received serious damage and was running for her life. Her career came to an abrupt end a few hours later, when she was sunk by the anti-submarine trawler HMS *Vascama*. If there was to be a major battle in this area, it was evident that the U-boats would not have it all their own way.

2

A Merchantman at War

While U-501 marked time maintaining her station off Iceland, 1,500 miles to the southwest the Norwegian steamer *Einvik* fretted at her anchor cable in the port of St. John's, Newfoundland. Loaded with a full cargo of pit props for the coal mines of South Wales, the *Einvik* was bound for the Bristol Channel, and her master, Captain Wetteland, was anxious to be on his way before the approaching autumnal equinox added a vicious sting to the North Atlantic's turbulence.

Owned by Skibs A/S Einvik of Trondheim, the 2,000-ton *Einvik* was far from her home waters. Built in Toronto in 1918 and originally named *War Taurus*, she was one of a number of "D" type standard ships hurriedly turned out to replace Allied losses in the First World War. Taken under the Norwegian flag, she had eked out a living between the wars in the North Sea timber trade, and only now, after an absence of 23 years, was she back in the Atlantic.

When German troops overran Norway in June 1940, Norway had a merchant fleet of almost 4 million tons, consisting mainly of ships between 1,500 and 2,000 tons gross, engaged in the carriage of timber. Fortunately, when Norway fell, most of these ships escaped capture and, by courtesy of the Norwegian Government in exile, came under the control of the Ministry of War Transport. In effect, although they still flew the Norwegian flag and were Norwegian-manned, they became part of the British merchant fleet.

The *Einvik* was among the escapees, and a year later her crew of 23, once all Norwegian, now contained a sprinkling of British, French and Canadians, but, in true Scandinavian style, she remained proudly aloof, ever immaculate and resolutely efficient. However, her 175-horsepower, coal-fired steam engine had only ever been just barely adequate for her tonnage, and would never again drive her through the water at the 11.5 knots she had achieved on her acceptance trials. Given a fair wind, conscientious firemen and best Welsh steam, coal, a combination rarely achieved, she could manage no more than 5 knots. The *Einvik* was small and vulnerable, and whatever the weather Captain Wetteland had no illusions but that the long passage ahead would be difficult.

With her loading completed and her bunkers filled with Nova Scotian slack—a far cry from Welsh steam coal—the *Einvik* was under orders to sail that evening to rendezvous some 280 miles north of St. John's with convoy SC41, which had already sailed from Sydney, Cape Breton. Captain Wetteland was in all respects ready for sea, except that three of his firemen had not yet returned from shore leave. With every hour that passed with no sign of the missing men, Wetteland grew ever more anxious. His total crew was small enough, and to take the ship to sea with three firemen short was out of the question.

While Wetteland fumed, the three missing men, the cause of his anxiety, were oblivious to the crisis they were creating. Firemen in coal-burning ships were always, by necessity and tradition, tough, independent and hard-drinking; the men in question, Thomas Dwyer, a Canadian, Joseph Bebb, British, and Andrew Dwyer, a British West African, were no exception to the rule. Mindful of the long, hazardous voyage ahead of them, they had slipped ashore to seek out and sample the fleshpots of St. John's, such as they might be.

St. John's, Newfoundland, was not, as the pleasure-bent firemen soon discovered, New York or Rio de Janeiro. Even today, it is described by the guide books as ". . . a blend of England and Ireland as they were in the last century . . ." In the 1940s St. John's was a town fighting tooth and nail to avoid being dragged out of the Victorian era by the spreading ripples of the Battle of the Atlantic. Its sheltered harbour was still home to a large cod-fishing fleet, with its attendant stink of fish and flocks of squabbling seagulls, but it now also played host to ships of another breed altogether. The wharves that once held only salt-stained fishermen were lined two and three deep with grey-painted corvettes, sloops and destroyers of the British and Canadian Navies, under repair, storing or resting between convoys. In the bay a collection of merchant ships lay at anchor, awaiting their turn to be shepherded across the Atlantic.

Yet, in spite of the demands of an influx of war-toughened seamen with apparently unslakable thirsts, St. John's still held fast to the strict principles of its Scottish Presbyterian founders. It offered only one cinema, a handful of frontier-type stores and a "Flying Angel" club, where seafarers gathered under the watchful eye of the Church to drink watery beer. There were no pubs, and spirits were strictly rationed, available solely at the Government Liquor Store, and then only on the production of a liquor licence. The Prohibition Act may have been repealed in the United States more than eight years before, but its ghost still lingered on in St. John's. Although it was legal to buy a bottle of spirits at the Government store, it was against the law to consume it in public or take it back aboard ship. In consequence, St. John's was a port where visiting merchant seamen drank themselves into a stupor in back alleys, in dingy hotel rooms and, as a last resort, on the slopes of the hills overlooking the town.

The two Dwyers and Bebb had sampled the weak beer at the "Flying Angel," ignored the cinema and, after investing 25 cents in a liquor licence, joined the queue at the liquor store. In due course, they each came away clutching a bottle of high-proof spirits, to which they were in no way accustomed, and which they lost no time in pouring down their dry throats. An hour later, they were maudlin drunk and indulging in the seaman's time-honoured practice of bemoaning their lot.

Despite the alcoholic haze, the three firemen did not deny that they enjoyed far better conditions aboard the Norwegian-flag *Einvik* than they would have done in a British tramp. The pay was more, with a cost of living allowance for every day spent in North American ports—the latter being regarded as a ludicrous extravagance by British shipowners—the food was good and plentiful, and the accommodation generally of a higher standard. Yet, no matter which flag they sailed under, the lot of a fireman in an old coal-burner like the *Einvik* was a hard one. A four-hour watch in the stokehold of such a ship was akin to a brief sojourn in Hell itself: four hours spent in the service of a bank of insatiable furnaces that threatened to fry him alive every time their heavy iron doors clanged open. Stripped to the waist and covered in thick coal dust, the colour of a man's skin became an irrelevance; only sheer muscle and guts mattered. Come what may, the back-breaking rhythm must be maintained, lest the steam pressure fall, and with it the ship's speed. When eight bells rang to signal the end of the watch, the ladders leading up from the depths of the stokehold to the deck resembled the road to Everest. On deck lay another world, often cold, wet and inhospitable. A hard straw mattress in a dank forecastle that heaved and thumped with every wave was scant reward for four tons of coal shovelled in as many hours. Little wonder then, that when blessed sleep finally came these weary men dreamt only that one day every ship would be an oil-burner, every watch a joy to stand.

As if that was not enough, in 1941 there was also the enemy. The sheer pressure of work in the stokehold was not conducive to idle speculation, but at the back of a fireman's mind was always the frightening thought that between him and the speeding torpedo lay only 3/8 of an inch of steel plate. The engine space, being the largest single watertight compartment in the ship, was invariably the primary target of the man behind the U-boat's periscope. A torpedo striking in the engine room or stokehold caused maximum destruction of a vessel's buoyancy, and very few caught below survived the catastrophic flooding, the scalding steam and the exploding boilers.

The maudlin talk of the *Einvik's* shore-going firemen centred on the dubious privilege of crossing the North Atlantic in convoy, as their ship was soon destined to do. The theory was good—to sail in company with other ships under the guns of escorting warships must be safer than attempting to cross alone. However, in 1941 the reality of the convoys was in stark contrast to the concept. A convoy made progress only at the speed of the slowest ship, escorts were in short supply, and the enemy appeared to be everywhere. The fate of convoy SC26 only four months previously bore witness to this. SC26, consisting of 22 merchantmen escorted by the armed merchant cruiser HMS *Worcestershire*, was steaming at 7 knots when it was set upon in mid-Atlantic by a wolf-pack of eight U-boats. The *Worcestershire*, a 16-knot ex-passenger liner armed with ancient 5.9s, was completely impotent in the face of the fast and highly manoeuvrable Type VIIC U-boats, and was soon put out of action. In the unearthly glow of the Northern Lights, convoy SC26 was brutally savaged, with no fewer than 11 ships out of 22 going down.

When the three men, their bottles empty and having no money to buy more, finally returned to the *Einvik*, they were determined they would not be sacrificed in this mad ocean conflict. It was on their fuddled minds to demand that the ship be held in port, but they were not given the opportunity to put their case. When they reached the foot of the gangway, an irate Captain Wetteland ordered them to be bundled aboard without ceremony. Within the hour, the *Einvik* weighed anchor and left St. John's in company with six other merchantmen—three British, one Greek, one Polish and one Dutch.

The wage-earners of St. John's were making their way home at the end of the day when the seven grey-painted tramps steamed in line astern through the narrow bottleneck at the head of the harbour between Chain Rock and Pancake Island. A century before, a heavy iron chain had stretched between the two to keep out pirates and enemy fleets, but on this dark August night in 1941 the way was clear. Inside the harbour it was relatively calm, but when they cleared the narrow channel which leads out to the open sea past precipitous cliffs the ships met the full fury of the North Atlantic. The low-pressure area which so troubled U-501, patrolling to the south of Iceland, was of massive proportions, its effects reaching as far as Newfoundland's eastern shore in the form of a gale-force northerly wind.

Venturing out into the open Atlantic, the heavily laden merchantmen immediately rolled their scuppers under to the accompaniment of groaning plates, protesting rigging and the crash of unsecured crockery; this was their first taste of things to come. Ahead lay 1,500 miles of open ocean, the nearest land over the far horizons being Ireland's rocky west coast.

The North Atlantic, said to have been first crossed by the Norse explorer Erik the Red at the end of the tenth century, is a perpetually angry ocean, where the transition from winter to summer is evidenced only by a barely perceptible lessening of the rampant waves. It is an ocean violently hostile to ships and men; yet, when it had been established that to sail westwards would not entail falling off the edge of the earth, it became the world's busiest ocean, and remains so even now. In 1941, bounded on one side by the Old World at war, and on the other by the New World with an abundance of food and weapons to sell, the North Atlantic was the ocean which would decide the fate of nations.

Awaiting the merchant ships outside the port was their escort to the Western Rendezvous Point north of St. John's, where they would join convoy SC41. The escorts were exclusively Canadian, the fourstacker, ex-US destroyer HMCS *St. Croix* and the corvettes *Pictou*, *Buctouche* and *Gait*, all en route to take over the protection of the main convoy.

For the next two and a half days the *Einvik* and her unfortunate companions battled northwards against heavy seas whipped up by a wind blowing unhindered down the Davis Strait, and carrying with it the icy lash of Greenland's glaciers. For much of the time the ships were out of sight of each other, hidden by spray and rain, each engaged in its own lonely battle for survival. Progress was painfully slow, and there seemed little chance of joining up with the convoy before it sailed past into the Atlantic. Then, on the morning of the 28th, the weather eased, the clouds lifted, and there on the horizon ahead were the tall masts and smoking funnels of SC41.

The convoy was an impressive sight: 61 merchant ships, steaming in 11 columns, and escorted by the British armed merchant cruiser HMS *Ranpura* and the Canadian corvettes *Matapedia*, *Arvida* and *Chicoutimi*. The St. John's ships, on the instructions of the convoy commodore, who flew his flag in the British steamer *Wanstead*, attached themselves to the starboard side of the convoy, the *Einvik* ending up at the rear of column 13. This was not an ideal position to occupy, for she would always be vulnerable to U-boats stalking the convoy. There were those on board the Norwegian who crossed themselves, whereas the more secular fingered their rabbits' feet. This was not an auspicious start to the voyage.

In the not-so-distant past, when peace reigned, Captain Wetteland would have followed the shortest route across the Atlantic—an arc of the great circle to within sight of Fastnet Rock, and thence due east into the Bristol Channel. The distance by this route to Barry Roads was some 1,900 miles, a long enough haul for a ship of the *Einvik's* size at the best of times. However, being under Admiralty direction, Wetteland now had no jurisdiction over his route. The U-boats were known to be out in force and SC41 was to follow a much more indirect track, reaching up as far as latitude 61° north, before curving down towards the Outer Hebrides and into the North Channel. This would add at least another four days to the passage, four extra days of exposure to the vagaries of the North Atlantic, to German U-boats, and, as they moved east, to the attentions of patrolling Focke-Wulf Kondors. There was no alternative, however. Statistics showed that a merchant ship in convoy, no matter how thinly escorted, was considerably less at risk than when sailing alone.

Once the new arrivals had been shepherded into position, the corvettes *Matapedia*, *Arvida* and *Chicoutimi* turned back, leaving SC41, now 14 columns strong, in the charge of HMS *Ranpura* and the newly arrived Canadian ships St *Croix*, *Pictou*, *Buctouche* and *Galt*. Given that the *Ranpura* was no more than a clumsy ex-passenger liner inadequately armed, and the St *Croix* was of 1917 vintage and totally unsuited for work in the North Atlantic, this could hardly be described as an adequate escort for 68 fat merchantmen steaming at between 6 and 7 knots.

The next 24 hours passed without incident, with the weather moderating until it was almost favourable. Unfortunately, by the evening of the 29th, the *Einvik* was already in trouble, straggling several miles astern of the convoy. This prompted an angry exchange of signals with the commodore, who was understandably concerned. The *Einvik* was a danger not only to herself but also to the other ships, for no escort could be spared to cover her. Trailing astern unattended, she might well be the means of revealing the presence of the convoy to any U-boat casting around for prey.

The *Einvik's* problem was simple and not uncommon in a ship of her calibre: she was unable to maintain a full head of steam. Wetteland sent for his chief engineer, who explained that the bunkers taken in Sydney were of poor quality, and also grudgingly admitted there was unrest in the stokehold. Wetteland immediately investigated and discovered that the same three firemen, Joseph Bebb and the two Dwyers, who had come near to holding the ship in port in St. John's, were in a state of outright mutiny. They were, in fact, deliberately refusing to feed the boiler furnaces adequately and openly demanding that the ship return to port.

Had the *Einvik* been a naval ship or a passenger liner, Wetteland would have had the option of putting the men in irons and replacing them with other ratings–and he would have been fully justified in doing so. However, the small Norwegian tramp carried a crew of only 23, and every man had to be made to count. In the end, Wetteland had to content himself with giving the mutineers a thorough tongue-lashing, ending with the threat to hand them over to the authorities when the ship reached the UK. This approach worked, and the recalcitrant firemen returned to their shovels, although with little enthusiasm. Meanwhile, the *Einvik* had fallen so far astern that the convoy was out of sight. What had begun as a drunken revel in St. John's and culminated in a bad-tempered attempt at mutiny was to cost the Norwegian ship dear.

To the south of Iceland the wolves were assembling in force. News had reached Dönitz of the sailing from Halifax of the fast, UK-bound convoy HX145, and Förster's U-501 had been joined by U-38, U-82, U-84, U-202, U-207, U-553, U-567, U-569 and U-652. Others were on the way. The weather in the area had improved slightly, making life more bearable in the U-boats, but as the sea flattened so they became more visible to patrolling British aircraft, which were very much in evidence. It was clear that the C-in-C Western Approaches was every bit as well informed as Admiral Dönitz. In fact, at this stage of the war, both sides were happily reading each other's coded signals without being aware that they had been compromised. The Germans broke the Admiralty codes soon after the outbreak of war, but the Enigma coding machine, capable of producing 22 billion different code combinations, had defied the best of the Allied Intelligence brains until May 1941. Then, during an ill-timed attack on convoy OB316 off the Hebrides, U-110 was damaged and forced to the surface by the destroyers HMS *Bulldog* and *Broadway*. The U-boat was boarded before she sank and her Enigma machine and code books seized. Within a few days, all signals between Lorient and the U-boats were being read. The capture of U-110's Enigma machine was one of the best-kept secrets of the war, not being revealed until 1966.

The British aircraft were many and persistent, Catalinas and Hudsons continually sweeping up and down at low altitude, so that any German submarine foolish enough to linger too long on the surface was in for a very rough ride. U-82, commanded by Kapitänleutnant Siegfried Rollmann, had already been slightly damaged in an attack, and Förster's wireless operator Gerhard Wunderlich was receiving reports that U-570, on its way to join in the hunt, was in serious trouble.

Unknown to Förster and his fellow commanders, convoy HX145 had already slipped through their net, and the troubled U-570 had fought its first and last battle for the Third Reich.

Commanded by Korvettenkapitän Hans Rahmlow, U-570, like Förster's U-501, was on her first wartime patrol when Dönitz ordered her to join the *Markgraf* group south of Iceland. She was also Rahmlow's first command, and most of his crew were inexperienced beginners suffering cruelly from the curse of seasickness. Little wonder that on 27 August, when 70 miles south of Iceland, U-570 was caught on the surface by a Hudson of 269 Squadron Coastal Command. Rahmlow crash-dived, but when he surfaced four hours later, it was only to see a second Hudson, piloted by Squadron Leader Thompson, swooping in with its bomb doors open. Rahmlow attempted to dive again, but it was too late. Four depth charges straddled the U-boat, smashing all her instruments, extinguishing all lights in the boat, and causing several serious leaks in the pressure hull. Sea water reached the batteries, and choking chlorine gas rose from beneath the floor plates. U-570's young and inexperienced crew panicked, and when the spray from the depth charges cleared, Thompson was amazed to see the submarine still on the surface, with several German sailors on deck waving a large white cloth. Rahmlow was offering surrender. At this point, the Hudson was joined by a Catalina of RAF Squadron 209, and the two aircraft circled the surfaced submarine for two hours, until the arrival of the armed trawler HMS *Northern Chieftain*. The trawler took off Rahmlow and his crew, then stood by the U-boat throughout the night. Next morning, the destroyers HMS *Burwell* and *Niagara* arrived on the scene, and U-570 was taken in tow. She reached Iceland, where she was repaired and later re-entered the war under the White Ensign as HMS *Graph*.

Having had no communication with U-570 for some days, BdU became suspicious and ordered Förster to search in the vicinity of Rahmlow's last-known position. Förster, of course, found nothing. *Markgraf* group continued its dreary and highly dangerous waiting game, not a little disturbed by the knowledge that, even before the battle was joined, one of their number was missing.

3

Prepare for Sea

The news of the capture of U-570 had not yet filtered through to the briefing room of the Naval Control Service at Sydney, Cape Breton, where the talk was all of containment and defence. The pre-sailing conference for convoy SC42 was in progress and the large room with its bare, whitewashed walls was filled to capacity. Through the south-facing windows the late afternoon sun struggled without success to penetrate the tug of tobacco smoke emanating from dozens of pipes, cigarettes, and even the odd cigar. The shuffling of chairs and clearing of throats indicated a general air of impatience.

On a raised dais at one end of the room, the convoy commodore, Rear-Admiral W. B. MacKenzie, RNR, flanked by a clutch of Royal Canadian Navy officers, looked around at the men he would shortly lead into battle on the high seas. The masters and senior officers of the merchant ships making up the convoy were not an impressive sight. A few were in uniform, but most wore sober blue-serge suits, which like their scuffed leather briefcases were weathered by countless forays ashore on ship's business in the four corners of the globe. Beside each man rested a bowler, trilby hat or, in a few cases, a salt-stained uniform cap. This was an age when to venture abroad with out suitable headgear was to walk naked with the devil himself.

Rear-Admiral Mackenzie spoke at length on the need for good station-keeping, the evils of making smoke, dumping

Convoy SC42 (Order of Steaming)

1	2	3	4	5	6
Δ	Δ	Δ	Δ	Δ	Δ
Baron Pentland (Brit) 3,410 Lumber	Trefusis (Brit) 5,299 General/ Grain	Empire Springbuck (Brit) 5,591 Phosphates	Thistleglen (Brit) 4,748 Steel/ Pig-iron	Dundrum Castle (Brit) 5,259 Steel	Sarthe (Brit) 5,271 General
Δ	Δ	Δ	Δ	Δ	Δ
Stargard (Nor) 1,113 Lumber	Regin (Nor) 1,386 Lumber	Jedmoor (Brit) 4,392 Iron Ore	Titus (Du) 1,712 Phosphates	Caduceus (Brit) 4,364 Steel/ Pig-iron	Inger Elisabeth (Nor) 2,166 Steel/ Lumber/ Pulp
Δ	Δ	Δ	Δ	Δ	Δ
Bretwalda (Brit) 4,906 Flour	Makefjell (Nor) 1,567 Lumber	Campus (Brit) 3,667 Steel/ Lumber	Scania (Sw) 1,980 Lumber	Waziristan (Brit) 5,135 Wheat	Atland (Sw) 5,203 Phosphates
Δ	Δ	Δ	Δ	Δ	Δ
Vestland (Nor) 1,934 Lumber	Garm (Sw) 1,231 Lumber	Maplewood (Brit) 4,566 Steel/ Lumber	Empire Crossbill (Brit) 5,463 Steel	Kingsbury (Brit) 4,898 Grain	Trompenberg (Du) 1,995 Phosphates
Δ	Δ	Δ	Δ	Δ	Δ
Baron Ramsay (Brit) 3,650 Steel/ Lumber	Winterswijk (Du) 3,205 Phosphates	Nicolas Piancos (Grk) 4,499 Steel/ Lumber	Empire Hudson (Brit) 7,456 Grain	Askeladden (Nor) 2,496 Pulpwood	Mariston (Brit) 4,557 General
	Δ	Δ		Δ	Δ
	Bestum (Nor) 2,215 Pulpwood	Hampton Lodge (Brit) 3,645 Iron Ore		Joannis (Grk) 3,667 Iron Ore	Lorient (Brit) 4,737 Iron Ore

7	8	9	10	11	12
Δ	Δ	Δ	Δ	Δ	Δ
Everleigh	**Gypsum**	**Empire**	**Kheti**	**Stonepool**	**Sally**
(Brit)	**Queen**	**panther**	(Brit)	(Brit)	**Maersk**
5,222	(Brit)	(Brit)	2,734	4,815	(Brit)
Pig-iron/	3,915	5,600	General	General	3,252
Scrap	Sulphur	General/	Δ	Δ	Grain
Δ	Δ	Mail	**Lancing**	**Mount**	Δ
Gullpool	**Peterton**	Δ	(Nor)	**Taygetus**	**Arosa**
4,868	(Brit)	**Nailsea**	7,866	(Grk)	(Nor)
Sugar	5,221	**Meadow**	Whale Oil	3,286	5,043
Δ	Sugar	(Brit)	Δ	General	Lumber
Yearby	Δ	4,962	**Bulysses**	Δ	Δ
(Brit)	**Miguel de**	General	(Brit)	**Storaas**	**Michalis**
5,666	**Larrinaga**	Δ	7,519	(Nor)	(Grk)
Phosphates	(Brit)	**Tachee**	Gas Oil	7,886	5,685
Δ	5,231	(Brit)	Δ	Fuel Oil	Wheat
Southgate	**Phosphates**	6,508	**Randa**	Δ	Δ
(Brit)	Δ	Fuel &	(Can)	**Agia**	**Wigry**
4,862	**Zypenberg**	Diesel	1,558	**Vervana**	(Pol)
Lumber/	(Du)	Δ	General	(Grk)	1,859
Steel	4,973	**Rio Blanco**	Δ	2,433	General
Δ	Phosphates	(Brit)	**Gunvor**	General	Δ
MacGreqor	Δ	4,086	**Maersk**	Δ	**Bascobel**
(Brit)	**Barwick**	Sugar	(Brit)	**Berury**	(tug)
2,498	(tug)	Δ	1,984	(Brit)	(Brit)
Phosphates	(Brit)	**Muneric**	Paper	4.924	418
Δ	418	(Brit)	Δ	General	(tow)
Knoll	(tow)	5,229	**Wisla**		Socony VIII
(Nor)	C. H.	Iron Ore	(POL)		
1,151	spedden		3,106		
Lumber	Δ		General		
	PLM 13				
	(Brit)				
	3,754				
	Iron Ore				

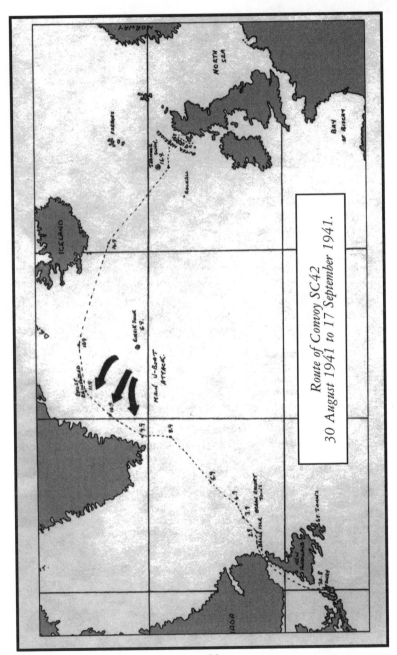

Route of Convoy SC42
30 August 1941 to 17 September 1941.

refuse, showing lights at night, of straggling and romping. As he did so, he studied the rows of faces before him and speculated on how these men would stand up to a 15-day passage across the North Atlantic which might well develop into a full-scale battle for survival

Recalled from retirement at 68, apart from service with the Royal Navy during the First World War, MacKenzie had spent his seagoing career in the élite passenger ships, a world far removed from the realities of life in the old tramps in which the vast majority of his audience sailed. Theirs was not a well-ordered round of decks scrubbed white, and pink gins when the sun crossed the yard arm, but a harsh, often drab existence dictated by the constraints of commerce and the whims of penny-pinching shipowners. They were by necessity tough, practical seamen, more concerned with cranky engines and chronic shortages of fuel, fresh water and food than with the dangers posed by the U-boats. There were those among them who were concerned that their ships were deliberately overloaded. Relaxed wartime regulations allowed for an extra 6 inches' sinkage below the load line, which in a large convoy could mean an extra 10,000 tons of precious cargo carried. For the bigger ships, the 5,000-tonners, 6 inches' less freeboard made very little difference, but for others it might prove too much. The tiny Norwegian timber-carriers *Stargard*, *Regin*, *Makefiell* and *Knoll*, and the Swedish *Garm*, none of them much over 1,000 tons gross, were in this category. By rights, they should never have ventured beyond the Skagerrak, but these were desperate times.

SC42, a slow convoy with a designated speed of 7.5-8 knots, was to be made up 63 ships, of which 40 were British, 12 Norwegian, four Dutch, three Swedish, two Greek, one Polish and one Canadian. It was a cosmopolitan mix and Rear-Admiral MacKenzie had real fears of confusion arising when there were signals to be passed. On the subject of escorts, MacKenzie had little cheer to offer his audience. For the first leg of the voyage, across the Gulf of St. Lawrence and through the Belle Isle Strait, only three Royal Canadian Navy corvettes, HMCS *Napanee*, *Barrie* and *Arvida*, would provide protection for the merchantmen. Fortunately, this sector presented no serious dangers, other than the weather. When the convoy was north of Newfoundland, where the Atlantic proper began, *Napanee, Barbie* and *Arvida* would hand over to another RCN group, the corvettes *Alberni, Kenogami* and *Orillia,* led by the destroyer HMCS *Skeena.* Air cover was to be given in the first instance by Catalinas flying from Newfoundland, and then by Sunderlands, Liberators and Catalinas based in Iceland. MacKenzie warned, however, that the air cover would not be continuous. To the south of Greenland there was a 600-mile-wide gap, the infamous "Black Pit," out of range of aircraft from either side. At SC42's best speed, this meant three and a half days of empty skies, 84 hours in which the U-boats were free to roam unmolested on the surface.

Most of the merchantmen were armed to some degree, but, in spite of Hitler's declaration of unrestricted submarine warfare, the Allies were still sticking strictly to the letter of the Geneva Convention. Four-inch and 12-pounder guns, where carried, were mounted aft and incapable of being trained forward of the beam, lest they be deemed to be offensive, rather than purely defensive, weapons. Nevertheless, MacKenzie urged that these guns be used to good effect. When the U-boats came—and come they surely would, he assured his audience—they could be expected to remain at periscope depth during the hours of daylight, picking off ships, preferably stragglers, as the opportunity arose. The escorts, with their asdics and depth charges, would deal with the daylight attacks, but at night, when the enemy's standard practice was to surface and penetrate the columns of the convoy, then it was up to the merchantmen to defend themselves. "If you see a U-boat on the surface, do not hesitate to open fire—even at the risk of hitting other ships," Mackenzie urged. This caused more than a few wry smiles, and even a guffaw of cynical laughter from the back of the room. The majority of heavy guns fitted were of First World War, or even Boer War, vintage, and manned largely by sailors, stewards and firemen, whose only training, if any, consisted of a three-day gunnery course held in a dockside shed.

With a final word on the need to keep complete radio silence at all times and a curt "Good luck!," Rear-Admiral Mackenzie closed the conference. There was a loud hubbub of conversation as those assembled rose and prepared to return to their ships. There was not a man amongst them not fully aware of the importance of this convoy, and they were anxious to get on with the job. Between them, the ships were carrying more than half a million tons of cargo: iron ore, sugar, grain, phosphates, timber, steel, oil, guns and ammunition, all urgently needed by a Britain entering her third year of total war. Only three months earlier, after one last vicious air raid on London, killing 1,500 civilians and injuring 1,800, Hitler's blitzkrieg had finally eased off, leaving the nation stunned and bleeding. Food, clothing and fuel were strictly rationed, and morale was clearly on a downward curve. After the massacre of convoy SC26, Churchill warned: "Everything turns upon the Battle of the Atlantic, which is proceeding with growing intensity on both sides. Our losses in ships and tonnage are very heavy and, vast as our shipping resources which we control, the losses cannot continue indefinitely without seriously affecting our war effort and our means of subsistence." The challenge to those who sailed the merchant ships was plain.

Churchill had another cause for concern, one which he hesitated to express in public. British dockers, suddenly finding themselves holding immense industrial power, had in the midst of this most desperate war decided the time was right to redress all the wrongs, real or imagined, they had suffered in the past. They stopped short of strike action, but demands for "danger money," "dirty money" and arguments over working conditions resulted in vast numbers of man-hours being lost, and ships lay idle in port long after they should have been at sea. A similar thing was happening in the overcrowded repair yards, where the patching up of the battle-weary merchantmen was dragged out to ridiculous lengths. In the eyes of the men who faced death every day at sea to feed these people, such selfishness was nothing short of treason—yet it went unpunished.

When the sun dipped below the plateau of the Cape Breton Highlands that evening, its dying rays briefly silhouetted the vast fleet of merchantmen anchored in Sydney harbour. At the stern rail of the British motor-vessel *Jedmoor*, 26-year-old Able Seaman Dan Hortop tugged idly at his fishing line as he watched the spectacular display of steam and fire on the nearby shore, where molten slag from the steelworks tumbled down the hillside into the sea. Hortop gave an involuntary shiver and fingered the silver whistle he wore on a lanyard around his neck. The chill of approaching autumn was in the air, but it was the "Dante's inferno" on shore that made Dan Hortop's blood run cold. It brought back chilling memories of another convoy in another place.

Six months earlier, Hortop was in the steamer *Clunepark* when the German heavy cruiser *Admiral Hipper* caught up with the unescorted convoy 270 miles north of Madeira at dawn. Within an hour six ships had gone down under the *Hipper's* 8-inch guns, and the *Clunepark*, although undamaged, had lost eight of her crew. It was following that narrow escape from death that Dan's father had given him the whistle, urging him to never be without it, for it might one day save his life. Hortop Senior had seven sons serving at sea and his advice was not to be ignored.

Dan Hortop joined the *Jedmoor* in his home town of Barry, South Wales, on 15 May 1941. Owned by Walter Runciman and Company of Newcastle and built in Sunderland in 1928, the 4,392-ton *Jedmoor* was a typical Northeast Coast tramp, broad in the beam and blunt in the bow. However, under 58-year-old Captain Robert Collins, who commanded a crew of 36 with a firm but benevolent hand, she was kept scrupulously clean and in a good state of repair. Unusually for a tramp of her day, she was a motor-ship, powered by a 417-horsepower diesel, which gave her a reasonable service speed of 9.5 knots. Having no labour-intensive boilers or steam machinery, her owners, renowned in the field of cost-cutting, took the opportunity to dispense with the services of all engine-room ratings. The *Jedmoor's* entire engine-room staff, led by Chief Engineer Robert Adamson, consisted of eight engineer officers who, in addition to watchkeeping, performed all the menial duties in the engine room. This arrangement was both feasible and permissible, but it was hardly to the liking of those (so-called) engineer officers, saddled with the extra work. For Dan Hortop and his fellow sailors on deck, however, the change was an unexpected bonus, giving them full possession of a fo'c'sle designed to house twice their number.

At that time the port of Barry had gained an unsavory reputa-

The Clunepark *at anchor off Funchal in Febuary 1941, after escaping the guns of the* Admiral Hipper.
(Photo: Fred Hartop)

tion amongst seamen, for the records showed that one in three ships that sailed from the dock fell victim to the enemy. It was therefore amid an air of some trepidation that the *Jedmoor*, loaded with a full cargo of coal, set out for the Brazilian port of Santos, half a world away. The 5,200-mile passage was to be made unescorted and "at best possible speed," which at 9.5 knots amounted to 23 days of high-risk exposure. In terms of defensive armament, the *Jedmoor* was well endowed, carrying a 4-inch anti-submarine gun and a HA/LA 12-pounder mounted aft, with a brace each of Hotchkiss and Lewis machine-guns amidships. These were manned by a team of five DEMS gunners, supplemented by those of the ship's crew not otherwise occupied, and led by Gunlayer Andrews, RN, with Second Officer William Evans acting as gunnery officer.

Much of the voyage south passed without incident, the weather being fine and the horizon empty. Once the thick coating of coal dust acquired during loading had been hosed away from the decks and superstructure, the chipping hammers and paint pots came out. If it had not been for Captain Collins insisting on daily gun drill, this might almost have been a normal peacetime voyage. Before sailing, Collins had been warned that German surface raiders were at large in the South Atlantic and, futile though the gesture might be, he intended to fight back if attacked.

It all went too well, and nobody was surprised when a day south of the equator the *Jedmoor's* engine coughed to a halt and she was left rolling awkwardly in the long swell. Chief Engineer Adamson diagnosed a blockage in the oil fuel pipe line, necessitating a dirty, painstaking job, which in view of the shortage of hands in the engine room was likely to take some considerable time.

Two hours later, with the *Jedmoor* still drifting beam-on to the swell, and the clang of heavy hammers echoing up from below, the masts of another ship were sighted coming up over the southern horizon. They were soon followed by two funnels and the unmistakable fighting top of a large warship. Robert Collins was now faced with one of the hardest decisions of his long career at sea. If the approaching vessel was a German raider—and in these latitudes it could well be—the engineless *Jedmoor* was trapped. She was unable to run away, but should she fight? The odds against her would be astronomical—guns of 8-inch calibre, or larger, manned by trained, disciplined naval gunners. The merchantman's ancient 4-inch and the insignificant 12-pounder would be blasted from their mountings, along with their scratch crews, long before the enemy came within their range. Yet it did not seem right to let the *Jedmoor* go without a fight. Collins sent his men to action-stations.

A tense half-hour passed, during which the unidentified ship, her bow-wave frothing, bore down on the *Jedmoor*. Collins, with his binoculars clamped to his eyes and cold sweat soaking his thin tropical shirt, counted a dozen 6 or 8-inch guns, and as many again of 4-inch calibre, most of which were trained on his ship. He waited for the rain of high explosive but, to his great surprise and relief, the "raider" swept past and around the *Jedmoor's* stern, her signal light flashing. She was the British cruiser HMS *Sheffield*, scouring the Atlantic for the enemy, and not at all interested in the plight of a broken-down old tramp. Shortly after the *Sheffield* disappeared over the horizon from which she had come, Chief Engineer Robert Adamson report-

LEFT: Sverre Karlsen, Gunner, DS Vestland, *convoy SC42, September 1941. (Photo: Sverre Karlsen)*

Jedmoor *in her pre-war colours, alongside in Cardiff Docks to load. (Photo: Welsh Industrial & Maritime Museum)*

ed the engines ready to use, and the *Jedmoor* followed on the cruiser's heels. The incident was made light of on board the merchant ship, but few were not aware that the cold hand of war had been laid upon them, even if only lightly.

The *Jedmoor* reached Brazil in mid-June, and spent a languid seven weeks in the port of Santos discharging her coal, and subsequently taking on a cargo of manganese ore for the UK. Santos was an unreal world, far removed from the trials of war, where a large colony of British expatriates, perhaps as a salve to their consciences, took great pains to entertain the *Jedmoor's* crew, both officers and ratings. Before the war, it would have been unheard of for a merchant seaman below the rank of master to cross the threshold of Santos' exclusive English Club, but now even lowly cooks, stewards and cabin boys were made welcome. Cricket matches, dances and lavish meals were laid on at every opportunity. Consequently, for her crew, the *Jedmoor's* long stay in Santos was a memorable one.

As ever, there was a price to be paid for the good things in life. When the *Jedmoor* steamed out of Santos in the first week of August, she carried in her holds 6,000 tons of manganese ore, a deadweight cargo in every sense. At best, she would be stiff and unyielding in her response to the sea and liable to roll her guts out in even a moderate beam swell; at worst, she would go to the bottom like a stone if torpedoed. Furthermore, instead of steering a direct course for Land's End when clearing the breakwaters at Santos, Collins was under Admiralty orders to go north. The *Jedmoor* was to take on oil fuel at Port of Spain, Trinidad, and then proceed unescorted to Sydney, Cape Breton, to join a convoy across the North Atlantic. The plan seemed nonsensical, but could not be questioned.

Cape Breton Island, separated from the peninsula of Nova Scotia by the narrow Canso Strait, is a craggy, scenic land, much like the highlands of Scotland, whence many of its early inhabitants came. Sydney, the island's principal city, was in the 1940s the centre of Nova Scotia's considerable coal-mining and steel-making industries. Its fine, deep-water harbour, sheltered from the worst of the North Atlantic's excesses, formed an ideal assembly place for large convoys forming up to cross the ocean under escort. When the *Jedmoor* entered Sydney harbour on 28 August, it was soon obvious to her crew that this cold, grey place was in sharp contrast to the Santos they had left three weeks earlier. Rumour had it that the local inhabitants were in the habit of arranging parties ashore for ships' crews and that the hospitality was contrastingly warmer than the climate, but this could not be put to the test. In the interests of security, no shore-leave was allowed, so there remained only the idle contemplation of the fiery slag-heaps and the fishing—the latter, for those who appreciated it, was excellent.

The rank of rear-admiral in the Royal Navy is a senior one, and commands a great deal of respect. When a man of such rank boards a naval ship the gangway is fully manned, bosun's pipes trill and smart salutes are snapped. This was not the case when Rear-Admiral MacKenzie boarded the commodore's ship *Everleigh* at her anchorage in Sydney. Apart from the curious stares of a couple of seamen in weathered denims and shapeless roll-neck jumpers, the arrival of the commodore and his staff went unnoticed. The lack of protocol MacKenzie was prepared to disregard, for this was a hard-working tramp and not a man-of-war. He was not expecting, however, to find a British ship in such an appalling state. The *Everleigh* was a rust-bucket, and dirty and foul-smelling to boot. Previous policy had been to choose the smartest and fastest ship in the convoy to carry the commodore's flag, which made good sense; however, it was said that some devious mind at the Admiralty, despairing at the state of many British tramps, had suggested the policy be reversed and the commodore be placed in the most disreputable ship the convoy had to offer. Presumably the hope was that those on board would be overwhelmed by the honour accorded them, and quickly mend their ways. In the case of the *Everleigh*, this theory obviously did not apply.

To be fair to the *Everleigh's* master, Captain W. H. Gould, and his crew, the state of their ship was not entirely of their making. Owned by the Atlantic Shipping and Trading Company of London (otherwise the notorious Tatems of Cardiff masquerading under a fanciful name) the 5,222-ton steamer was not old, having been built at Haverton-on-Tees in 1930, but she was certainly well worn. Over the years since she left the yard she had been run on the thinnest of shoe-strings, pushed beyond all reasonable limits and battered into degradation by the punishing cross-trades. Gould and his men gave their utmost to keep the ship in a reasonable state, but starved of resources they had made little visible progress.

Before boarding, Mackenzie had learned that his "flagship," armed with a 1913 vintage 4-inch and two .303 Lewis guns, carried a cargo of pig-iron and scrap, and boasted a top speed of 8 knots. Ignoring her state of repair and cleanliness, this seemed hardly the ideal vessel in which to lead 63 ships steaming at 7.5 knots over 2,000 miles of U-boat-infested waters. On the other hand, appearances were not everything. Mackenzie still retained painful memories of his previous merchantman, the 5,108-ton Liverpool steamer *Colonial*. A smart 12-knotter, she was blown from under him 100 miles northwest of Freetown, and he spent 20 hair-raising hours on a small raft, surrounded by hungry sharks, before being rescued.

Having discussed the coming voyage briefly with Captain Gould, MacKenzie climbed to the *Everleigh's* upper bridge and ran his eyes over the convoy. The ships were anchored in orderly rows, filling the harbour from shore to shore, and as far as the eye could see to seaward—an impressive sight which put Mackenzie in mind of the Spithead Reviews he had attended between the wars; but the resemblance was in numbers only. Here there was no gaily-coloured bunting, no immaculate paintwork and gleaming brass, only forlornly drooping, tattered ensigns and slab-sided hulls streaked with rust. It was a mixed gathering, all sizes, all shapes, but the majority of the ships small, aging and heavily loaded. The three oil tankers stood out like the prime targets they would surely be for the U-boats. Two of them, the 6,508-ton, London-registered *Tachee* and the 7,886-ton Norwegian *Storaas*, were loaded with heavy fuel oil, and the third, Anglo Saxon's 7,519-ton *Bulysses*, carried 9,300 tons of gas oil. This was the most vulnerable ship in the convoy, and she would need to be zealously guarded. There was a fourth tanker in the anchorage, but she carried a non-volatile cargo of whale oil, precious but not dangerous. She was the 7,866-ton *Lancing*, Norwegian-owned and a long way from the Antarctic whaling fleet of which she was part. Built in 1898, she was the oldest ship in the harbour, and showed all of her 43 years of hard steaming. MacKenzie could not help wondering if she might not prove to be a heavy liability, even in a convoy as slow as SC42.

Resting his gaze on the 7,465-ton *Empire Hudson*, MacKenzie felt a twinge of envy. Here was the ship in which he should surely have been flying his flag. She was a handsome wartime replacement out of Sunderland, and on her maiden voyage. She was also SC42's main arm of defence against enemy aircraft, being a CAM (Catapult Aircraft Merchantman) ship. On her foredeck she carried a modified Hurricane fighter aircraft mounted on a catapult, the primary role of which was to deal with Focke-Wulfs spotting for U-boats. However, for the pilot any launch would invariably be a one-way mission; his only way of returning to the parent ship was by baling out or ditching in the sea alongside. It was an extremely hazardous job, but the CAM ships had so far proved their worth. The *Empire Hudson* had yet to be tested in battle.

Far out, close to the entrance to the harbour, Mackenzie was comforted to see the stark, no-nonsense lines of the *Stonepool*, one of Ropner's famous "gunboats." The 4,803-ton West Hartlepool tramp had earned her title early in the war, when she fought a seven-hour gun battle with a U-boat—and won! It went without saying that the *Stonepool* would look after herself. Could the same be said, however, of the five Greeks anchored close by? The *Agia Vervana*, the *Joannis*, the *Michalis*, the *Mount Taygetus* and the *Nicolas Piancos*—these were the unpredictable ones, prone to straggling, romping, making smoke, and all the other unforgivable convoy sins, yet, at the same time, capable of feats of brilliant seamanship. And what of the lone Polish ship, the *Wisla*? A 3,000-ton, ex-British vessel, she was an unknown quantity and would require watching.

With a shrug, MacKenzie swung his binoculars around to the vice-commodore, anchored within easy signalling distance of the *Everleigh*. The 4,748-ton *Thistleglen* was also an East Coast ship, and was similarly loaded with scrap and pig-iron from New York. Her master, Captain Gordon Dobson, was to act as MacKenzie's deputy, and would take control of the convoy in the event of the *Everleigh* being sunk. MacKenzie had discussed tactics with Dobson at the convoy conference and was confident that the 42-year-old Scot was well able to shoulder any responsibility thrust upon him. In the event of having to take charge of the convoy, however, Dobson would inevitably have problems with communications. Unlike Rear-Admiral MacKenzie, he did not have a staff of six naval signallers at his disposal.

MacKenzie could not see the escorts, but he knew them to be the Royal Canadian Navy corvettes *Napanee*, *Barrie* and *Arvida*, the latter only lately returned from escorting SC41.

The Empire Hudson
Catapult Aircraft Merchantman or CAM (Sepember 1941).

These "Flower" class corvettes, each of 925 tons' displacement, and armed with one 4-inch, one 20-mm Oerlikon and depth charges, would accompany the convoy as far as the Western Rendezvous Point to the north of Newfoundland, where the ocean escort would take over. MacKenzie anticipated the RCN trio might have little defensive work to do while they were with him, but he would have to rely heavily on them to keep an eye on the merchant ships until they settled down to the convoy routine.

4

The Wolves Gather

The smell of frying bacon still lingered on the air when, shortly before 0900 on Saturday 30 August, convoy SC42 began to stir. Thermals of grey smoke curled skywards from the forest of tall funnels as furnaces were stoked in earnest, multi-coloured flags snapped in the breeze, and last-minute launches scurried across the ruffled waters of the bay. Here and there ships' foredecks disappeared under clouds of white steam, and the clank of labouring windlasses echoed back from the surrounding hills. The order had gone out to shorten anchor cables, a sure sign that this motley armada would soon be on the move. It was a fine, sunny day, but there was a chill in the wind sufficient to warrant thick jerseys and duffle coats on deck. For interested observers ashore, Sydney harbour on that autumn morning was a sight not easily forgotten. Sixty-three ships, totalling 290,000 tons gross, carrying half a million tons of cargo, and manned by some 2,700 men from seven nations, were preparing to challenge the wartime perils of the North Atlantic.

At 0930 the *Everleigh*, as befitting the commodore's ship, led the way out past the headlands, her funnel belching black smoke and her scarred hull curtsying stiffly as she felt the latent power of the open sea. On her bridge, Captain Gould was for once uneasy in his command. Spare hands are at a premium in merchant ships, and when leaving port he was accustomed to having with him on the bridge only the officer of the watch and a helmsman. On this occasion, with Rear-Admiral MacKenzie and his staff of six Royal Navy signallers, all immaculately uniformed, crowding the tiny wheelhouse, Gould felt some of his authority slipping away. Yet the rules were quite clear. The command of the ship was at all times with him, whereas MacKenzie was concerned only with the direction of the convoy. It remained to be seen how this arrangement would work in practice.

The other ships followed the *Everleigh* out one by one, and at intervals dictated by the efficiency of their windlasses. Hard on the heels of the commodore's ship came one of "Hungry Hogarth's" of Glasgow, the 3,410-ton *Baron Pentland*, Clyde-built and manned, as solid as Dumbarton Rock, and only marginally more mobile. Commanded by 40-year-old Captain Alexander Campbell, she carried 1,512 standards (that is almost 3 million board feet) of timber from St. John's, New Brunswick, for West Hartlepool. In her wake came the *Muneric*, a 5,229-ton, oil-burning steamer owned by the Bright Navigation Company of London, weighed down with a full cargo of iron ore loaded in Rio de Janeiro for the blast furnaces of Middlesbrough. Also on board the *Muneric* from Rio were two stowaways, who were causing Captain Prank Baker difficulties he could well have done without. The men had no papers, and Sydney had refused permission for them to land. Unless the authorities in Britain took a more lenient view, the *Muneric* might be forced to carry these unwanted passengers for a long time to come.

Following the *Muneric* out through the headlands was the 5,591-ton *Empire Springbuck*, built at the end of the First World War as the *San Angelo*, now managed for the Ministry of War Transport by W. A. Souter and Company of Newcastle-upon-Tyne. She carried in her holds a lethal mix of steel and explosives, consigned to Leith and London. Manned by a crew of 42, mainly Glasgow Scots, she was commanded by Captain Walter O'Connell, who hailed from South Shields and was no stranger to the North Atlantic, or the perils of the war at sea. Only five months previously, when in command of Chapman and Willan's four-year-old steamer *Hylton*, O'Connell had been torpedoed when homeward bound 200 miles south of Iceland. The *Hylton* was the unlucky recipient of one of a spread of four torpedoes fired by Kapitänleutnant Herbert Schultze in U-48. The four torpedoes hit four ships in quick succession, sending to the bottom at one fell swoop 17,299 tons of Allied shipping and earning Schultze the distinction of being the first U-boat commander to be awarded the coveted Knight's Cross. O'Connell was not aware of his attacker's good fortune, and it is doubtful that, if he had known, he would have cared, but on this August morning he was acutely conscious that he was, for the second time in less than six months, treading a very dangerous path. He tried not to dwell on the tightly packed cases of explosives forming part of the *Empire Springbuck's* cargo.

Side by side, and jockeying for position as they reached the open sea, came two of the smaller vessels making up SC42. The 3,205-ton, 27-year-old *Winterswijk*, owned by Erhardt and Deckers of Rotterdam, was another veteran of the seas. She carried a crew of 33, was loaded with foul-smelling phosphates, and was armed with a stern-mounted 4-inch and four machine-guns. Her companion, struggling to keep abreast, was the tiny Norwegian *Vestland*, of 1,934 tons. Built in 1916, she was a long way from home waters, but the cargo of timber she carried was familiar enough to her crew. Owned by Dampsk A/S Vestland of Haugesund, the *Vestland* was commanded by Captain Leonard Terjesen and armed with a 4-inch gun. Despite her maximum speed of 7.5 knots, the Norwegian was destined to play a major part in the fortunes of SC42.

Behind the two North Europeans came another British tramp. The 5,666-ton *Yearby* was one of Sir Robert Ropner's notorious "coffin" ships, dedicated to maximum profit for minimum cost. Built at her port of registry, West Hartlepool, in 1928, she was far from ancient, but living conditions on board were reminiscent of the "wooden walls" of an earlier century. Whereas her master and deck officers enjoyed a modicum of comfort in cabins beneath her bridge, engineers lived over the engine room in a block of accommodation through which ran the archaic rod-and-chain system connecting the steering engine aft to the bridge. The clank of the auxiliary steam engines driving the system, and the rattle of the rods and

The ill-fated Muneric *at the buoys awaiting a cargo.*
(Photo: Welsh Industrial & Maritime Museum)

chains occasioned by the slightest movement of the helm, made life abaft the funnel an absolute Hell, day and night, while the ship was at sea. The deck and engine-room ratings, when off duty—which was not often—eked out a drab existence in a Colditzlike fo'c'sle right in the bows of the ship, which in heavy weather was undoubtedly the most uncomfortable spot on board. The *Yearby* carried only a small supply of domestic fresh water, necessitating continuous water-rationing at sea, and a bath in a bucket of hot water filched from the engine-room hotwell was luxury indeed. Half-rotten meat and weevil-infested dried vegetables were the common fare for both the officers' saloon and the crew messroom for much of any voyage. The *Yearby's* owners were clearly not in the business of feather-bedding their crews. She was, in other words, a typical British tramp, but none the less worthy for that. When, in the summer of 1940, she was attacked by a German bomber in the River Thames, her gunners had summarily blown the aircraft out of the sky, and the *Yearby* proceeded on her way to Surrey Commercial docks, contemptuous of this crude attempt to interrupt her voyage. Captain G. M. Hudson, eight years in command of the *Yearby*, was that sort of man.

In the *Yearby's* wake came a ship whose name suggested she did not belong in this ragged assembly of has-beens and have-nots. She was the 5,259-ton *Dundrum Castle*, owned by the prestigious Union Castle Line, famed for its graceful lavender-hulled passenger liners that in pre-war days sailed from Southampton for Cape Town every Thursday afternoon, but the *Dundrum Castle* belonged to her famous sisters in name only. She was an aberration, a no-frills, coal-burning cargo ship built on the Clyde at the end of the First World War. For 20 years she had plied the New York to Cape Town run, earning good freight, but sadly neglected because of her mundane role in the Union Castle fleet.

So the long UK-bound procession filed past the headlands of Sydney Bay. Sallying forth into the unknown were, among many others: the *Sally Maersk*, British flag, Danish crew; the bulk-carrier *Gypsum Queen*, incongruous with her bridge situated right forward, only a few feet away from her bows; the *Nailsea Meadow*, one of Evans Reid's of Cardiff; the Greeks *Nicolas Piancos*, *Mount Taygetus*, *Michalis*, *Joannis* and *Agia Vervana*; the *Bretwalda*, Newcastle-built and only three years old. Well to the rear were the ocean-going tugs *Bascobel* and *Barwick*, the former towing the damaged tanker *Socony VIII*, and the latter had the *C. H. Spedden*, another deep-sea tug, at the end of her long towline. This hampered quartet was certain to have an eventful voyage.

It was 1400 before the last ship cleared the bay, leaving only the 1,558-ton Canadian motor-vessel *Randa* at anchor. This sole representative of her country's merchant fleet, loaded with general cargo for Liverpool, was plagued with engine problems which her engineers had not yet been able to remedy. She would either have to wait for the next convoy or brave the Atlantic alone, a voyage not to be undertaken lightly.

With a great show of threshing propellers and asthmatic wheezing of steam whistles, the 62 ships formed up in three straggling columns, with a distance of 5 cables, or half a mile, between columns and two cables between ships in line astern. The *Everleigh* was at the head of the centre column, and, as the cavalcade was nearly six miles long, the 2,734-ton Liverpool motor-vessel *Kheti*, commanded by Captain O. H. Turner, had been appointed as rear commodore to oversee the tail end. When comparative order had been established, Rear-Admiral MacKenzie set course to the north, into the Gulf of St. Lawrence. Thus convoy SC42 embarked upon the first leg of its passage across the North Atlantic, a long, devious journey that, over the weeks to come, would take it almost to the Arctic Circle, and seemingly into the very mouth of Hell itself.

On that penultimate day of August 1941, the dawn seemed to come reluctantly to those on watch in the conning tower of U-82, patrolling 300 miles south-southwest of Reykjavik. The gales that had been blowing without let-up for almost a week had at last moderated, but the sea was still lumpy, and the northeasterly wind had a bitter chill that came direct from the polar icecap. Despite the improvement in the weather, the general uplifting of morale that usually follows this event was not in evidence. On the contrary, a marked air of frustration pervaded the boat.

U-82 was in latitude 60° north, halfway between Cape Farewell and the Outer Hebrides, and had been so for six days. It was now obvious that the much-heralded eastbound Allied convoy, HX145, had somehow eluded the *Markgraf* group, either under the cover of the bad weather, or by some wide diversion of course undetected by Lorient. This being so, the long period of waiting, interrupted by the frequent and most unwelcome attentions of prowling British aircraft and warships, had been in vain. To date, U-82's first operational patrol was proving to be a bitter disappointment for her crew, who had come to sea with the scent of impending glory in their nostrils.

U-82 was a Type VIIC, displacing 769 tons and having a top surface speed of 17.2 knots and top submerged speed of 7.3 knots. She had a maximum range of 8,500 miles and was armed with five 21-inch torpedo tubes, an 88-mm deck gun, and one 20-mm anti-aircraft cannon. Being just 220 feet long by 20 feet in the beam, the VIIC was small and cramped compared with the later Type IX, but with its low silhouette it had proved ideal for operations against convoys, and was consequently the mainstay of Dönitz's North Atlantic arm.

Launched at the Bremer Vulkan shipyard on the River Weser in March 1941, U-82 was commissioned on 4 May that year, and then moved to Kiel for basic training. Appointed to command was 27-year-old Kapitänleutnant Siegfried Rollmann. His watchkeeping officers were the aristocratic Oberleutnant-zur-See Hans-Georg von Carlowitz-Hartitzsch, 26, Leutnant-zur-See Hans Fricke, 21, and Oberfahnrich-zur-See (Senior Midshipman) Ulrich Wentz, 20. Rollmann's first command, U-82 was in all respects a "young" boat, the average age of her 48-man crew being only 22 years, and the oldest on board being her chief engineer, 34-year-old Oberleutnant (Ingineur) Alfons Elbing. As was common practice, the boat had been "adopted" by a German town, in this case the Bavarian town of Coburg, once the seat of the Dukes of Saxe-Coburg-Gotha and, ironically, birthplace of Prince Albert, consort of one of the originators of British naval power, Queen Victoria. Perhaps unaware of the British connection, U-82 proudly carried the coat-of-arms of Coburg on her conning tower.

On completion of her working-up, early in July, U-82 was transferred to Norway for operational exercises with the 25th Training Flotilla in Oslo Fjord. When, after a gruelling month of rigorous training, she left the fiord in the early hours of 10 August on her first war cruise, Kapitänleutnant Rollmann was confident there was no possible situation his boat and his men were not equipped to deal with. His confidence was to be put to the test far sooner than anticipated. Less than half an hour after leaving port, when passing abeam of the island of Leksen, U-82 ran aground. Fortunately, the bottom was soft, and she came afloat again quickly The incident was minor, but it was a poor beginning for a maiden voyage, and regarded by all on board as a bad omen.

Satisfied that no major damage had been caused, Rollmann decided to continue the patrol and the next five days passed without incident. The weather was fine and U-82 made good speed on the surface, passing north of the Faeroes and joining the Markgraf group to the south of Iceland on the 15th. Then began a long, monotonous spell of watching and waiting, sweeping the seas between the 60th parallel and Iceland and as far west as 200 miles off the Greenland coast. It was grim, painstaking work, rewarded with nothing but bad weather and the persistent attentions of British aircraft.

On the 24th, Rollmann closed the west coast of Iceland in the vicinity of Reykjavik in order to fix the position of his boat accurately. With the sky being solidly overcast for many days, giving no opportunity for sun or star sights, navigation had been largely a matter of guesswork for too long. Lying stopped on the surface within sight of Stoerihoefti lighthouse, Rollmann was puzzled at the lack of shipping in the area. Even the inshore fishing boats were not in evidence, but this was perhaps not surprising, for the weather was deteriorating rapidly.

It was soon blowing a full gale from the east, with a vicious 15-foot sea running that made the U-boat difficult to handle on the surface. Rollmann was debating whether or not to submerge, when the decision was made for him by the approach of an enemy aircraft. Then what should have been a routine crash dive, practised so often in the Baltic and the Norwegian fjords, almost turned into a disaster. Owing to the rough sea, even with full buoyancy tanks and engines running full ahead, U-82 was agonisingly slow in slipping below the waves. Fortunately for Rollmann, the aircraft's lookouts must have been poor, for there was no attack.

Next day, Rollmann received a signal from BdU reporting two Allied convoys approaching from the west. With the tension on board increasing, U-82 moved clear of the land and that night took up a position in the expected path of the convoys. Close at hand, unseen but in radio contact, were U-202, U-38, U-652, U-569, U-84, U-567, U-553, U-207 and U-501. The stage was set for a major battle.

The weather remained in the favour of the U-boats, the wind being easterly Force 6 and the sea rough; uncomfortable for their crews, perhaps, but ideal conditions in which to operate on the surface with little chance of being spotted. Certainly in U-82, despite her recent experience, this must have encouraged some complacency, for Rollmann was again caught on the surface, this time by a Bristol Blenheim of the RAF. The consequences were almost fatal.

The Blenheim was less than two miles off when it was seen coming in from the sun with its bomb doors open. Rollmann dived immediately, levelling off at 20 metres—but this was not deep enough. Two depth charges exploded close by, the shock waves slamming the hull of the U-boat like giant sledge-hammers on an empty drum. Glass shattered, men screamed, and the boat was plunged into complete darkness. Now the long months of intensive training bore fruit. There was fear and apprehension but no uncontrolled panic.

Rollmann took the boat down to 40 metres, and made off to the east at all possible speed, while more depth charges exploded astern. In the light of the emergency lamps a quick check around revealed no serious damage, only broken gauge glasses and blown fuses. Three hours later, when Rollmann judged it safe to surface again, it was found that some of the wooden deck gratings had been smashed, but the boat was otherwise intact. All the same, it had been a near thing, and Rollmann resolved never again to be caught napping. Next time danger threatened from the air, he resolved to dive deep without hesitation, a policy he soon had ample opportunity to implement. Over the following four days, while still patrolling to the south of Iceland on BdU's orders, U-82 was forced to play a constant cat-and-mouse game with enemy aircraft. As to the expected convoys, Rollman saw nothing. The intensive Allied air activity had achieved its purpose.

A kindly sun shone down on the long crocodile of SC42 as it steamed across the Gulf of St. Lawrence with the three corvettes *Arvida, Barbie and Napanee* fussily in attendance. Thanks largely to constant patrols by aircraft of the RCAF, no U-boats had yet been seen in the Gulf, but it must have occurred to the senior officer escort, in HMCS *Barrie*, that in the event of an enemy attack his tiny force could muster no more than a token defence. In reality, the corvettes were on hand merely as sheepdogs, to snap at the heels of stragglers, to be at the beck and call of a shepherd, sailing in what appeared to be the scruffiest ship in the convoy.

On the bridge of the *Everleigh*, the "shepherd," Rear-Admiral MacKenzie, gave scant thought to the U-boats. The convoy was now heading for the east coast of Newfoundland, moving into waters where there were other and more immediate dangers.

The Gulf of St. Lawrence comes under the influence of two powerful bodies of moving water, the Labrador Current and the Gulf Stream, a clash of warm and cold that bodes no good for the seaman. The Labrador Current, originating in the Arctic Ocean beyond the frozen shores of Spitzbergen, sweeps down through the Denmark Strait and brushes along the east coast of Greenland, whose glaciers are estimated to carve more than 5,000 icebergs in a year. The current carries many of these bergs into the Labrador Sea and then south to the waters off Newfoundland. Bergs of up to 250 feet high and 1,700 feet long have been seen off the north coast of the island, and occasionally drift down through the Belle Isle Strait into the Gulf of St. Lawrence.

The benign Gulf Stream, whose warm kiss is so welcome on the western shores of Britain, also brings with it a threat of danger when it enters the Gulf of St. Lawrence from the south. When the wind is light and the warm, moist air carried on the Gulf Stream flows over the cold water of the Labrador Current, dense fogs form off the coast of Newfoundland, particularly in the narrow Belle Isle Strait, which separates Newfoundland from the Canadian mainland.

To lead a convoy of 62 slow-moving ships into an area possibly blanketed by dense fog, in which giant icebergs might lie hidden, was a daunting prospect for Rear-Admiral MacKenzie. Nevertheless, if MacKenzie and many others in SC42 harboured fears for the immediate future, they kept their own counsel, and outwardly all was normal. Taking advantage of the fine weather, the crews of the ships were on deck, scaling rust, painting, splicing ropes and generally maintaining ship as though this was just another routine day. At the same time, MacKenzie's signallers, anxious to test the ability of the merchantmen, enlivened the morning with a series of flag hoists, and Aldis lamps flashed from ship to ship, giving the convoy an air of purpose and efficiency. Not to be outdone, DEMS gunners, Navy men living the good life in the merchant ships, polished their ancient 4-inch guns, and shook their experienced heads at the antics of the tiny Canadian corvettes.

That night, those off watch slept soundly, while the watch-keepers, wary but relaxed, passed the long hours in contemplation of the voyage to come. In the British ships many thought of the homes and families they would soon see again, whereas in the others—the Norwegian, Swedish, Greek, Dutch and Polish—there was an inevitable sadness, for years must pass before there was any homecoming for them.

At 0300 on 31 August, the flash of the lighthouse on Cape Ray, southwestern corner of Newfoundland, pierced the darkness to starboard, and the long procession of ships eased around to the northeast to run parallel to the coast. At first light, the missing Canadian merchantman *Randa* clawed her way over the horizon and tagged on astern. Having completed her repairs in Sydney, she had run her engine bearings hot in an heroic effort to avoid being left behind. Now complete, and with the first 90 miles of the long voyage covered without incident or alarms, SC42 steamed confidently on.

5

Ocean Escort

At 15 minutes before sunrise on the morning of 1 September, three ships of the 24th Escort Group, Royal Canadian Navy, slipped quietly out of St. John's, Newfoundland, and steamed north to rendezvous with SC42. It was a cold, grey morning, and those unfortunate enough to be on duty in the port sought the warmth of the nearest bogie stove as soon as the ships pulled away from their berths, leaving only the wheeling gulls to witness the early sailing.

Once clear of the harbour, the destroyer HMCS *Skeena* and the corvettes HMCS *Alberni* and *Kenogami* formed up in loose line abreast, with *Skeena* in the centre and slightly in the van, as befitted the senior ship. *Skeena*, with the senior officer escort, Commander James Hibbard, RCN, on her bridge, was a "River" class destroyer of 1,337 tons' displacement and a unit of Canada's small peacetime Navy. Like most destroyers of her day, she was ill-equipped for convoy work, having no radar or HF/DF, but among her complement of 138 were a fair proportion of experienced men. With five 4.7-inch guns, two 2-pounder anti-aircraft cannon, eight torpedo tubes and a good supply of depth charges, *Skeena* was a match for most U-boats. Her two consorts were "Flower" class corvettes, fat and ugly in comparison with the sleek destroyer, but designed with the North Atlantic in mind.

The "Flower" class corvette, based on a pre-war Antarctic whale-catcher, had for some time been the Royal Navy's workhorse of the North Atlantic convoys. As simple in design as the merchant ships it was charged with protecting, the "Flower" class was of 925 tons' displacement and powered by a 4-cylinder, triple expansion reciprocating steam engine and two Scotch boilers, giving it a top speed of 16 knots. It carried a crew of 47, was armed with a single 4-inch gun and depth charges, and had a remarkable range of 4,000 miles on 200 tons of fuel. Unfortunately, the "Flower" class was a poor weather ship, being reputed to "roll on wet grass," an attribute unlikely to improve its fighting capabilities in the turbulent North Atlantic. As to the Canadian-built corvettes, of which the *Alberni* and *Kenogami* were two, they were even more primitive, having no gyro compass, and with asdic equipment so basic as to be considered obsolete in the Royal Navy.

On the other side of the St. John's peninsula, in Conception Bay, the fourth member of the 24th Escort Group assigned to SC42 waited impatiently at anchor. HMCS *Orillia*, also a Canadian-built "Flower" class corvette, and commanded by Lieutenant-Commander Edward Briggs, was to play nursemaid to a small convoy under orders to join up with SC42 for the Atlantic crossing. The British ships *Hampton Lodge*, *Lorient*, *PLM 13*, and the Greek *Joannis* were, between them, loaded with nearly 30,000 tons of iron ore from the terminal at Wabana, on Bell Island, and the Norwegian-flag *Bestum* carried a cargo of wood pulp, also from Wabana. The rendezvous point with SC42 was 20 miles to the east of the north point of Newfoundland, a steaming distance of 280 miles. With *Joannis* being 32 years old, and not one of the others capable of much more than 8 knots, it was obvious, even with *Orillia* urging them on, that they would be hard-pressed to meet up with the main convoy before it disappeared into the great void of the Atlantic.

To the northwest, in the Gulf of St. Lawrence, SC42 had come through its first night at sea without mishap. Here and there clouds of black smoke indicated the struggle some of the older ships were having to maintain station, but, by and large, the three long columns were remarkably neat. Rear-Admiral MacKenzie gazed astern from the bridge of the *Everleigh* with a growing admiration for this collection of shabby tramps of diverse flags and discipline. Given that the ships were sailing in close order for the first time, the fact that they had survived the night without mayhem breaking out was a remarkable achievement.

It is possible many of the ships' masters and officers were even more surprised than MacKenzie that they had come through the hours of darkness unscathed, but if this was so it was not evident. In fact, there was an air of unexpected normality over the convoy. The weather continued fine, and maintenance work on deck went ahead with enthusiasm. The war might just have well been a million miles away, instead of close over the horizon. Sadly, it was all too good to last. By noon, although the sun was as high as it would go, there was an ominous, icy chill in the air. Very soon, the first of the growlers came drifting past. Being relatively small chunks of ice broken off from large bergs, the growlers presented no real threat to the convoy, but they warned of a greater menace that might be lurking ahead. The "ice mountains" spawned by the glaciers of Greenland, having drifted on the current, first north into Baffin Bay, then down the Canadian coast, lose a great deal of their volume by the time they reach the seas off Newfoundland. Yet many are still huge, up to 200 feet high and 1,500 feet long, and floating with three-quarters of their dangerous mass hidden below the surface.

Shortly after the leading ships of SC42 had entered the Belle Isle Strait, the narrow channel between the coast of Labrador and the northwestern shoulder of Newfoundland, they steamed into a wall of dense fog. Bearing in mind the known effect of the meeting of the Gulf Stream and the Labrador Current in the area, this was not entirely unexpected, but was nevertheless unwelcome.

MacKenzie immediately reduced the speed of the convoy to 4 knots and ordered fog buoys to be streamed. Very soon, the whole 6-mile-long procession, three columns wide, was in the fog, with each ship cocooned in a separate world of opaque whiteness, the awesome silence of which was broken only by the steady beat of the ship's engines and the hushed voices of those on the bridge. Radio silence being in force, there could be no communication between ships, the only warning of an impending collision being given by a looming shadow in the whiteness, or the sight of a fog buoy, a simple but ingenious device which, when towed astern of a ship, kicked up a tall fountain of water. The ships of SC42, being committed to the Belle Isle Strait, a channel 15 miles wide and 80 miles long, flanked on either side by steep, rocky shores, were about to be tested to the limit.

On the bridge of the *Baron Pentland,* close astern of the *Everleigh,* 23-year-old Second Officer John Dewar, who had the watch, experienced a chill of apprehension as the fog closed around his ship. Dewar was young for his rank, and relatively inexperienced, but typical of many officers in the convoy.

Of all the fronts on which Britain and her allies were fighting, it was at sea that their losses were greatest. From the outbreak of war until the end of August 1941, a total of 2,068 merchant ships of nearly 8 million tons had been sunk, most of them by the U-boats in the North Atlantic. The point at which replacements could be turned out to match, ship for ship, those being sunk, was long past.

For the men who manned the ships, the merchant seamen, it was a war in which the odds were weighted heavily against them. Long used to fighting the ritual battle with the forces of nature, they now found themselves crossing the wide oceans in thinly defended convoys, threatened and harassed day and night by hostile submarines, surface raiders and aircraft. It was a battle so one-sided as to border on the ludicrous. The casualty rate was appalling, more than 500 men a month dying, more often than not without the remotest opportunity to defend themselves.

The wonder of it all was that men had the courage to endure such sustained punishment. Yet they came back voyage after voyage, like punch-drunk boxers re-entering the ring convinced that just one more round was all that was needed to sway the fight. There were a few exceptions, who could take no more and crept away to hide, but no ship was ever held in port for lack of a crew to sail her. One inevitable effect of the high casualty rate was rapid promotion, especially among deck officers. Second Officer John Dewar was a product of the times, as was the *Baron Pentland's* third officer, 20-year-old John

McNichol, a time-serving apprentice elevated to watchkeeping officer only a month earlier.

Captain Alexander Campbell, called to the bridge, was at Dewar's side as the ship entered the fog. Campbell, a 40-year-old Glaswegian, was well used to these waters and realised he was in for a long vigil. Fog at the southern end of the Belle Isle Strait invariably meant fog all the way through. Before another dawn came he would be tired and jaded, prowling the bridge with every nerve on edge as he strained his bloodshot eyes to distinguish alien shapes in the baffling whiteness. As his eyes searched, so would his ears be listening for the muted beat of another ship's engines, or the warning blast of a siren. He would by then also be calling on the extraordinary sixth sense that a master mariner develops over the years—the ability to sense when immediate danger threatens. Nevertheless, if, and when, the challenge came, Campbell was confident that his ship would respond to his hand, for she was of good lineage.

When Hugh Hogarth of Ardrossan purchased the brigantine *Fearless* in 1868, it was a small and tentative beginning for shipping on Scotland's west coast. Other sailing vessels followed, to be followed in their turn by steamers, until, by the outbreak of war in 1939, the Baron Line, as the enterprise had become known, consisted of 39 ships, and was the largest privately owned tramping fleet in the world. This distinction was not gained without cost, for although Hogarth's ships were solid and dependable, conditions on board for their crews were, to say the least, not of the best. Suffice to say, the Baron Line was known worldwide as "Hungry Hogarth's."

The *Baron Pentland* was typical of the Hogarth stable. Registered, as were all Hogarth's ships, at Ardrossan, she was Scottish-built, Scottish-engined, and for the most part Scottish-named. At 3,410 tons gross, she was not a big ship for her day, but big enough to brave the deep oceans, and not too big for the rivers and shallow-water ports she was called upon to visit in the course of her tramping voyages. She would normally carry a total crew of 33, but this had been increased to 41 by the addition of eight DEMS gunners, who manned her armament of one 4-inch, a Bofors anti-aircraft gun and four machine-guns. At this stage of the war, for an old tramp, she was well armed. Her cargo on this voyage was for her not an unusual one: steel in the bottoms of the holds from Sydney, Nova Scotia, topped off with 4,000 tons of timber from Quebec. This, as her canny owners well knew, was the optimum way to load a ship; full cubic and full deadweight, with not a cubic inch of space below or above decks which had not been used to good effect. Her port of discharge in the UK was Middlesbrough, a choice not appreciated by the many Scots on board.

Some way astern of the *Baron Pentland*, and feeling her way through the fog with considerable apprehension, was the British motor-tanker *Bulysses*. Owned by the Anglo-Saxon Petroleum Company of London, the 7,519-ton *Bulysses* was carrying 9,300 tons of gas oil, loaded in New York and consigned to Liverpool. Discounting the hazards of war, the tanker was an extremely vulnerable ship. A spark, such as might be generated by the grating of steel on steel in the most minor of collisions, would be sufficient to turn her into a raging inferno. This scenario was uppermost in the mind of Captain Bertram Lamb as, with the officer of the watch, Second Officer Robert Walker, he kept a sharp lookout on the bridge. Lamb had under his command a well-found ship, crewed by British officers, whom he knew would rise to any emergency, but he was also aware that his Chinese ratings were liable to panic when under pressure.

Only slightly less apprehensive was Captain William Bannan, master of the tanker *Tachee*. This 6,508-ton motor-vessel, owned by Socony Vacuum of London, had on board 8,500 tons of heavy fuel and diesel oil, a cargo hazardous enough, but much less volatile than that of the *Bulysses*. Short of being put to the torch by an outside source, the *Tachee* was relatively safe. She also had an experienced British crew, but suffered the disadvantage of being 27 years old. Even for a dry cargo ship this is a very full lifetime, but in a tanker carrying mainly corrosive oils such long service is tempting Providence.

As the day went on the fog grew thicker, and the night that followed was long and filled with peril for SC42. Men grew tired and careless, and the cumbersome merchantmen, reduced to the equivalent of a brisk walking pace, blundered through the confined waters of the strait like a herd of blind elephants. The carefully streamed fog buoys lost their usefulness, for those navigating could see no further than the foremast of their own ship. As the threat of the enemy was temporarily brushed aside by more immediate dangers, lights burned brightly and sirens wailed indiscriminately as ships manoeuvred to avoid one another. Hanging over all this tense confusion was the awful threat that, at any time, one or more icebergs of titanic proportions, shrouded in fog, might drift down on the convoy.

At daylight on the 2nd, SC42 broke free of the Belle Isle Strait and, as suddenly as it had come down, the fog cleared. The columns were ragged but there had been no collisions, no ship had run ashore, and there were no reports of damage by ice, although there were those who swore they had seen shadowy shapes as tall as houses slipping by in the murk.

The euphoria brought on by the deliverance from the fog and ice was short-lived, for, as so often happens in these waters, the transition from eerie calm to howling gale was swift. By the time the rendezvous was made with HMCS *Skeena*, *Alberni* and *Kenogami* 15 miles east of Belle Isle, the wind was in the north and blowing down the Davis Strait with ever-increasing ferocity. It was no doubt with considerable relief that the corvettes *Arvida*, *Barrie* and *Napanee* handed the convoy over to Commander Hibbard and headed for home.

Rear-Admiral MacKenzie now passed the signal for the ships to take up their ocean steaming formation of 12 columns abreast. Perversely, as he did so, the vacuum left by the dispersed fog was filled by drizzling rain. Visibility fell to 1 1/2 miles, which succeeded in making an already complex operation into a nightmare. The low-powered, single-screw merchant ships, always slow to answer to the helm, and further hampered by heavy seas and poor visibility, milled around in a state of total confusion. Near-collisions were frequent and the air was filled with invective, but within the hour the task was completed. The disorganised jumble of 63 ships became 12 orderly columns, with 3 cables between columns and 2 cables between each ship and the one ahead. When complete, the formation covered an area of 25 square miles, about which the destroyer *Skeena* and the corvettes *Alberni* and *Kenogami* took up defensive positions. It is not recorded what Commander Hibbard thought of the impossible task assigned to his ships, but it is certain that, even to the lowliest boy seaman in the most insignificant old tramp in the ranks, the escorting force for convoy SC42 was purely symbolic. To Captain Robert Collins on the bridge of the *Jedmoor*, second ship in the third column, the situation was plainly ludicrous, confirming his conclusion that he would have been wiser to have defied Admiralty instructions and sailed direct to the UK from Santos unescorted. The risks would surely have been no greater, and the weather undoubtedly more kindly.

The *Everleigh*, lead ship in the middle column, now set course to the northeast for the Mid-Ocean Meeting Point, where ships of the Royal Navy based in Iceland would reinforce the escort. The rendezvous lay deep in the Denmark Strait, over 1,000 miles' hard steaming away, and a mere stone's throw from the Arctic Circle. The course would take the convoy to within 50 miles of Cape Farewell, southernmost point of Greenland. This area, lately christened "Torpedo Junction," was outside the range of aircraft operating from Newfoundland and Iceland, and therefore a favourite ambush spot for the U-boats.

Steaming with the wind on the port bow, gale force and still rising, the smaller ships, in particular the Swedish *Garm* and the Norwegians *Knoll*, *Regin* and *Stargard*, none of them much over 1,000 tons, were finding the going hard. As the wind continued to increase, so the convoy's speed dropped, until it was down to a mere 4.5 knots. This may have been fortuitous, for midway through the morning an iceberg the size of a small mountain loomed up out of the rain and sailed majestically through the centre columns of the convoy. It was back in the murk before the horror of this registered on many who saw it, but where there was one there might be others. The chill already in the air became an icy portent of the danger abroad.

There was still no sign of HMCS *Orillia* and the five ships from Wabana, and MacKenzie was beginning to fear for their safety when *Skeena* established contact with *Orillia* by radio-telephone. It transpired that, in the poor visibility, the newcomers were hopelessly lost and steaming by dead reckoning towards the rendezvous point. *Skeena* carried out a search ahead, and more by good luck than design, stumbled on the missing ships as they crossed 9 miles ahead of the convoy. The destroyer guided them back to SC42, and while the merchantmen took up positions at the rear of the convoy *Orillia* joined the defensive screen, thereby increasing it by 25 percent. The rendezvous had been made just in time, for darkness was closing in and the visibility was down to 1 mile.

Predictably, the weather worsened further during the night, and when the grey light of dawn filtered through the thick canopy of cloud on the 3rd the ships were barely making steerage way. Rolling crazily and with decks awash with foaming green water, some were unable to steer at all and had slewed out of the ranks. Shortly before noon, the tug *Barwick* broke radio silence to inform the commodore that she had been forced to slip her tow and was dropping back to stand by it. Twelve hours later, the *Bascobel*, with the *Socony VIII* in tow, passed a similar message. It was thought that both the *Socony VIII* and the *C. H. Spedden* would be able to raise sufficient steam to reach St. John's. As for the tugs, they had to be left to their own devices, for there was no one to come to their aid.

Still the weather deteriorated, the wind racking up to storm force and the great Atlantic rollers marching in from the far horizon to the beat of the Storm God's drum. The drizzle turned to driving rain and all the while the thermometer fell steadily. Ships rolled their bulwarks under, climbed invisible mountains and plummeted into dark valleys where the wind was momentarily stilled, each fighting a life-and-death battle in isolation with the raging ocean. For the bridge watchkeepers, oilskinned and huddled in whatever shelter offered, the slowly passing hours were a hell they would have gladly sold their mortal souls to escape. Those off watch below fared little better. Fo'c's'les and cabins were awash with icy water, and the bruising, shock-like movement destroyed all hope of sleep. That a deadly enemy might be lurking beneath the waves seemed a total irrelevance. The suffering was worst in the tiny corvettes, manned mainly by Canadian volunteer reservists on their first deep-sea voyage. Appalled by the fury of the sea, and weakened by seasickness, they were in no condition to fight.

Fortunately, the enemy was at this time a long way off, the assembling units of the *Markgraf* group being 150 miles south-west of Iceland and also experiencing heavy weather. Hurrying to join them from the east was U-652, a Type VIIC command-ed by Oberleutnant-zur-See Georg-Werner Fraatz.

A product of the Howaldt Shipyard in Hamburg and commissioned in April 1941, U-652 was one of the few boats in the area which had already seen action, albeit on a limited scale. She had the distinction of being the first U-boat to sink a Soviet ship in this war, having torpedoed the armed trawler *SKR-70* on 6 August in the Barents Sea. Three weeks later, while passing between the Faeroes and Iceland, Fraatz claimed to have hit a 9,000-ton ship of indeterminate name and nation-ality, but there was no confirmation of this sinking. In all, U-652's record to date was not remarkable, but Fraatz was deter-mined to alter this state of affairs.

It was his eagerness to join the Markgraf group that almost brought about Fraatz's undoing. Motoring on the surface in daylight and within range of British aircraft operating from Iceland was, to say the least, unwise, and this was brought home to the Oberleutnant very forcibly on the morning of 4 September. An RAF Hudson appeared unannounced, guns blazing, and U-652 was forced into an undignified crash dive. Had the matter ended there, it would have done no more than provide a topic of conversation in the conning tower for some days to come. Unfortunately for, and unknown to, Fraatz, the Hudson had earlier sighted the American destroyer USS *Greer*, on her way from Newfoundland to Reykjavik. Although the United States was not then at war with Germany, the enter-prising British pilot sought out the destroyer and informed her that there was a U-boat in the vicinity. He then flew off and proceeded to circle the spot where U-652 had dived. The *Greer* followed, but her commander, Captain Laurence Frost, USN, was under orders not to attack unless his ship was first attacked, which left him in something of a dilemma. There was no guarantee that the U-boat would not mistake the *Greer* for a British warship, with disastrous consequences, but, for the time being, Frost decided to use his sonar to track the "enemy." If nothing else, this would provide a valuable exercise for his crew.

The exercise turned into unpleasant reality when, as the *Greer* obtained a contact with her sonar, the Hudson dropped a pattern of depth charges close to U-652. Fraatz, unaware that the aircraft was still overhead, assumed he was being attacked by a British destroyer, and came to periscope depth. He fired two torpedoes at the American ship, which missed their target. Having been attacked, the *Greer* was now perfectly justified in defending herself, and this she did with vigour. U-652 escaped from her depth charges only by going very deep, and staying there for some hours. Unwittingly, Fraatz had scored another "first" by being in command of the first U-boat involved in action with a United States warship in the Second World War.

6

A Chance Meeting

Duming the short time the *Einvik* spent with convoy SC41, however inadequate its ocean escort, Captain Wetteland was comforted by an illusion of security. At the very worst, if his ship was sunk, other ships were on hand to pick up survivors. When, on the evening of 29 August, the convoy left the *Einvik* trailing astern, and then disappeared over the horizon, the Norwegian captain could be forgiven for experiencing a momentary surge of panic. In the light of the setting sun, the Atlantic, although unusually calm, was grey and unfriendly–openly hostile to a ship sailing alone.

Limping along at 6 knots, and armed only with a single Lewis gun and a second-hand Thompson submachine-gun–the latter more suited to a Chicago back street than a merchant ship–the *Einvik* presented a threat to no one. She would most certainly be completely at the mercy of the first U-boat to spot her. Wetteland's only real defence, such as it was, lay in keeping rigidly to the courses laid down by the commodore of SC41. This added considerable distance to the passage, and reached far north of the normal shipping lanes, but it was said to be a "safe" route, away from the known hunting grounds of the U-boats. How safe remained to be seen.

On 1 September the *Einvik* was 220 miles south of Cape Farewell, still in unusually fair weather, and forging ahead at 6.5 knots. In view of the churlish attitude of some of her firemen and the inferior coal she burned, this was as good a progress as could be expected. Nevertheless, the courses she was following would take her to within one and a half days' steaming of the Arctic Circle, and with every hour the temperature edged lower. In order to maintain steam on the main engine, Wetteland had dispensed with all accommodation heating, a desperate measure, which only served to increase the misery of all but those lucky enough to be on duty in the engine room or galley. Later in the day, minds were temporarily diverted from the steadily falling thermometer by the appearance of an American destroyer, which exchanged signals by lamp with the *Einvik* before going on her way. This was probably the USS *Greer*, soon to be inadvertently drawn into the confrontation building up in the lower reaches of the Denmark Strait.

Perhaps fortune was smiling too kindly on the Norwegian tramp, or it may have been just that she had been pushed too hard and for too long, but the inevitable happened early on the 3rd. The *Einvik* was in latitude 60° north and 200 miles due east of Cape Farewell, when her chief engineer reported to Wetteland that one of the bearings of the main crankshaft was running hot and must be renewed. Under the circumstances, Wetteland was reluctant to heave-to, for then his ship would be even more vulnerable than ever, but he had no real alternative. So, for the next 12 hours the *Einvik* lay stopped, rolling uneasily in the long Atlantic swells, while her engineers worked feverishly to replace the worn bearing. In true trampship style, at the same time the opportunity was taken to clean the *Einvik's* boiler tubes thoroughly, as they were thick with soot from the dirty Nova Scotian coal she had been burning.

The hours spent drifting helplessly in an area of great danger stretched Wetteland's nerves to breaking point. It was with much relief therefore that, late that evening, he was able to ring full ahead on the engine-room telegraph and once again feel the deck pulsating beneath his feet. The effects of the boiler clean were immediately noticeable, and that, coupled with a sudden newfound enthusiasm amongst the firemen, soon had the *Einvik* bowling along at an unprecedented 7.5 knots. The bitter cold and the threat of the enemy were forgotten, and a new air of optimism spread through the ship.

The change for the better was short-lived. During the night the weather deteriorated rapidly, and by dawn on the 4th it was blowing a full gale, with the *Einvik* labouring in heavy seas. The additional strain proved too much for her aging machinery, and late in the afternoon a high-pressure steam pipe burst, filling the engine room with clouds of scalding steam. The engine slowed, and then ground to a halt, leaving Wetteland once again in command of a drifting hulk. Fortunately the damage was quickly repaired, and the *Einvik* was under way again within the hour, although at a reduced speed.

Two hours later, just as darkness was closing in, a Canadian corvette, one of SC41's escort returning to St. John's, came over the horizon and passed within hailing distance. Using a loud hailer, her commander informed Wetteland that the convoy was two days' steaming ahead of the *Einvik*, and steering even further to the north to avoid a reported concentration of U-boats. This grim news strengthened Wetteland's growing doubts of the advisability of following in the wake of SC41. The decision was made for him when, as the corvette rolled and pitched her way out of sight, he was presented with yet another dilemma. As a result of her frantic efforts to keep pace with SC41, the *Einvik* was running out of coal. On the figures given to him by his chief engineer, Wetteland calculated he had sufficient bunkers left for only another four or five days' steaming. As the nearest British port lay 750 miles away—or five days' steaming at 6 knots—the successful completion of the voyage now hung in the balance. There was no other choice open to Wetteland but to alter course to the southeast and take the shortest route to the Bristol Channel.

So the destinies of the *Einvik* and U-501 drew ever closer. As the Norwegian ship answered her helm to the new course, the German U-boat was only 160 miles to the southeast and motoring northwestwards on the surface to join the *Markgraf* group. The two vessels, unknown to each other, were on reciprocal courses and closing at a combined speed of around 17 knots.

The concluding days of August had not been happy ones for Hugo Förster and his men, being marked by continuous foul weather, unrelieved frustration, and the unwelcome and persistent attentions of the RAF. Acting on BdU's orders, U-501 had covered a 250-mile-long patrol line of the meridian of 20° west, steering first south, then north, up and down with monotonous regularity. At the southern end of the line the temperature rose a few degrees and the weather improved marginally, making life on board almost bearable. Otherwise, for much of the time the submarine was trapped in a frozen world of howling winds and crashing waves, from which there was no escape. She came near to an untimely end when, on the morning of the 28th, she was in latitude 60° north and heading north into a rising sea. An aircraft bearing RAF roundels suddenly dropped out of the low cloud, roared in at 50 feet above the waves, and straddled the submarine with a stick of bombs. As luck, or bad judgement, would have it, the bombs did no damage and U-501 escaped with nothing more than the shock caused by a hurried crash dive. When the crisis was past, Förster had only one wish, and that was to be swiftly delivered from this dangerous and monotonous patrol in which he was engaged. His wish was not to be granted for another week, when on the afternoon of 4 September BdU ordered U-501 to join up with the *Markgraf* group.

The last hour before another day dawns is the darkest hour of the night. It is also the hour when human metabolism is at its lowest ebb, the hour when ghosts walk abroad, and the deep caverns of the subconscious are filled with despair and foreboding. So it was with Oberleutnant-zur-See Werner Albring, U-501's senior watchofficer, as, at 0300 on the morning of the 5th, he willed his tired eyes to pierce the darkness. Ripples of green phosphorescence arrowed away from the submarine's bow and an indistinct shading of grey and black showed where the sea and sky merged, otherwise the world around him was a dark void without substance. Albring shivered and pulled the collar of his leather watch coat higher, grateful for the presence of the petty officer and two ratings of the watch in the conning tower.

In the preceding 24 hours, there had been a welcome change in the weather, the wind easing down to a gentle Force 2, matched by a calm sea and a slight rise in temperature. U-501's powerful 6-cylinder diesels were driving her through the water at 14.5 knots on a northwesterly course, BdU having warned of a large eastbound convoy, towards which all units of the *Markgraf* group were moving. It was hoped that U-501 would be within striking distance of the convoy by mid-morning, and then all the long months of training and the weeks of fruitless patrolling might at last come to a useful conclusion. The thought of being in on the U-boat's first kill, and an almost imperceptible lightening of the sky indicating the imminent arrival of dawn, sent Werner Albring's spirits soaring. It was then he saw the dark shadow ahead and to port. He moved quickly to the captain's voice pipe.

On the bridge of the *Einvik*, Albring's opposite number had for some time been puzzled by a smudge on the greying horizon in the east. It had the appearance of a small ship, about the size of a fishing trawler, yet they were too far from land for a fisherman to be operating. When, after examining the silhouette through his binoculars for some time, the *Einvik's* chief officer realised he was looking at a U-boat, it was too late. He ordered the helm hard to starboard to put the ship's stern to the enemy, but as the *Einvik* began her slow turn U-501's 50-cm torpedo, packed with 300kg of TNT, slammed into the forward hold of the Norwegian's port side. There was a dull rumble that grew into a roar, and a huge column of water and debris shot high into the night sky. The *Einvik* staggered drunkenly.

Having spent the best part of ten days since leaving St. John's without proper sleep and under great stress, Captain Wetteland had retired to his bunk late on the 4th mentally and physically drained, ready to sleep around the clock. He was in a deep slumber when Förster's torpedo brought him rudely awake. Pausing only for a moment to gather his wits, he dashed for the bridge, reaching it as the *Einvik* took a heavy list to port.

It was still very dark and difficult to assess how seriously the ship had been hit, but the deck cargo of pit props forward of the bridge was a smoking shambles, indicating complete devastation below decks. The U-boat was nowhere to be seen—obviously lurking beneath the surface, waiting to deliver the *coup de grace*. With the *Einvik* listing alarmingly as the sea poured into her breached hull, Wetteland saw no point in postponing the inevitable. He ordered his crew to abandon ship while there was still a chance.

In a providentially calm sea, and with the *Einvik's* largely Norwegian crew conducting themselves in their usual phlegmatic manner, the ship's two lifeboats were lowered without incident. Only when the boats had pulled away from the sinking ship was it discovered that the wireless operator was missing. He had last been seen making for the wireless room, with the obvious intention of sending an SOS, although Wetteland had not ordered him to do so.

Hugo Förster was angry. He had used six torpedoes on the *Einvik*, five of which had missed, and when U-501's operator reported the merchant ship to be sending a distress, Förster lost no time in bringing his boat to the surface. Whoever was transmitting the SOS must be silenced quickly, before it was picked up by any British warship listening. As soon as U-501's gratings were clear of water, the 105-mm deck gun was manned and fire was opened on the *Einvik*, concentrating on her bridge.

In spite of the shells bursting around the ship, the *Einvik's* chief officer decided to take his lifeboat back to search for the missing wireless operator. It was a brave attempt which came to nothing, for as the lifeboat neared the *Einvik* it came under fire and was forced to withdraw to avoid being severely damaged or sunk.

The shelling went on for more than half-an-hour, during which time the *Einvik's* survivors lay back on their oars and watched their ship systematically reduced to a burning hulk by the U-boat. When the first rays of the rising sun were reaching up over the horizon, the *Einvik*, ex-*Rendal*, ex-*Fermund*, ex-*Cormount*, ex-*War Taurus,* veteran of two world wars and countless battles with the sea, lifted her stern high and slipped beneath the waves to her last resting place. There were tears in the eyes of many in the lifeboats as they watched their floating home–the only home some of them knew–go under.

As soon as full daylight came, it was apparent that, contrary to usual practice, the U-boat had fled the scene of her crime without bothering to question the survivors. Wetteland, in particular, was greatly relieved, for the Germans had the nasty habit of taking the master of a sunken vessel prisoner, thereby removing a key man from circulation. There was a further surprise a few minutes later, when a small gig was sighted rowing towards the lifeboats. At the oars was the *Einvik's* wireless operator, who had lowered the small boat single-handed and escaped as the ship sank. The operator, a Canadian on his first trip to sea, had acted in the best traditions of ship's radio officers down through the ages by sticking to his post transmitting an SOS until the very last minute.

Much later, it was learned that the Canadian's courageous act had been in vain, for no ship or shore station picked up the repeated SOS call. However, at the time, the men in the lifeboats were not to know this and they held on to the hope that help would soon be at hand. Wetteland was less optimistic, although he did not voice his thoughts. He was aware of the parlous state of the British Navy in the area and thought there was little chance of a warship being sent to look for the survivors of an old Norwegian timber-carrier, even assuming their SOS had been heard. Convoys passed this way, but usually well to the north, so there was little hope of succour from that source.

Although his command had gone, Wetteland was still responsible for the safety of his men, and the next move was up to him. He was faced with the alternatives of waiting for a rescue ship that might never come, or trying to reach land. The two lifeboats were small and adrift in the world's most inhospitable ocean, and although the sea was calm it was unlikely to remain that way for long. At any time the wind might be whipped up into a howling gale, with seas big enough to swamp the boats.

The *Einvik* had gone down 330 miles southwest of Iceland, and much the same distance from Greenland. The latter, a largely uninhabited land of snow-covered mountains and glaciers, offered no refuge. As for Iceland, this was more hospitable, as the coastal areas were well populated, Allied ships and aircraft were based on the island, and there was a large and very active fishing fleet. It was a long haul for the small boats, however, at least nine days' sailing, and all the time they would be going north, deeper and deeper into bitter sub-Arctic waters. Their survival, if it was to be, would be hardwon, but Wetteland could see no other choice but to head for Iceland. At sunrise he ordered the sails to be hoisted, and with the two boats roped together they set course for the northeast, and Iceland.

The foolish but brave action of the *Einvik's* wireless operator had caught Hugo Förster unawares, and as soon as the Norwegian ship sank he took U-501 on northwestwards at all possible speed. Like Wetteland, he had no means of knowing whether the SOS had been picked up, and he certainly had no intention of waiting to find out. The sighting and sinking of the merchant ship had been a welcome boost for the morale of the U-boat's jaded crew, even though it had cost six torpedoes and 40 105-mm shells—a high price to pay for one 2,000-tonner loaded with timber. As to the future, Förster was more optimistic. Where there was one ship, there were others, and U-501, now fully operational and blooded, would find them.

As the *Einvik's* survivors embarked on their perilous journey north and U-501 made good her escape, in St. John's harbour two corvettes of the Royal Canadian Navy, HMCS *Chambly* and *Moosejaw*, were preparing for sea. The ships, both newly commissioned, and commanded respectively by Commander J. S. D. Prentice and Lieutenant Frederick Grubb, were about to set off on their first deep-sea training exercise. Prentice and Grubb were regular Navy officers, but their crews were mainly new recruits lately snatched from civilian life: bank clerks, lumberjacks, factory workers, farmers and coal miners, none of whom had ventured into deep waters before. Commander Prentice, recalled from retirement after 22 years of service with the RCN to become Senior Officer Canadian Corvettes, had the unenviable job of licking these men into shape in as short a time as possible, for the corvettes were sorely needed for convoy escort. When they sailed from St. John's at noon on the 5th, Prentice was aware of the progress of SC42 and set course for the area through which the convoy was expected to pass in the next few days. He had no remit to protect the convoy but, if and when the torpedoes began to run,

Prentice intended to have *Chambly* and *Moosejaw* within supporting distance. There could be no better tutorial for his untried men than to be pitched straight into the thick of the action.

Convoy SC42 was at this time 300 miles southwest of Cape Farewell and continuing its unending battle with the weather. The northerly wind funnelling down the Denmark Strait was savage and relentless, and before it all ships, merchantmen and escorts, were hove-to and fighting for survival. In driving rain and flying spray the visibility was down to a few hundred yards, and all too often ships lost sight of those nearest to them, thus creating a major hazard. The consequences of collision in such weather did not bear thinking about.

Skeena was making a brave effort to scout ahead, but her slim hull, designed to slice through calmer waters at high speed, was totally unsuited to riding the mountainous seas she now faced. The more ungainly merchantmen astern of her, broad in the beam and purpose-built to wallow their way across the face of the oceans, lifted to the waves, however reluctantly. The sharp-bowed destroyer would have none of this, preferring to cleave-dig her bows in even at slow speed, with the result that her foredeck, from fo'c'sle to bridge, was constantly buried under tons of foaming green water. The jerky, corkscrewing motion she affected was punishing to both mind and body, and any man who failed to have one hand for the ship and one for himself was courting serious injury.

Commander James Hibbard, firmly wedged at the fore end of *Skeena's* open bridge, wiped the spray from his eyes and cursed roundly. The practical seaman in him urged that he heave-to, but the demands of war were greater. An Admiralty signal received earlier warned of a large concentration of U-boats to the southwest of Iceland, but the position given was only approximate. There was also the danger that other U-boats, the vanguard of the wolf-pack, were already past Cape Farewell and closing on the convoy. Hibbard had no way of knowing the true situation and must at all times be prepared for the worst.

Adding to the commander's worries was a report from *Skeena's* wireless office of suspicious radio signals emanating from a source close by. The distinctive note of the unidentified transmitter indicated that it was made by a spark-gap transmitter, as carried by some of the older tramps in the convoy. The signal, which lasted for some two minutes, consisted of a series of long dashes, followed by the letters "TU," being the abbreviation commonly used by wireless operators for "Thank you." It could be that this dangerous breach of radio silence was only the work of a bored operator in one of the tramps, but Hibbard could not shake off the awful suspicion that one of the ships in the convoy was acting as a homing beacon for the U-boats. The thought sent cold shivers racing up and down Hibbard's spine, but in view of the weather he was powerless to investigate. In any case, the signals had not continued for long enough for the wireless office to take a bearing of the source, so he would not know where to begin the investigation.

In reality, the U-boats of the *Markgraf* group were still some 600 miles northeast of SC42, but moving slowly to the south and west. BdU had informed them of a large Allied convoy leaving Sydney, but could give no clear idea of its position or course.

By weight of numbers, the *Markgraf* group, 15 boats strong and more coming in, presented a terrifying threat to the lightly escorted SC42. However, the U-boats and the men commanding them were very short on experience, with a few exceptions.

U-38, which sank its first ship, the British tanker *Inverliffey*, only eight days after the outbreak of war, had a long string of successes to its name under Heinrich Liebe. Her new commander, Korvettenkapitän Heinrich Schuch, who succeeded Liebe in August 1941, was not an experienced U-boat man, but had already showed some promise by sinking the 1,700-ton Panamanian tanker *Longtaker* within a few days of leaving base. U-105, with Kapitänleutnant Georg Schewe in command, was one of the larger Type IXBs, and had chalked up some notable victories off the coast of West Africa earlier in the year. Kapitänleutnant Robert Gysae's first command, U-98, was also not without a claim to fame, having sunk the 10,549-ton armed merchant cruiser HMS *Salopian* and acted in support of the ill-fated *Bismarck*. There was also U-569, a new boat commanded by the veteran Kapitänleutnant Hans-Peter Hinsch, late of U-4 and U-140.

Others with limited experience were U-202, Kapitänleutnant Hans-Heinz Linder, responsible for the sinking of the 500-ton Russian-armed trawler *Kapitan Voronin*, and Förster's recently successful U-501. The rest were: U-81, Kapitänleutnant Friedrich Guggenberger; U82, Kapitänleutnant Siegfried Rollmann; U-84, Kapitänleutnant Horst Uphoff; U-85, Oberleutnant-zur-See Eberhard Greger; U-207, Oberleutnant-zur-See Fritz Meyer; U-372, Kapitänleutnant Heinz-Joachim Neumann; U-432, Kapitänleutnant Heinz-Otto Schultze; U-433, Kapitänleutnant Hans Ey; and U-652, Oberleutnant-zur-See Georg Werner Fraatz. These were all as yet completely unproven in war. For both sides, the battle, when it came, would be a matter of learning the hard way.

LEFT: U-boat commander
Kapitänleutnant Hans Ey
takes the con.
(Photo: Horst Bredow)

BELOW: Type VIIC class U-
boat entering harbour. The Type
VIIC, which was the mainstay
of the U-boat Arm, had a range
of 8,500 miles and was capable
of maximum speeds of
17.3 knots surfaced and
7.6 knots submerged.
(Photo: Bundesarchiv, Koblenz)

7

The Other Enemy

For SC42 the threat of the U-boats had now become an irrelevance. Throughout that day the weather grew steadily worse, and as it did so the temperature dropped sharply. Then the driving rain turned to sleet, adding misery to discomfort and danger. There were few in the convoy who did not rue the day they had walked up the gangway of their ship.

Aboard the *Empire Springbuck*, lead ship in the third column, the suffering was intense. She was an old ship, her hull strained by carrying heavy cargoes over the years, her plates and frames wasted through lack of maintenance, her engine a miracle of make-do and mend. Weighed down under a full load of steel, the Newcastle-managed tramp was in dire trouble, groaning in every rivet each time she lifted to an oncoming wave, her propeller racing out of control as she dropped into the follow- ing trough. In continuing the struggle to maintain station in the convoy, Captain Walter O'Connell knew he was asking too much of his ship. Soon, something must give way, most prob- ably the engine. Then, unable to steer, she would be at the complete mercy of the waves, it being only a matter of time before she broke up. At 1900, O'Connell decided he had had enough and pulled the *Empire Springbuck* out of the convoy. With the wind and sea fine on the port bow, and with just sufficient way on her to steer, the ship rode more easily; but she also fell astern and became a straggler, a tempting morsel for any marauding U-boat

On the far side of the convoy, in column 9, the 5,229-ton *Muneric*, just a year younger than the *Empire Springbuck* and staggering under the burden of 9,000 tons of iron ore, was faring only marginally better. With the bulk of the ore stowed low down in her lower holds, she was "stiff" and responded to the waves with a quick, jerky motion, putting a great strain on hull and engines, not to mention those on hoard. However, being an oil-burner, the *Muneric* had an advantage over the *Empire Springbuck* in that her engineers had no difficulty in keeping a decent head of steam. Like every other ship in the convoy, though, she was taking a heavy pounding. The wind howled in her rigging like all the demons of hell let loose, spray soared over her bridge, coating her funnel white with salt, and the shock-like crash of her blunt bows into each advancing wave was felt and heard throughout the ship.

In the *Muneric's* wheelhouse, where a brace of inadequate steam radiators fought to keep the icy cold at bay, Captain Frank Baker thrust his hands deeper into the pockets of his duffel coat and bit hard on the stem of his empty pipe. Like Collins of the *Jedmoor*, he was amazed and angry at the stupid policy that had brought his ship 6,000 miles north from the waving palms of Rio de Janeiro into this dangerous Arctic wilderness on the pretext that she would enjoy safe conduct across the North Atlantic at the hands of the Navy. Baker put his face close to the wheelhouse window and peered out into the impenetrable darkness. Somewhere out there in the turmoil of this violent night—only God and their commanders knew where—were a destroyer and three corvettes of the Royal Canadian Navy. Brave and resolute though they might be, they lacked the experience of war and mustered between them only a handful of 4-inch guns and a few racks of depth charges. So armed, they were expected to defend this huge armada of merchant ships. Some safe conduct, indeed! If this had not been the stark reality of the situation it would have been laughable. Yet, if the Admiralty's statistics were to be believed, the *Muneric's* chances of reaching British waters intact were far greater in convoy than if she had made a dash from Rio unescorted.

The night that followed was for all the ships like a bad dream with no ending. The wind increased to Force 9, a strong gale, with the tops of the relentlessly marching waves tumbling into foaming white crests and filling the air with flying spume. Dark and forbidding clouds scudded past at mast-top height, and rain and sleet, borne horizontal on the shrieking wind, reduced visibility to a few hundred yards. All pretence of station-keeping was abandoned and ships fought merely to hold their bows up into the wind so that each advancing wall of water struck them only a glancing blow. Now was the time for pure, dogged seamanship. Nothing else mattered.

When a grey, reluctant dawn came on the 6th, it was esti-mated—and any talk of accuracy was farcical—that the convoy had made good only 15 miles in the past 24 hours. The destroyer *Skeena* had fared worst of all. Unable to ride the waves, Commander Hibbard had been forced to cut back to minimum revolutions in order to avoid reducing his ship to a heap of tangled metal. In consequence, *Skeena* ended up well astern of the rear ships of the convoy and powerless to close the gap. The corvettes *Alberni*, *Kenogami* and *Orillia* reported by R/T to Hibbard that they were still on station but unable to deviate from their course. The tiny warships were in fact slid-ing from trough to trough in a dark tortured world that was all their own, with all but a few hardy individuals on board prostrate with seasickness. As a fighting unit the 24th Escort Group had been rendered impotent by the awesome power of the North Atlantic.

At 1300, Admiral Sir Percy Noble, C-in-C Western Approaches, far removed from the fury of the sea in his Liverpool bunker, signalled a change of course which would take SC42 deeper into the Denmark Strait and, coincidentally, right into the heart of the storm. This did nothing to help morale; indeed, there were those who argued it was no longer worth prolonging this terrible trial by storm to avoid the U-boats. That nerves were stretched as taut as bow strings was graphically illustrated that night, when the Dutch ship *Trompenberg* inadvertently showed lights and was subjected to a fusillade of rifle shots from her nearest neighbour, the West Hartlepool tramp *Yearby*.

The torment went on and on, with every wretched, storm-racked hour stretching into an eternity; then, on the morning of the 7th, after five days of continuous gales, the weather finally relented. The barometer, after levelling out during the night, began slowly to rise again, the wind lost its power, and the waves no longer threatened. Overhead, the massed clouds showed signs of lifting, but the rain still fell, although much of the sting had gone out of it. The convoy's speed, which had averaged only 3 knots over the past four days, gradually moved up towards 5 knots. The waves were no longer breaking aboard the ships and men appeared on deck again, but treading warily, for the swell was still high. Tentative wisps of smoke issued from a forest of galley funnels, signalling the tantalising prospect of the first hot meal for days. Before that, however, there was a considerable amount of weather damage to be patched up, and soon the crisp, cold air resounded to the ring of hammers and the rasp of saws. At noon, *Skeena*, showing the scars of her prolonged battle with the elements, rejoined the convoy and passed through the ranks of the high-sided merchantmen. Commander Hibbard was relieved to see that, with the exception of a few gaps left by stragglers, SC42 was largely intact.

The wind and sea continued to subside during the night, and when daylight came on the 8th the weather was almost benign. A detailed count of the ships revealed that the *Empire Springbuck* was missing, and the 4,862-ton *Southgate* and the small Norwegian timber-carrier *Makefiell* were tagging along 6 miles astern. The others, at the commodore's urging, were slowly increasing speed.

In the late afternoon, *Skeena* received a signal from C-in-C Western Approaches giving the rendezvous point at which additional escorts from Iceland could be expected to join. This lay 400 miles to the northeast, no more than three days' steaming if the weather held. When the good news was passed around the convoy there was a visible surge of hope. SC42 had been at sea for nine days without a sign of the enemy. Was this to be an uneventful passage after all?

The mood of optimism was short-lived. At 2000, when the convoy was approximately 90 miles south of Cape Farewell the

Admiralty reported U-boats massing in the path of the convoy and recommended an emergency alteration of course to due north. Signal lamps flashed, and at 2005, following the *Everleigh's* lead, the 12 columns turned as one to head for the southern point of Greenland. Rear-Admiral MacKenzie passed the order to all ships to man their guns and post extra lookouts.

MacKenzie's intention, acting on Admiralty advice, was to steer for Cape Farewell until the land was sighted, some time on the morning of the 9th, and then to steam parallel to the coast of Greenland until the danger from the U-boats was passed. The plan was feasible, but the convoy had been without sights for five days, and its position was largely a matter of guesswork, possibly being out by as much as 20 miles. To steam north blindly through the night was to run the risk of the whole convoy piling up on the steep shores of Greenland. It therefore fell to *Skeena*, being the most manoeuvrable, to remain 3 miles ahead of the other ships during the hours of darkness. Commander Hibbard's thoughts on the use of his ship as a sacrificial lamb are not on record, and neither are his reactions on the receipt of an urgent signal from the C-in-C Western Approaches soon after *Skeena* moved into the van. The signal read: "On 8th September 64 ship in convoy SC42 intercepted a series of 20 dashes followed by 6 short breaking through on 353 kcs per second. Signals very loud and operator considers they emanated from ship in convoy. Signal your remarks." Ship no. 64 was the Norwegian tanker *Storaas*, and, had he been in a position to do so, Hibbard would have demanded an explanation of her master as to why he chose to break radio silence by reporting to Liverpool, instead of using his signal lamp to inform the commodore. Meanwhile, with danger drawing ever nearer, Hibbard was once again faced with the possibility of a renegade ship in the convoy. As before, however, he was powerless to take action.

The foul weather that had plagued SC42 for so long moved on across the North Atlantic. Some 350 miles east of Cape Farewell, the *Einvik's* lifeboats were already feeling the full lash of the wind and waves, but faring comparatively well. As the boats were each capable of carrying 30 men, they were not overcrowded, having only 11 men in one and 12 in the other, and, thanks largely to the foresight of Captain Wetteland, they contained ample clothing and provisions. Very wisely in these high latitudes, in addition to American-made rubber survival suits, Wetteland had stocked the boats with oilskins and heavy woollen jerseys, while, also at his urging, every crew member carried with him a "panic bag" packed with a few extras. Each boat contained 20 gallons of drinking water, 18 boxes of tinned Icelandic meatballs, biscuits, 500 cigarettes and a primus stove. Well clothed, sustained by a diet of meatballs and biscuits heated on the stove, and with cigarettes to round off each meal, the survivors were in good shape. The onset of bad weather made life that much more uncomfortable, but the sturdy boats sailed well and Wetteland anticipated reaching Iceland within seven days. Having seen no fewer than four U-boats hurrying westwards on the surface since the *Einvik* sank, he feared many others might not be as lucky as he and his men.

One of those sighted by Wetteland was another untried hopeful, U-81, commanded by Kapitänleutnant Friedrich Guggenberger. This Type VIIC was the first U-boat deployed off the north Russian coast following the outbreak of war between Germany and the Soviets in the previous June. Her initial patrol proved fruitless, and she returned to Trondheim in mid-August, leaving again for the North Atlantic on the 27th of that month. Now, five months after commissioning on the River Weser, U-81 carried the marks of her punishing training schedule and her subsequent service in the cold waters of the Barents Sea. Her once-immaculate grey paintwork was peeling and streaked with red rust, her hull dented by countless minor collisions with quays and wharves, and green weed grew from the wooden duckboards of her deck. Yet, in spite of her well used look, U-81 had not yet fired a shot in anger, a shortcoming Guggenberger, recently promoted from Oberleutnant and in command for the first time, fervently hoped would soon be rectified. Since receiving orders from BdU on the 5th to join up with the *Markgraf* group off Greenland, U-81's diesels had run hot.

When Captain Walter O'Connell took the *Empire Springbuck* out of convoy SC42 on the evening of the 5th, he did not do so lightly, for he had been down this road before. He remembered vividly the price his previous command, the *Hylton*, paid for straggling from her convoy. O'Connell had only just escaped with his life then and was not anxious to repeat the experience. His intention now was to rejoin SC42 as soon as the weather permitted, and when the wind and sea calmed down on the 7th O'Connell called on his chief engineer, 55-year-old Quintin Bell, to push the *Empire Springbuck's* engine to its utmost limits. Unfortunately, as it transpired, Bell and his engine excelled themselves, producing speeds in excess of 10 knots. This would have been fine, had not the convoy in the meantime altered course 45 degrees to port. O'Connell, unaware of this alteration, continued on a northeasterly course, with the result that, by the early hours of the 9th, the *Empire Sprlngbuck* was 140 miles ahead of SC42 and still chasing an empty horizon.

Unhappily for the *Empire Springbuck* the horizon was not as empty as it seemed. By pure chance, her path was converging on that of U-81, then on her way to join Dönitz's assembling wolf-pack. They met at a little before 1500 on 9 September in position 61°38' north 40°40' west. Guggenberger's salvo of two torpedoes caught the merchantman just forward of her bridge and she stopped dead in her tracks. Seconds later, her part cargo of explosives went up in a sheet of flame and the *Empire Springbuck* was torn apart. The steel in her holds took her to the bottom like a stone, and with her went captain Walter O'Connell and the 41 men who sailed under his command. By a cruel combination of circumstances, first blood in the battle for SC42 went to the *Markgraf* group.

Sunrise is always a time for reflection on the bridge of a merchant ship, time to take stock after a long night's vigil, time to prepare for a new day. When the sun came up on the morning of the 9th, the *Jedmoor's* bridge was no exception to the norm. Captain Robert Collins, up and about since before dawn, and Chief Officer Leslie Moller, on watch from 0400, were both unshaven and jaded, yet in a buoyant mood. This was not surprising, for it was a morning of breathtaking beauty. Gone were the grey skies, the keening wind, the angry waves; the sky was blue, the sea calm and the air crisp and still.

ATTACK & SINK

To port lay the mountains of Greenland, the world's largest island, discovered by Erik the Red in AD 982 and said to have been so named to attract potential settlers. The reality must have been a great disappointment for these unfortunates. Greenland is a frigid land, with 85 per cent of its 840,000 square miles covered by a permanent icecap, where the thermometer falls to -23°C. in winter, and rarely exceeds 10°C. at the height of summer. Nevertheless, the view from the sea was impressive as SC42 steamed parallel to, and 15 miles off, the coast, having by the grace of God and clever dead reckoning sighted the shore at first light.

The sheer beauty of the scene was not lost on Dan Hortop as, well muffled against the cold, he turned to on deck with the watch below. The soaring white mountains with their sparkling glaciers running right down to the blue sea were a breathtaking sight, and it was with some reluctance that Hortop turned his mind to the mundane task of painting ship. After being confined so long in a world that alternated between a bridge where the wind and rain beat a man almost senseless, and a damp, ill-lit fo'c'sle reeking of carbolic and stale cigarette smoke, the morning was like the glimpse of Paradise itself. Then there was also the mouthwatering smell of early breakfast cooking in the galley. At that precise moment, war or no war, Dan Hortop, humble sailor in a British tramp, would not have changed places with the King himself.

Looking down from the bridge, Captain Collins, having enjoyed the luxury of a hurried wash and shave, shared Hortop's sentiments. That is until, without warning, the steady beat of the *Jedmoor's* engine slowed, and then stopped altogether. Chief Engineer Robert Adamson came to the bridge a few minutes later with bad news. The trouble which had plagued them on the outward passage had returned; the fuel lines were again blocked, and it would take some time to clear them. Meanwhile, the *Jedmoor* was engineless and drifting.

Two black balls were hoisted at the masthead, indicating that the *Jedmoor* was "not under command," and 15 minutes later the last ship of the column, the ore-carrier *Hampton Lodge*, steamed past with a reassuring wave from her bridge. Some time after her came the two stragglers, *Southgate* and *Makefjell*, hurrying to rejoin the convoy. And then the *Jedmoor* was alone.

If there were U-boats about, and Collins had no illusions that this was the case, then his ship was in great danger. Once again, he had occasion to send his men to man their guns.

Rear-Admiral MacKenzie watched the *Jedmoor* drop astern with an anxious frown. During the past night HMCS *Skeena* had reported a great deal of wireless activity in the vicinity, clearly identifiable as chatter between U-boats searching for the convoy. Much as he would have liked to send a corvette to watch over the *Jedmoor*, MacKenzie knew this was impossible, for the pitiful size of the escort would not allow for such extravagance. The Newcastle tramp must fend for herself, just as MacKenzie assumed the missing *Empire Springbuck* was doing. The commodore was still unaware of the fate of this ship, for so abrupt had been her end that she had gone down without sending an SOS.

There was, as yet, no sign that SC42 had been sighted by the enemy, but MacKenzie knew this was now only a matter of time. In a convoy of 63 ships, many of them old coal-burners, some smoke was inevitable, but on this fine, clear morning SC42 resembled a large industrial city on the move. Dozens of long plumes of black smoke reached slywards, to merge and spread out into a dark cloud, which was undoubtedly visible for many miles in all directions. The worst culprits were the 43-year-old Norwegian whale-oil tanker *Lancing* and the smaller Dutchman *Zypenberg*, but all the coal-burners were guilty to some degree. In their defence, it must be said that the majority of them, being old, poorly maintained and too long out of dry dock, were hard-pressed to maintain steam. Added to this, inferior coal and firemen who were overtired or not experienced enough with the shovel and

Able Seaman Dan Hortop, MV Jedmoor. *(Photo: F. C. Hortop)*

slice resulted in funnels (which would normally trail only a harmless wisp of smoke) belching like factory chimneys. After days of complaining, threatening and cajoling with no sign of improvement, MacKenzie had resigned himself to the inevitable.

That Admiral Dönitz knew of the existence of SC42 is beyond doubt but, up until that morning, he had only a hazy idea of its whereabouts. Certainly, he would not have been inclined to search for the convoy so close to the coast of Greenland. The patrol line of the *Markgraf* group was at this time some 60 miles to the east of Cape Farewell, and it seems likely that the diversion of the convoy to the north would have taken it around and out of sight of the northernmost unit of the *Markgraf* group Had it not been for the arrival of U-85 on the scene, the subsequent fate of SC42 might have been quite different.

8

First Contact

The gathering canopy of smoke over SC42, rising on the morning thermals to several thousand feet, was visible from afar, and it was this that U-85's lookouts sighted low down on the horizon at daylight.

U-85, a Type VIIB, built at Lübeck and commissioned only three months earlier, was at the time more concerned with making contact with the rest of the *Markgraf* group than searching for potential targets. By chance, or poor navigation, she had strayed further north than intended and, so it turned out, changed the course of history.

Oberleutnant-zur-See Eberhard Greger, U-85's commander, at first judged the smoke to be a patch of cloud, but as the sight strengthened he decided it was worth investigation. Under full power, the submarine surged forward, her twin exhausts belching black smoke. For the next hour she raced northwards at 17 knots, the distant "cloud" becoming more obviously man-made as she closed the gap.

Ironically, it was the U-boat's own exhaust smoke that in turn attracted the attention of a lone British aircraft operating at the extreme limit of her range. The aircraft came roaring in at low level and was almost on top of the U-boat before being sighted. Greger, fearing the worst, took his boat below the waves at a rush. He was not to know that the aircraft carried no bombs.

It was another hour before Greger felt it safe to bring U-85 back to the surface, by which time the skies were empty. Only a faint grey smudge on the horizon to the northeast indicated that the convoy–and Greger was now convinced it must be a convoy–had passed by and was pulling away rapidly. He estimated it to be already 35-40 miles off, and assuming she was able to stay on the surface U-85 would take at least four hours to intercept it. Once again Greger spoke urgently to his chief engineer, Hans Sanger, and the submarine's 3,000-horsepower diesels began working up to full speed. Meanwhile, U-85's radioman tapped out a terse message to BdU reporting the convoy's position.

In accordance with standard wolf-pack practice it was now Greger's task to shadow the convoy, at the same time acting as a homing beacon for the other boats of the *Markgraf* group. When the pack had gathered in sufficient strength, a concerted attack would be made under the cover of darkness. Until then, it was incumbent on Greger not to alert the convoy in any way.

U-85 pressed on at full speed for another hour, during which time the masts and funnels of SC42 lifted over the horizon. Greger was jubilant, for he had obviously stumbled on a huge fleet of slow-moving enemy ships. Keeping them in sight until other U-boats arrived on the scene would not be difficult. He called for reduced speed and settled down to a long, tedious pursuit. Darkness was still more than ten hours away.

Greger soon became aware that, in spite of his reduction in speed, U-85 was steadily overtaking a lone ship, which seemed to be straggling astern of the convoy. Half-an-hour later and the ship was only 10 miles off, completely alone, and quite plainly stopped. She appeared to be a freighter of about 5,000 tons and heavily loaded–the proverbial sitting duck. Using his powerful Zeiss binoculars, Greger carefully searched both the sea and sky for signs of an escorting warship or aircraft, but could see neither. For a moment–only a moment–he wrestled with his conscience; his orders were to shadow and not attack the convoy. Did this ship, however, drifting on her own, constitute part of the convoy? The temptation to make U-85's long overdue kill was too much. With a determined movement, Eberhard Greger pressed the button of the diving klaxon and slid down Into the control room, slamming the hatch behind him.

The *Jedmoor* had been lying stopped for two hours, and the convoy was hull-down on the horizon to the northeast. Captain Robert Collins, a normally unexcitable man, paced the bridge with a step that was becoming increasingly impatient. The lookouts were doubled up and all guns manned, and that was the limit of Collins' options. Now he could only wait and worry, conscious all the time that with a flat-calm sea and excellent visibility his stationary ship was an easy target for even the most inexpert of U-boat commanders. To add to his discomfort, black whales were blowing all around the *Jedmoor*, each one a potential U-boat to the jumpy lookouts. Collins silently cursed the engine that had once again let him down, at the same time admiring the cool bravery of Chief Engineer Adamson and his men labouring in the bowels of the ship. Robert Adamson, a survivor of a torpedoing in the First World War, more than anyone knew the fearful risk they were taking. Collins halted his anxious pacing to accept a mug of hot coffee from his third officer, 28-year-old John O'Neil, who appeared to be impervious to the threatening danger. Approaching 60, and with ten stress-filled days behind him, Collins was beginning to feel age pressing down on him, and envied the younger man's nonchalance. The indulgence lasted only for seconds, being wiped away by an urgent shout from the lookout man in the port wing of the bridge.

Instantly alert, Collins followed the man's outstretched arm and saw the twin tracks of torpedoes streaking across the *Jedmoor's* bows from port to starboard. Surely the gods must have been watching over the *Jedmoor* on that September morning, for even though she was stationary the torpedoes missed the ship by 50 yards or more.

The alarm bells, triggered by O'Neil, were ringing as Collins snatched up his binoculars and scanned the horizon to port. He was not surprised to see, amongst the spouting whales, the thin stalk of a periscope. He quickly alerted his gun's crew, standing by at the 4-inch on the poop, and ordered O'Neil to fire distress rockets to inform the convoy of the attack.

That the *Jedmoor* escaped an abrupt and violent end there and then was due to a combination of circumstances. When, at precisely 0959, having manoeuvred into a favourable position on the *Jedmoor's* port side, Eberhard Greger fired his first torpedo; it proved to be a tube-runner, sinking deep and passing below the merchantman's keel. This was disappointment enough, but when inexperienced hands were slow in filling ballast tanks to compensate for the loss of weight incurred by firing the torpedo the U-boat porpoised. This upset Greger's aim when he fired the other three bow tubes, all of which consequently missed. It was the tracks of two of these latter torpedoes that Collins sighted. Greger now turned U-85's stern to the *Jedmoor* and fired a final shot–which also went wide. Thoroughly disgusted at his bad luck, and with all tubes empty, he then dived deep to reload.

At 1150, having reloaded his tubes, Greger brought U-85 up to periscope depth, only to find his window of opportunity closed. The destroyer *Skeena* and the corvette *Orillia* had abandoned the convoy and were standing guard over the *Jedmoor*. For the next 40 minutes the two warships circled the lone merchant ship dropping depth charges, and Greger was obliged to retire to a safe distance.

Rear-Admiral MacKenzie, viewing matters from the bridge of the *Everleigh*, was sceptical of the reported attack on the *Jedmoor*, being of the opinion that her crew had mistaken one of the many whales in the vicinity for a U-boat. However, the commodore did consider it prudent to warn all ships to man their guns and keep a sharp lookout for signs of the enemy. Even if the convoy had not yet already been discovered, it was making so much smoke that it could only be a matter of time before this happened.

The C-in-C Western Approaches in Liverpool, Admiral Sir Percy Noble, on the other hand, took very seriously the *Jedmoor's* wirelessed SSS (submarine attack), relayed to him by Iceland. His plot showed at least twelve U-boats in the area of SC42, which could only indicate that a mass attack was imminent. He informed MacKenzie and Hibbard of his opinion, and ordered the Royal Navy's 20th Escort Group to sail at once from Reykjavik to reinforce Hibbard's tiny Canadian force. Additionally, HMS *Douglas* and other ships of the 2nd Escort

Group, then with the fast westbound convoy ON13, were instructed to break off from the convoy and return to Iceland to refuel, before going to SC42's aid. It was clear to Sir Percy that neither force would reach the convoy in time to prevent the impending massacre, but this was the best he could do with the meagre resources at his disposal. For some unexplained reason, the admiral had not been informed of the presence of the corvettes *Chambly* and *Moosejaw*, carrying out training exercises in the Denmark Strait only 400 miles ahead of SC42. Fortunately, the Northern Forces commander in St. John's had already taken the initiative and ordered *Chambly* and *Moosejaw* to join Commander Hibbard's hard-pressed team with all dispatch. Again, for no apparent reason, St. John's omitted to inform Hibbard that help was on the way.

The news of the *Jedmoor's* narrow escape spread through the convoy like wildfire, prompting a general tightening-up all round. Lookouts watched the horizon with renewed diligence, guns' crews checked their ready-use ammunition and lifejackets were kept closer at hand. It was unlikely that there would be any major attack in daylight, but the coming night promised to be filled with danger.

On board the vice-commodore ship *Thistleglen*, leading the fourth column of SC42, Captain Gordon Dobson had little need to call for increased vigilance. The Sunderland ship was carrying 7,640 tons of steel and pig-iron, and there was not a man on board who dared to forget this. With this solid mass in her holds one torpedo would be enough to take her to the bottom in seconds.

Owned by Allan Black and Company and built at Sunderland in 1929, the 4,748-ton *Thistleglen* carried a crew of 49, including six DEMS gunners. Tramp though she might be, and built at a time of great economic depression, she was a good ship to sail in. Her accommodation was basic, but clean and comfortable, and the food her galley served was of a reasonable standard. Her crew, who hailed mainly from the east coast of England, from the ports of Sunderland, Grimsby and Newcastle, were a tough, resourceful bunch, closely welded together by 42-year-old Gordon Dobson, a Scot from Gretna Green.

ATTACK & SINK

The *Thistleglen* had sailed from Hull in ballast in early July, crossing the North Atlantic in convoy without harassment. Two weeks spent in New York loading cargo were a fairy-tale interlude for men used to the blacked-out austerity of wartime Britain, the long stress-filled watches on a hostile sea, and to cat-napping fully dressed with lifejacket close to hand. The United States was not yet committed to the war, the lights shone brightly in her cities, the shops were full of undreamt-of luxuries, and the open-hearted Americans treated British merchant seamen with astonishing warmth. This was so different to the reception they received in their own country, where merchant seamen were often regarded as lower-deck cousins of the Royal Navy, to be tolerated in the interest of the prosecution of the war, but not to be indulged. That these men were dying in their thousands to keep the sea lanes open was either unknown to the people of Britain or of no concern to them.

On the far side of the convoy, leading column 12, was the 3,252-ton Danish motor-vessel *Sally Maersk*, commanded by Captain J. K. Lindberg. The *Sally Maersk*, like most of the merchantmen in SC42, was no stranger to the hazards of war. Caught in the West African port of Dakar when France capitulated in June 1940, she was seized by the Vichy authorities and seemed destined to see out the war under Axis control; but Captain Lindberg and his crew of 33 had ideas to the contrary. When on her way into the Mediterranean under escort by the French Navy, she escaped under cover of darkness and reached a British port. She was then taken under the Red Ensign, being managed for the Ministry of War Transport by the Liverpool shipowners Moss Hutchinson, but she retained her Danish crew. A few months later, while off the coast of Portugal, she was attacked and damaged by German aircraft, and was towed into Gibraltar with a number of her crew wounded by cannon shells. On this, her third voyage under the British flag, she was loaded with 4,527 tons of wheat from the Canadian port of Three Rivers, to be discharged at Sharpness, in the Bristol Channel.

When the commodore gave the word to man the guns, little action was required in the *Sally Maersk*. The Danish ship was armed with only two Hotchkiss .303 machine-guns and a

Holman Projector, a crude grenade-thrower operated by pressurised steam and designed for use against low-flying aircraft. In theory, the Holman Projector hurled a hand-grenade 300-400 feet in the air, where it was intended to explode with devastating effect in the path of an attacking aircraft. In practice, a merchant ship's steam pressure being what it was, the bomb usually rose only a few feet in the air, before falling back to the deck and threatening the projector's operator with a messy end. The Holman Projector was the only "secret weapon" ever supplied to British merchant ships, and its only recorded success was in mock battles involving rotten potatoes waged between ships in convoy.

While the farcical Holman Projector defended the head of column 12, at the rear of column 4 was the very latest in merchant ship protection. The *Empire Hudson* carried a catapult-launched Hurricane on her foredeck, a desperate measure designed to deal with desperate circumstances. For some time North Atlantic convoys had been under attack from long-range Focke-Wulf Kondors operating from bases in France and Norway. These huge aircraft, with a range of over 2,000 miles and a bomb load of 4,626 lbs., were able to strike well beyond the cover of British land-based fighters. In the first five months of 1941 the Focke-Wulfs sank over 500,000 tons of Allied merchant shipping, this being 13 per cent of all losses during that time. In addition, these planes acted as spotters for the U-boats, circling a convoy out of range of its guns while radioing directions to the wolf-packs. It was to combat the threat of the Focke-Wulfs that the CAM (Catapult Aircraft Merchantmen) ship was born.

The CAM ship, usually a newly-built merchant ship, carried a Hawker Sea Hurricane Mark 1 launched by a simple rocket-propelled catapult mounted in the bows of the ship. The Sea Hurricane, developed from the famous land-based Battle of Britain aircraft, was a single-seat fighter powered by a 1,030-horsepower Rolls-Royce Merlin engine. It carried eight .303 Browning machine-guns, had a top speed of 300 miles per hour, a ceiling of 30,000 feet and a range of 450 miles. As with every new innovation, the CAM ship had its weaknesses. To outside observers, the flash and smoke of the catapult resembled a bomb-hit on the ship, and the aircraft often came under fire from nearby ships as it climbed skywards. Despite this, the Sea Hurricanes, flown by Fleet Air Arm pilots, were an immediate success, shooting down their first Focke-Wulf on 3 August 1941, some 200 miles west of Cape Finisterre. Unfortunately for the Hurricane pilots their mission was one-way only. Once catapulted off, unless within reach of land, they had the unenviable choice of either baling out or crash-landing on the water, for they could not return to their parent ship.

SC42's CAM ship, the *Empire Hudson*, was one of the new wartime replacements then coming down the slipways of British shipyards in growing numbers. As such, she was of a very basic design in all respects, being little more than a large steam-propelled barge with accommodation added. Her builders claimed she was capable of a service speed of 10.5 knots, but the very most she ever achieved was 10 knots, and that only when she was flying light and in calm weather. Like all her class, she was grossly underpowered for her size, and, loaded as she now was with 9,562 tons of Canadian wheat, she was reduced to a little over 8 knots.

Commanded by Captain John Cooke, a 34-year-old Londoner, and managed for the Ministry of War Transport by Stanley and John Thompson Ltd. of London, the *Empire Hudson* mounted, in addition to her Hurricane, a 4-inch, two Hotchkiss, two Marlin and two Lewis machine-guns. She carried a crew of 58, which included six DEMS gunners, a Fleet Air Arm pilot, a flight directing officer, four RAF mechanics, a naval catapult hand and two RDF operators, who manned her early-type radar. She was, then, part-warship, part-merchantman, with the potentially fatal handicap of being too slow and cumbersome to be really effective as either.

U-85's sighting signal was followed two hours later by a general call from BdU to all U-boats in the area to close in on SC42. Dönitz had by this time established that the convoy was only weakly defended, and was anxious to mount an attack before the Royal Navy was in a position to bring in reinforcements.

One of those to receive Dönitz's signal was U-432, then only 100 miles to the east of SC42. U-432, a Type VIIC built at

Danzig and commissioned in April 1941, was, like the majority of the *Markgraf* group, on her maiden patrol and had yet to prove her worth. In command was 26-year-old Kapitänleutnant Heinz-Otto Schultze, a courageous and resourceful officer. On receipt of BdU's signal, Schultze headed for the convoy at all possible speed on the surface. At 1445, he sighted the conspicuous pall of smoke, and then patiently began to work ahead of the enemy ships, being careful not to betray his presence. As he did so, other members of the group moved in from all sides.

Following the *Jedmoor* incident and warnings from C-in-C Western Approaches, Rear-Admiral MacKenzie and Commander Hibbard had little doubt that the convoy was being shadowed, but there was nothing they could do to alter the situation. The ships were making a good 6 knots, which was as much as could be expected of them, and the four escorts were spread to best advantage around the long perimeter they were required to protect. The coming of the night, which promised to be fine with a full moon, was awaited with some trepidation.

At 1714, one hour before sunset, and with the convoy 80 miles NNE of Cape Farewell, *Skeena's* wireless office, listening on 500 kcs, again picked up very strong signals similar to those heard on the 5th and reported by the Norwegian tanker *Storaas* on the 8th. This time it was possible for *Skeena* to take a quick bearing on the signal with her W/T direction-finder. The bearing was found to pass through the leading ship of the starboard outer column, which was the Danish ship *Sally Maersk*. The inference was that someone on board that ship might be deliberately transmitting in order to betray the convoy and provide a beacon for the U-boats to home in on. However, bearings taken with a W/T direction-finder are affected by atmospheric conditions and are notoriously inaccurate around sunrise and sunset. The signals could have been emanating from any one of half-a-dozen ships in the vicinity of the *Sally Maersk*, and there was no way of pinpointing the culprit.

9

The Wolves Close In

Soon after 1830, the sun dipped behind the snow-capped peaks of Greenland, momentarily turning them blood-red. It was an awesome sight, seen by those on watch on the salt-stained bridges and at the guns of SC42 as a precursor of events to come. There were few who, despite layers of thick clothing piled on to combat the numbing sub-Arctic cold, did not give an involuntary shiver.

As a grey twilight set in on the orderly ranks of the convoy, still steaming on a course parallel to the coast, Rear-Admiral Mackenzie reached a decision to alter to the northeast towards the arranged rendezvous with the destroyers of the Iceland Force, 300 miles into the Denmark Strait. He was of the opinion that the *Jedmoor* incident earlier in the day, if not the work of over-active imaginations, must have been caused by an isolated U-boat. Had he known of the sinking of the *Empire Springbuck*, he might have been of a different opinion. As it was, he was satisfied he had pushed far enough north to avoid the wolf-pack reported by Liverpool. At 1900, he gave the order to alter course to the northeast. SC42 had by then reached latitude 61° north, and was 35 miles southwest of the position where the *Empire Springbuck* went down. MacKenzie was unwittingly taking the convoy directly into danger.

Coloured signal lights burned briefly in the gathering dusk, and the 12 columns of ships wheeled slowly to starboard under their attendant cloud of smoke. It was with a certain sense of relief that they at last set out to cross the broad Atlantic. All that had gone before, the nervous traverse of the Gulf of St. Lawrence, the trauma of the Belle Isle Strait, and the horrors and discomforts of the storm that seemed to have no end, were only a prelude to the main drama to come. Ahead lay 1,200 miles of open ocean, in which another page of history must he written.

Two hours passed before all the ships had settled down on the new course, by which time the moon was high, shining full and brilliant in a cloudless sky. The wind was light and variable, the sea calm, with only a long, gently undulating swell to tell of the weather recently experienced. Visibility was excellent, the distant mountains of Greenland still showing up on the port quarter, sharply etched by the bright moonlight.

To Captain Harold Hudson, commanding the 4,906-ton *Bretwalda*, third ship in the port outer column, conditions were ideal for the U-boats, and being in a highly exposed position he was uneasy. Built in Sunderland in 1939, and owned by Hall Brothers of Newcastle, the *Bretwalda* was deep-loaded with 8,250 tons of bagged flour from Montreal for London. Northeast-Coast tramp though she might be, she was capable of 10.5 knots–4 knots faster than the convoy's present speed–and Hudson would have liked nothing better than to give her her head. But patience must prevail, and he could do no more than ensure that the ship was at a high state of readiness for whatever the night might bring. Glancing astern at the next ship in line, the Middlesbrough-bound *Muneric* staggering along under a full load of iron ore, Hudson took comfort in the thought that his problems were minor in comparison with those of the men who commanded the *Muneric.*

Unknown to Hudson, Heinz-Otto Schultze in U-432 was already in position on the port side of the convoy, submerged and running his periscope over the line of ships. It was a pretty sight for the U-boat commander. Leading the column was the 5,299-ton *Trefusis*, immediately behind her the diminutive Norwegian *Stargard*, followed by the *Bretwalda*, the *Muneric* and the 3,650-ton *Baron Ramsay*, carrying between them 30,000 tons of grain, flour, timber, steel and general cargo. Every single ton was vital to Britain's continued existence.

Another half-hour passed before Schultze was satisfied with his careful preparations, then, at 2130, he fired a fan of four torpedoes, aiming for the middle ship in the line, the unsuspecting *Bretwalda*. Unfortunately for Schultze, U-432 lost her trim following the discharge of the torpedoes and dived out of control. The German commander was unable to see the result of his salvo.

Captain Hudson, on the bridge of the *Bretwalda*, the main target of Schultze's attack, on the other hand, had a grandstand view he would undoubtedly remember for the rest of his life. Powerless to take avoiding action, he watched in horror as three torpedoes trailing phosphorescent bubbles raced towards his ship. Miraculously, one passed ahead, one astern, and one beneath the *Bretwalda*. Hudson shouted for rockets to be fired to warn other ships of the attack and, as he did so, two cables astern, a brilliant flash and a fountain of water and debris erupted from the *Muneric*. Schultze's fourth torpedo had found a victim.

In the confusion that followed, no one witnessed the ultimate fate of the *Muneric*, but it must be assumed that the torpedo broke her back and, weighted down by her cargo of iron ore, she sank within seconds. With her went 63 men, including two hopefuls who had stowed away in Rio de Janeiro in search of a new life.

U-432's action did not go completely unavenged. The track of one of her torpedoes was seen by the corvette *Kenogami*, at the time carrying out a speculative sweep astern of the convoy. Asdic contact was established and Lieutenant-Commander Jackson immediately moved in to attack, but before depth charges could be dropped the contact was lost.

The action did not finish there. *Kenogami* now sighted a U-boat on the surface, 1,000 yards off, heading at speed away from the convoy and into the darkness offered by the backdrop of the coast. *Kenogami* worked up to her maximum speed of 16 knots and opened fire with her 4-inch, but the U-boat—it was Eberhard Greger's U-85—made good her escape into the shadows. As *Kenogami* was not equipped with starshells, she could not illuminate her target, and Jackson reluctantly ordered his gun's crew to cease fire. Before returning to the convoy

Kenogami dropped a single depth charge as a somewhat futile warning to the U-boats.

Aboard *Skeena*, Commander Hibbard had received word from Iceland that the 20th Escort Group had sailed to rendezvous with SC42. The group was hardly an impressive show of force, consisting only of the corvettes HMS *Gladiolus*, HMS *Mimosa* and HMCS *Westaskiwin*, and the armed trawlers HMS *Buttermere* and *Windermere*. Meanwhile, the rendezvous point was still 48 hours away and the U-boats had begun their attack.

When Hibbard learned that *Kenogami* had made contact with the enemy, he took *Skeena* down the port side of the convoy and carried out a starshell search. This proved fruitless, and the brilliant light provided by the shells probably exacerbated the situation, serving only to expose further the slow-moving columns of merchantmen.

The *Everleigh's* signal lamp began to flash urgently and *Skeena* returned to the head of the convoy. The commodore reported that a surfaced U-boat had been seen on the *Everleigh's* port bow soon after the torpedoing of the *Muneric*. This may only have been U-85 or U-432 making good its escape, but the mere fact that the U-boat was on the surface showed the contempt with which the enemy regarded SC42's defences. Rear-Admiral MacKenzie was, quite rightly, alarmed.

At 2210, the *Dundrum Castle* and the *Sarthe*, lead ships of columns 5 and 6, both reported on W/T a U-boat on the surface ahead of the convoy. MacKenzie ordered an emergency turn of 45 degrees to starboard, which undoubtedly saved the two reporting ships from destruction. As the ships turned away from the danger, U-81, stealthily moving in on the convoy's port bow, loosed off a spread of four torpedoes. Friedrich Guggenberger later claimed hits on three ships, but in reality all his torpedoes missed, and as U-81 turned away to run parallel to the convoy, she came under fire from the guns of the *Dundrum Castle* and the *Sarthe*. Guggenberger quickly retired into the darkness to the west and submerged to reload his empty tubes.

Now, it seemed, the battle was to be joined in earnest. Flares and rockets soared into the night sky, whistles screeched, and tracer arced across the water as nervous gunners

Canadian "Flower" class corvette on
escort duty in the North Atlantic,
from a painting by Commander E. M. Chadwick.

fired at shadowy forms slipping silently through the ranks of
the convoy. It is not known exactly how many of the *Markgraf*
group were then in the vicinity of SC42, but it is certain that
at least eight U-boats were involved. The advantage the
Germans enjoyed could hardly have been greater. Adding to
the painfully slow progress of the merchantmen–6.5 knots is 8
miles per hour, or the speed of a frisky carthorse–and the paucity of escorts, nature was also ranged against them. The moon
was a great silver ball in a clear, star-filled sky, moonbeams
danced on the oily surface of a flat-calm sea, and, to complete
this unbelievable scene, the Northern lights had chosen this
night to put on a dazzling display. The unfortunate SC42 was
caught onstage in the full glare of a battery of lighting no
human hand could extinguish.

Then, just as the action appeared likely to move to a swift climax, all went quiet, and for more than an hour the convoy steamed on without harassment. During this time a veil of thin, high cloud spread across the sky, dulling the light of the moon and shortening the visibility. Rear-Admiral MacKenzie took advantage of the lull to move the Norwegian ship *Vestland* into the gap left by the sinking of the *Muneric*. The 1,934-ton *Vestland*, loaded with timber and commanded by Captain Leonard Terjesen, was to play a vital part in later events.

Following his torpedoing of the *Muneric* and *Kenogami's* rapid intervention, Schultze took U-432 deep. At 2258, being satisfied that the furore he had created had died down, he resurfaced and hauled ahead of the convoy for a surface attack. Unhappily for Schultze, the sky then cleared, leaving the surface of the sea bathed in the full glow of the moon. U-432 was sighted by the leading ships of the convoy and the alarm was raised. Urgent whistle blasts rent the air, rockets flared and machine-guns opened fire. Luckily for Schultze and his men, none of the merchantman's 4-inch guns would train far enough forward to be effective, or U-432 might well have been in serious danger.

Three-quarters of a mile astern in the tanker *Tachee*, rear ship of column 4, Captain William Bannan was a concerned witness to the dramatic events. Being situated directly on top of 8,500 tons of highly inflammable oil, he was uneasy, but had little time to dwell on the danger as the commodore had signalled for a 45-degree emergency turn to port.

Meanwhile, Oberleutnant-zur-See Georg-Werner Fraatz in U-652 was stealthily overtaking the convoy on the surface from the starboard quarter. Carefully matching the ships' alteration of course to port, Fraatz entered between columns 7 and 8, but had not progressed far when the submarine was seen by lookouts aboard the *Knoll* and *PLM 13*, the rearmost ships of these columns. Both ships sounded a warning with their whistles, and the Norwegian-manned *Knoll* opened fire with her only armament, a .303 Hotchkiss. The range was only 300 yards, and some 20 rounds were seen to strike the U-boat's conning tower, no doubt giving Fraatz a severe fright.

Fraatz would have been even more concerned if he had known that, at the same time, the nearby *Vestland's* gun's crew had U-652 in the sights of their 4-inch. The U-boat missed almost certain destruction when the first shell loaded jammed in the breech of the Norwegian's 1902-vintage gun, and could not be cleared. Several other ships opened fire with machine-guns, but the small-calibre bullets had little effect, other than to ensure that those in the conning tower of U-652 kept their heads well down.

While the bullets were flying in the rear of SC42, *Skeena* was ahead of the convoy, close on the *Everleigh's* starboard bow, tracking U-432, which had dived. The pandemonium taking place astern was a clear indication of a serious attack, so Commander Hibbard wasted no further time on the elusive U-432. Calling for full speed, he took *Skeena* across the *Everleigh's* bows and charged down between columns 6 and 7 towards the rear of the convoy. It was most inopportune that Rear-Admiral MacKenzie should choose this moment to throw the convoy into another emergency turn to port. Before Hibbard's horrified eyes, what had been an open lane of water suddenly became impassable as the slab-sided merchant ships swung ponderously across the speeding destroyer's path.

Skeena was hemmed in on all sides, and there was no way back. Now James Hibbard's long years of training and experience with the Royal Canadian Navy were put to the test. He was not found wanting. Using full helm and full power ahead and astern on the engines, he threw *Skeena* from side to side, scraping past the bow of one ship, skidding around the stern of the next, dodging and weaving in a nightmare high-speed dash that might at any minute end in disaster. Ship's whistles screamed in protest, disembodied voices bawled obscenities through megaphones, but Hibbard kept his nerve. There was no horrendous collision that would surely have wiped out the only really effective unit of SC42's escort.

While the destroyer was passing the 4,862-ton Northeast Coast tramp *Southgate*, fourth ship in column 7, U-652 was spotted on the surface close to starboard of the merchantman. Hibbard wrenched *Skeena* around the stern of the *Southgate*, intending to ram the U-boat, but his path was blocked by other ships in the column.

Apart from a few paint chips on her conning tower, U-652 was as yet unscathed, but Fraatz realised that it was only a matter of time before the attacking destroyer or one or more of the merchant ships brought their big guns to bear. He decided to dive, but before doing so he swung the U-boat to port and loosed off two torpedoes in the general direction of *Skeena*. Both missed the destroyer and carried on into the massed ranks of merchantmen.

From the bridge of the *Baron Pentland*, rear ship of column 4, Captain Alexander Campbell watched with undisguised admiration *Skeena's* efforts to come to grips with the U-boat. He failed to see the track of one of Fraatz's roving torpedoes, which having passed through two lines of ships homed in on the *Baron Pentland*. The torpedo slammed into the timber-carrier's starboard side abaft the bridge and exploded with a thunderous roar. Campbell swung around to see a tall column of water carrying hatchboards, tarpaulins and much of the contents of his ship's coal-bunkers erupting skywards. The *Baron Pentland* then listed heavily to starboard and there was a second explosion, which Campbell assumed to be one of his boilers blowing up.

The double explosion was clearly heard two ships ahead on the bridge of the *Tachee*, where Captain Bannan was concentrating on bringing his ship around 45 degrees to port, as specified by the commodore's order. Bannan glanced aft towards the sound just in time to see a long line of frothing bubbles racing in on the starboard quarter of his own ship. Fraatz's second torpedo had arrived.

It was too late for Bannan to take avoiding action and the torpedo struck the tanker in her aftermost cargo tank. The *Tachee* shook violently, as if in the grip of a giant hand, a gusher of oil shot high into the sky, and then the night was turned into day as the after part of the ship went up in flames.

U-652 was forced to dive, which should have given *Skeena* the opportunity to attack with depth charges, but owing to the churning wakes of so many ships manoeuvring in the area, asdic contact could not be obtained. Hibbard searched for 20 minutes, dropping a number of probing charges, but without result. Fraatz had escaped.

Both the *Baron Pentland* and the *Tachee* were still afloat, although obviously badly damaged. A hurried inspection below decks had shown Campbell that the *Baron Pentland's* engine room, boiler room and nos. 2 and 3 cargo holds were already flooded. A large hole had been blown in the deck forward of the bridge, and the starboard lifeboat was missing. Casualties were mercifully light—only the engineer of the watch and one fireman were missing. It seemed pointless to take the risk of the crippled ship sinking under them, so Campbell crammed the remaining 38 men of his crew into the port lifeboat and pulled away from the *Baron Pentland*, intending to stand off until daylight.

The situation aboard the *Tachee* was more serious. Although no one had been killed or injured, the after cargo tanks had been laid open to the sea, and the pump room was flooded with oil from the punctured tanks and was on fire. This, in turn, had set fire to the fuel oil in no. 8 tank, which was blazing fiercely. As with all tankers of her day, the *Tachee's* crew's accommodation was split, the master, navigating and radio officers having cabins amidships, under the bridge, and the engineers and ratings living right aft, over the engine room. The fire was between the two sections, leaping flames and dense clouds of smoke turning the intervening deck into an inferno, and effectively cutting off one end of the ship from the other. Bannan's immediate fear was that the fire would spread to the lighter-viscosity diesel oil in the forward tanks. If this happened the ship was doomed.

Pausing only to scoop up the ship's secret books and hurl them over the side in their weighted bags, Bannan gave the order to abandon ship. Fortunately, Third Engineer Taylor, who was on watch below, had the presence of mind to stop the main engine and circulation pump before leaving the engine room. His actions undoubtedly made the launching of the boats a lot less hazardous.

The starboard after lifeboat was missing, but the ship's four engineers and ten ratings who were trapped on the afterdeck launched the port-after-boat, while Second Officer Charles Cable took away the port forward boat with 20 men. Captain Bannan, Chief Officer Archie Canner and eight volunteers stayed aboard for another 30 minutes in the hope that they might save the ship, but were soon forced by the advancing flames to leave in the only remaining lifeboat. The three boats pulled away from the burning tanker to await daylight or rescue. The latter appeared to be unlikely, as the convoy was already out of sight.

Forty miles to the west, in U-82, Kapitänleutnant Rollmann had for many hours been listening in vain for directional signals from U-85, supposedly shadowing the convoy, but without success. Rollmann was on the point of searching elsewhere when a great flare showed up on the horizon to the east. The *Tachee* had become a beacon for the enemy, a funeral pyre for SC42.

10

The Slaughter Begins

Asilence that was complete and full of foreboding settled over convoy SC42. The gaps in the ranks left by the *Baron Pentland* and the *Tachee*, both now drifting forlornly astern, were filled without undue fuss and the orderly lines of ships sailed on across the untroubled sea, rolling rhythmically in the long, oily swell. No cloud marred the brightness of the moon, no friendly haze blurred the limitless horizon. The ships of SC42 were as exposed as plastic ducks on a fairground shooting range.

Three thousand yards ahead of the lead ships, *Skeena* pressed on cautiously, asdics pinging monotonously, gun's crews closed up and her lookouts quartering the horizon meticulously with their binoculars. On her open bridge, Commander Hibbard, his face showing the strain of eight consecutive days and nights with little rest or peace of mind, sat hunched in his high pilot chair staring into the night. Despite the crushing fatigue, his mind was grappling with the enormity of the problems facing him and his command. He had already lost one ship, the *Empire Springbuck* was missing and possibly also sunk, and two others were severely damaged, one of the latter on fire with 8,500 tons of irreplaceable fuel oil in her tanks. This was only the beginning, too—the initial probing of his defences by the vanguard of a gathering U-boat force. With *Orillia* astern looking after the two crippled merchant ships, his meagre resources were stretched to the absolute limit.

When the main attack came–and come it would–*Skeena*, *Kenogami* and *Alberni* could not alone hope to provide a credible screen for the convoy. However, for the next 48 hours or so, until the arrival of the 20th Escort Group from Iceland, that was just what they were expected to do.

Two hours passed, during which not a man in the convoy dared to relax, let alone sleep. With lifejackets lashed on over layers of thick clothing, they stood to their guns, manned bridges or stood around in groups on deck. In the surrounding darkness, shadowy growlers, outriders of the icebergs, slid silently past, a grim reminder of other dangers abroad. Despite the bitter cold, the warmth of the accommodation suddenly had no appeal, even for those with no specific station to go to. Those on watch in the engine rooms paid strict attention to the roaring furnaces and thrusting pistons, shutting out the world outside. They knew full well that no precaution they took would save their lives when the crash came. In the four escorts, *Skeena* ahead, *Kenogami* and *Alberni* on the wings and *Orillia* astern, the uninterrupted pinging of the asdics were loud on the still night air. No echoes came back.

U-432, forced to dive by *Kenogami* after torpedoing the *Muneric*, had resurfaced at 2300 and pulled ahead of the convoy ready for another surface attack from the port side. She was in a favourable position soon after 0200 on the 10th, waiting in the shadows for the first ships to come within range. In the U-boat's conning tower, Heinz-Otto Schultze, grateful for the warmth of his long leather watchcoat, gave his orders in a hushed voice, for the scene before him was breathtaking. The massed ranks of heavily laden ships, clearly silhouetted by the light of the moon, seemed to stretch out to infinity–and not an escort in sight. Encouraged by the ease of his earlier success, Schultze decided to use the same tactics, aiming for the middle of the nearest column. He fired three torpedoes from his bow tubes, then using both helm and engines turned the U-boat short round and loosed off a stern shot. While the torpedoes were still running, he called for full speed and raced back into the shadows, still on the surface.

The tiny, 1,113-ton Norwegian *Stargard*, second ship in the port outer column of SC42, had escaped Schultze's first attack nearly five hours earlier. This time she was not so lucky. One of U-432's torpedoes caught her squarely in the engine room, blasting her hull wide open in its most vulnerable section. Two of the engine-room watch died in the explosion and three men on the bridge, Captain Lars Larsen, Second Officer H. Jacobsen and the helmsman Walter Keys, were blown overboard. The 26-year-old ship, in spite of her cargo of timber, began to go down quickly, but the remaining members of her crew made good their escape in two lifeboats. One of the boats picked up the three men thrown into the water by the explosion, all still alive, then both boats pulled away from the sinking ship. As he watched his ship go down, Captain Larsen, who suffered a broken ankle and back injuries, sadly reflected that all the terrible pounding she had stood up to in the week-long storm had been for nothing. Ironically, if the *Stargard* had sailed with SC41, as had been the intention, she would have got through, for the *Einvik* was the earlier convoy's only casualty.

On the bridge of the *Winterswijk*, Chief Officer van der Moolen gasped in horror at the sudden, brutal end of the *Stargard*. The 3,205-ton Dutch steamer, loaded with a full cargo of phosphates and carrying a crew of 33, was fifth ship in the second column, and commanded a clear view of the little Norwegian's death throes. Van der Moolen had little time to dwell on the fate of the *Stargard*, however, for his own ship was the second victim of Schultze's randomly aimed torpedoes. It caught the *Winterswijk* in her no. 2 hold, immediately forward of the bridge, and the whole foredeck seemed to erupt in a huge geyser of phosphates, water and smoke, which climbed 200 feet in the air before falling back onto the bridge.

Van der Moolen dived for the shelter of the wheelhouse to escape the deluge. As soon as it was safe to emerge, he ran to the port wing to fire the distress rockets kept ready in chutes on the outboard bulwark. He was too late. The rockets had been swallowed up by the explosion. A quick glance over the fore end of the bridge showed the foredeck already under water. The *Winterswijk* was going down rapidly. It was time to leave.

Taking the ladders leading to the deck at a run, van der Moolen picked his way through the wreckage littering the after well-deck. His head was ringing and his mind was confused, but clear enough to notice that the hatchboards and tarpaulins of no. 3 hatch, along with the liferaft stowed on top of the hatch, had all gone.

When he reached the boat deck, it was deserted, except for two seamen, who were making a desperate, but ineffectual, attempt to clear away the port lifeboat. Van der Moolen went to their aid, using his knife to cut away the lashing securing the boat. While he was so engaged, there was a loud bang and the world went black. U-432's stern torpedo had also found its mark in the *Winterswijk*.

The explosion hurled the unconscious chief officer high into the air and clear of the ship. He came to his senses soon after hitting the sea to find himself being dragged down into a watery grave by a powerful suction. He fought back, but his lungs were almost bursting before he managed to break free of the merciless grip and kick his way to the surface.

Looking around him, van der Moolen saw that the *Winterswijk* had disappeared. The ship had, in fact, gone down in two minutes following the second torpedo hit, and had come very near to taking him with her. He looked around for something to support him, and was fortunate enough to find a large piece of wreckage floating nearby. Around him he heard cries for help and saw a number of tiny red beacons bobbing on the swell like ghostly will-o'-the-wisps. Van der Moolen was not alone, but the convoy had moved on, and as the chill of the sub-Arctic water seeped into his bones he was aware that unless rescue came soon be would die.

Third Officer L. Van Beusekom, who doubled as the *Winterswijk's* wireless operator, was also blown over the side when the second torpedo hit. He was lucky enough to find a liferaft, on board which he was joined by three other men, one of them severely injured. Two hours later, van der Moolen, van Beusekom and 11 other survivors from the *Winterswijk* were picked up by the corvette *Orillia*. No trace was found of the other 20 crew members, and it was assumed they had gone down with the ship.

Immediately after the torpedoing of the *Stargard*, *Skeena*, on station 3,000 yards ahead of the *Everleigh*, swept round to port and fired starshells to illuminate the exposed flank of the convoy. *Kenogami* raced in to support her, and both escorts began an antisubmarine search. At the same time, *Stangard's* fellow Norwegian, the 1,368-ton *Regin*, third ship in the adjacent column, altered course to port. Her master had seen men in the water and was going to their aid.

As the *Regin* answered her helm and sheered off to port, those on her bridge sighted a U-boat on the surface between the two columns. Unable to escape to the west owing to the arrival of *Skeenia* and *Kenogami*, Schultze was taking U-432 deep into the convoy, seeking a hiding place. She passed close astern of the Norwegian, whose machine-guns opened fire, spraying the U-boat's conning tower. It was fortunate for Shultze that the *Regin* was not fitted with a 4-inch on her poop, otherwise U-432's short career might have ended there and then.

Undeterred by her brush with the enemy, the *Regin* stubbornly continued to search for the *Stargard's* boats. This was a brave gesture, but strictly against convoy standing orders, which forbade merchantmen to break ranks to pick up survivors. Her perseverance was soon rewarded when she found a lifeboat containing nine men. A little later, the *Stargard's* other boat, with six men on board, was picked up by the corvette *Alberni*.

Following the chance sighting and sinking of the *Empire Springbuck*, it had not been difficult for Friedrich Guggenberger in U-81 to home in on SC42. The ether was by then thick with sighting reports from other U-boats—reports no longer necessary, for the pall of smoke hanging over the convoy was clearly visible to U-81's lookouts in the light of the moon, a signpost beckoning them on.

Unfortunately for Guggenberger, he was just drawing abreast of the leading ships in the port outer column when U-432 shattered the silence of the night with her salvo of torpedoes. With *Skeena* and *Ketiogami* quickly on the scene, Guggenberger was forced to sheer away and cross ahead of the convoy. Moving at her full surface speed of 17 knots, U-81 cleared the lead ships with ease, and by 0230 was off the starboard wing of the convoy.

The leading ship of the starboard outer column was the British-flag, Danish-owned *Sally Maersk*, commanded by Captain J. K. Lindberg. Uncomfortably aware of the exposed position of his ship, Lindberg had for some time been reflecting on the paucity of his ship's defensive armament. The Heath-Robinson-like Holman Projector and two .303 machine-guns were likely to be of little use in fighting off U-boats, and for a long time Lindberg had badgered the Admiralty to fit a 4-inch. Earlier in the year, the *Sally Maersk* had languished in Glasgow for more than three months with engine repairs, during which time Lindberg continued to press his case. The excuses and promises were plentiful but, needless to say, when the ship sailed in June she sailed without her big gun.

On arrival at Montreal, Captain Lindberg again pursued his case for a 4-inch, and was told bluntly that he would have to take his place in the queue. However, he was assured that the *Sally Maersk's* poop deck would be stiffened while she was loading at Three Rivers, and the gun mounted while she waited for a convoy at Sydney. It was, of course, all so much pie in the sky. In the summer of 1941, the Admiralty had simply run out of heavy guns for merchant ships, having pressed into service even those leftover from the Boer War. The *Sally Maersk* was destined to meet the challenge of the enemy with small arms for some time to come.

It was not just the lack of defensive equipment that troubled Captain Lindberg as he paced the bridge in the early hours of that cold September morning in 1941. The 18-year-old motorship's three generators, without which her engines could not function, were again giving trouble. The machines had been repaired during the long lay-up on the Clyde, and again at Three Rivers, but in both cases the cure was only temporary. On his return to the UK, Lindberg would have a number of accounts to settle.

Not all the heavy guns and smooth-running generators in creation would have saved the *Sally Maersk* that night. Her lookouts were distracted by the brilliant display of pyrotechnics on the far side of the convoy, where rockets and starshells continued to soar skywards and all the escorts were concentrated. It was an easy matter for Friedrich Guggenberger to manoeuvre U-81 into a favourite position to attack. The choice of targets on offer was mouthwatering. The *Sally Maersk*, sagging under the weight of 4,527 tons of wheat, led the column, followed by the 5,043-ton Norwegian timber-carrier *Arosa*, then the 5,685-ton Greek-flag *Michalis*, also down to her marks with wheat. Astern of them were the 1,859-ton Polish ship *Wigry*, carrying general cargo, and the *Lorient*, with iron ore from Wabana. After only a few seconds' deliberation, Guggenberger aimed at the *Arosa* and fired a spread of four torpedoes from his bow tubes.

All four torpedoes left the U-boat running true, but although Guggenberger watched and listened long after the prescribed time had elapsed, there was no blinding flash, no thunderous explosion—not even a dull thud to indicate a hit. The entire salvo had passed either between or under the merchant ships. Swallowing his disappointment, Guggenberger swung U-81 through 180 degrees and aimed his stern tube at the leading ship of the column. At 0253 he again gave the order to fire.

Captain Lindberg, blissfully unaware of the unseen threat to his ship, had left the bridge and was in his cabin. He was unable to relax, for his nerves were as taut as bow-strings, but the blessed relief of being able to put his feet up, even if only for a few minutes, was sweet indeed. The crash of U-81's torpedo slamming home put a cruel end to his rest exactly five minutes after he entered the cabin.

By the time Lindberg reached the wheelhouse again, the *Sally Maersk*, hit in her forward cargo hold, was listing heavily to starboard and her foredeck was awash. She was going down by the head with a rush. Lindberg gave the order to abandon ship and ran aft to the boat deck, where his crew were already assembling. A quick roll-call showed that only one man was missing and there were no injuries. Two lifeboats were lowered to the water and the ship was evacuated.

Lindberg and his wireless operator remained behind to make a last search for the missing man, intending to leave in the jolly boat. The man was located, but by this time the ship appeared to be in imminent danger of sinking. The jolly boat proved difficult to launch, and the only liferaft had been blown away, so Lindberg and his two companions were obliged to jump into the icy water and swim to the waiting boats. The *Sally Maersk* lifted her stern high and went down bow first just eight minutes later.

Captain Gordon Dobson, on the bridge of the *Thistleglen*, leading ship of column 9, had a clear view of the torpedoing of the *Sally Maersk*. A few minutes later, he caught sight of a U-boat on the surface to starboard of the stricken ship, and at once passed word aft for the 4-inch to open fire. However, by the time the gun was trained onto the fleeting shadow, Guggenberger had taken U-81 down to periscope depth. The *Thistleglen's* shell exploded on an empty sea.

Dobson ordered his wireless operator to break radio silence to report the U-boat. This alerted Rear-Admiral MacKenzie in the *Everleigh*, who ordered an emergency turn to port. Six minutes later, another U-boat having been spotted in the convoy's path, MacKenzie hauled the ships back to starboard. All the escorts were out of sight chasing shadows, and the commodore could do no more than dodge from side to side in the hope of spoiling the enemy's aim. With a large, slow-moving convoy of ships this was a most laborious business, fraught with the danger of collision and, so it seemed to a desperately tired MacKenzie, hardly worth the effort.

Six miles astern of the convoy, the *Regin*, having taken on board nine survivors from the *Stargard*, reversed course and piled on all steam in an attempt to rejoin the other ships. She had not been steadied on her new course for more than a few minutes when another submarine—probably U-432 again—surfaced close on her starboard side. It was difficult to deduce who was the more surprised, the Regin or the U-boat, but the little Norwegian's gunners were once again quick off the mark. The .303s opened up such a relentless fire that the unknown U-boat was forced to crash-dive. HMCS *Orillia*, also with *Stargard* survivors on board, was still in the vicinity and dropped depth charges, but with no apparent result. However, this must have served as a warning to the enemy that the convoy had sharp teeth, small though they may be.

In this, the last hour before the dawn, the U-boats withdrew. When the first flush of daylight came, the damage they had caused became all too apparent. Gone were the *Muneric*, her cargo of iron ore and 63 men, the *Winterswijk*, her phosphates and 20 men, the little *Stargard* with her timber and two men, and the *Sally Maersk* and her wheat. Without taking into account the *Empire Springbuck*, then only missing as far as the convoy was concerned, SC42 had lost 17,000 tons of priceless cargo and 85 men–and the attack was not yet 24 hours old.

On the credit side, the tanker *Tachee* and the *Baron Pentland* were still afloat, although abandoned by their crews and drifting many miles astern. *Orillia*, ordered by Hibbard to stand by the two torpedoed ships, circled warily around them. The tiny warship now had on board a total of 97 survivors, crammed into her limited accommodation and crowding her decks. Under less terrible circumstances, she might well have been mistaken for a Clyde excursion-steamer on a summer Bank Holiday. Certainly, as a convoy escort she had ceased to be of any real value, and Lieutenant-Commander Edward Briggs was uncertain as to how long he should remain in the area.

When full daylight came, Briggs was not pleased to receive a signal from *Skeena* ordering him to investigate the possibility of saving the damaged ships. This meant sending off boats with boarding parties, an unenviable task in view of the number of U-boats obviously skulking below the surface.

Briggs first approached the *Baron Pentland*, dropped a boat and put Captain Campbell and Chief Officer Forfar back on board their ship. The two men quickly established that the steamer's back was broken and her engine room flooded. However, as she was loaded with timber, it was Campbell's opinion that she could be salvaged, given that a tow was available.

Then it was the *Tachee's* turn. The fire that during the night had seemed about to turn the tanker into a blazing inferno had gone out, and Captain Bannan had little difficulty in reboarding his ship. He took with him his chief officer, chief engineer and third engineer, and between them they carried out a thorough appraisal of the tanker's condition above and below decks. The damage on deck was considerable, but not serious, the deck plating on the starboard side being peeled back in places. A small fire was burning near the pump room, but it took the party only a few minutes to extinguish this. They then went below, where they found a great deal of structural damage–but again not critical. The bulkheads in way of nos. 8, 9 and 10 cargo tanks were buckled and badly strained, but holding. The chief engineer reported the engine-room telegraphs and telemotor steering gear out of action, but the main engine was apparently undamaged. He was confident that he would be able to raise steam on the starboard boiler, possibly bringing in the port boiler later.

The reports brought back to *Orillia* by the two captains made the decision easy for Briggs. Although the *Baron Pentland* still floated, she was completely immobilised, and could only be saved if a salvage tug was available in Reykjavik. It was likely that the *Tachee*, on the other hand, would be able to make Iceland under her own steam. What really tipped the balance, however, was the tanker's cargo of 1.7 million gallons of oil, which appeared to be largely intact. Briggs could not afford to abandon such treasure. The *Baron Pentland* must be left to the mercy of the elements, while all efforts were concentrated on saving the *Tachee.*

Bannan called for volunteers to reboard the tanker, and most of his crew–the exception being a number of engine-room ratings–offered to go. In the end, Bannan selected 27 men, plus three volunteers from *Orillia's* engine room to make good the shortage below decks. They returned to the *Tachee* and commenced to raise steam. Meanwhile, Briggs rounded up two drifting lifeboats which were then hoisted aboard the tanker to provide some measure of security for the salvage crew. At the same time, Campbell took a party of men back to the *Baron Pentland* to collect more provisions for *Orillia*, which now had 70 extra mouths to feed.

It took less than half-an-hour to connect up the *Tachee's* emergency steering gear, but raising steam on the now cold starboard boiler would take many hours. She drifted, rolling gently in the long Atlantic swell, while *Orillia*, guns manned and asdics probing, circled her watchfully. Both ships were easy targets for the U-boats.

11

Confusion and Consternation

Whitten Siegfried Rollmann sighted the flare-up from the torpedoed Tachee, he knew his long search for convoy SC42 was over. Starshells arcing up into the night sky and the rumble of distant underwater explosions indicated a battle of first magnitude in progress—a battle for which U-82 was late on the scene. Rollmann submerged and, lying stopped at periscope depth, listened intently with the hydrophones. Faint propeller noises and the distinctive pinging of the asdics of searching escorts confirmed the convoy to be on a bearing between 210° and 290°, and at a distance of 40 to 50 miles.

Returning to the surface, Rollmann set off to the west at full speed, using the occasional bursting starshell as a guide. The moon, now high in the sky, was turning night into day, and very soon a dark shadow showed up on the horizon, which Rollmann took to be the smoke from a large number of ships; but, in the elation of the chase, his imagination was taking charge. As the submarine ate up the miles, her sharp prow cleaving a foaming path through the silver sea, the cloud hardened and became the icecapped mountains of Greenland. No more starshells climbed into the sky. There was no sign of the enemy ships.

The hours passed, and U-82 raced on, with a tension that was partly fear of the unknown and partly anticipation of the thrill of battle permeating throughout the boat, above and below deck. As the first light of the coming dawn died with the dying moon to herald another day, U-82's lookouts sighted ghostly white streaks on the horizon ahead that could only be the bow-waves of a fleet of ships. The klaxon blared and the adrenalin surged as men tumbled to their diving stations, but it was yet another false alarm. As they drew nearer, the frothing bow-waves became a field of growlers, miniature icebergs that bobbed and curtsyed as U-82 threaded her way through them.

It was after 0430 before the dawn came and vindicated Rollmann's determination to keep moving in towards the coast. Four dark smudges, clearly identifiable as smoke, showed up in the sky to the southwest, and beneath them a few indistinct blips on the horizon. Then, as the curve of the horizon flattened, a forest of masts and smoking funnels came into view. He had found SC42.

U-82 would soon be in a position ahead and to the north of the convoy. Assuming that, owing to the close proximity of the land, the ships would not take up a zigzag pattern at daylight, Rollmann decided to use a classic method of attack perfected by the U-boats. He would submerge and drift back into the middle of the convoy, then carry out a daylight attack at periscope depth.

At 0345 that morning, while Rollmann was still searching for the convoy, Captain John Cooke, master of the CAM ship *Empire Hudson*, felt the need to freshen up, even if only with a quick wash and a scrape with a razor. A look around at the quiet, orderly progress of the convoy reassured him, and he concluded that it would be safe to leave the bridge for a short while. He went below, leaving Second Officer W. R. Harrison in charge of the watch.

No watchkeeping officer of a ship is entirely at ease when the master is on the bridge. By virtue of the senior man's lonely position, the conversation is usually stilted, and although there may not be the intent, the officer cannot but feel that his competence is being challenged by the mere presence of the man. Harrison, aged 24, was no exception to this rule, and he walked the wing of the *Empire Hudson's* bridge with a more confident tread when Cooke had gone below.

Trimmed down and running at full speed.
(Photo: Horst Bredow)

The visibility was excellent, the sea calm, the ship on a course of 043°, steaming at 6.5 knots and holding her position at the head of column 2. To port, 40 miles off and silhouetted in the light of the moon, the mountain ranges of Greenland's King Frederick VI Land appeared strangely comforting. In reality, the precipitous, frozen shores they overlooked would offer sanctuary to no ship. Much closer to hand, a few hundred feet forward of the bridge on the *Empire Hudson's* fo'c'sle head, Harrison drew reassurance from the dark outline of the Hurricane fighter poised on its catapult. He was proud to be sailing on the only ship in the convoy capable of tipping the scales in the event of an air attack.

At 0400, Harrison was relieved by Chief Officer John Forrest. The two men talked for a few minutes, then Harrison went below, leaving Forrest warming his hands on a steaming mug of tea and running his eye over the ships on either side of the *Empire Hudson.* The sky in the east was already paling into that short period known as Civil Twilight, when the sun is 6 degrees below the horizon and it is still dark enough for the stars to be visible, yet light enough to give a sharp horizon. It would soon be time for Forrest to take morning sights.

While Forrest went through the daily routine with his sextant, Siegfried Rollmann had positioned U-82 on the port side of the convoy and was preparing to attack. The two outer columns, led by the *Trefusis* and *Empire Hudson*, were incomplete, having lost the *Muneric*, *Stargard* and *Winterswijk* during the night, but there was still plenty of easy targets on offer.

At 0457, it being now almost full daylight, Rollmann raised U-82's periscope and gave the order to stand by for a double torpedo spread, using tubes 1 and 3. He had little need to aim precisely, for the remaining five ships of columns 1 and 2 overlapped, bow to stern, presenting a solid wall of slow-moving, heavily laden vessels. The rang was 2,000 metres.

As if Rollmann's advantage was not then sufficient, the commodore chose this moment to make good the gaps in the column. This involved a number of flag hoists, which for the *Everleigh*, with her naval signallers, presented no problem. For the sparsely manned merchantmen, it was a different matter. At 0500, Forrest and his two lookouts on the bridge of the *Empire Hudson* were so occupied with the flags that they failed to see U-82's torpedo streaking towards the ship.

The unseen missile slammed into the steamer's port side, penetrating her stokehold and exploding, with catastrophic results. Smoke, debris and water shot into the air, the port-side lifeboats were reduced to matchwood, the mainmast buckled and the funnel, all its securing rivets blown out by the upward force of the explosion, toppled and fell with a crash. Water poured into the engine room, and the ship began to settle bodily.

Captain Cooke reached the bridge seconds after the explosion, and having assessed the damage ordered his crew to abandon ship. By the time the starboard lifeboats were lowered, the sea was lapping at the upper deck rails, and abandoning ship was a simple matter of stepping from the deck into the boats.

Once the boats were clear of the ship, a head count revealed that the second engineer and the three firemen of his watch were missing, and it was accepted that they had been killed when the torpedo struck. However, Cooke sent a boat to search around the ship and one of the missing firemen was found alive in the water. This man, who was slightly injured, had had a miraculous escape from the flooded stokehold, swimming out through the hole in the ship's side made by the torpedo.

Skeena was the only escort screening the convoy when the *Empire Hudson* was hit. *Orillia* was well astern, standing by the crippled *Tacheee* and *Baron Pentland*, while *Alberni* and *Kenogami* were also astern, occupied with picking up survivors. This left SC42 terribly exposed, and Rear-Admiral MacKenzie took the only course of action open to him, ordering an emergency turn 45 degrees to starboard to run away from the perceived danger. At the same time, *Skeena* reversed her course and began a sweep on the port side of the convoy in the vicinity of the *Empire Hudson*.

U-82 porpoised under after the discharge of her torpedoes, and it was four minutes before Rollmann succeeded in bringing her back to periscope depth. Encouraged by his hit on the *Empire Hudson*, he fired a third torpedo at the flank of the convoy, now turning away from him. Although the range was now down to less than 1,000 metres, the torpedo missed, probably through being set too deep. There was no time for post-mortems, however. *Skeena's* avenging bow-wave was filling the periscope and Rollmann was obliged to act quickly. It was too late to run away or dive deep, so he took U-82 down another 10 metres, stopped engines and called for silent routine.

The seconds ticked by with every man, nerves on edge, listening to the thump-thump of the approaching destroyer's propellers and the searching ping of her asdic. Rollmann was tempted to go deeper, but feared that the rush of water into the ballast tanks would give away the boat's position. His dilemma was made worse when the underwater noises of the approaching enemy ship suddenly ceased. She had stopped–but why?

Ten agonising minutes elapsed, then, unable to stand the suspense any longer, Rollmann went back to periscope depth and took a quick look around He saw ships of the convoy ahead and to starboard, none of them posing a threat; but he had a rude shock when he swung the periscope to port. The destroyer was only 250 metres away, so close that the horrified Rollmann could clearly see the men on her open bridge.

The U-boat commander was momentarily stunned by his

first sight of the enemy at close quarters, and his first instinct was to crash-dive. Then the long weeks of intensive training in the Norwegian fjords, the cat-and-mouse games played with an escorting tug, paid off. Rollmann remained at periscope depth, turned bow-on to the destroyer, and loosed off a single torpedo. Only then did he flood tanks and take U-82 deeper.

Another tense half-minute passed, with Rollmann counting off the seconds as the torpedo sped on its way, but there was no satisfying thump. Then he heard the destroyer on the move again, and he knew he had missed. When U-82 was shaken by five separate explosions in quick succession as depth charges tumbled around her, Rollmann dived to 50 metres.

The waiting that followed was an ordeal not previously experienced by the majority of the U-boat's crew. The measured tread of the destroyer's propellers and the sinister probing note of her asdic filled the boat with the fear of impending death. First the enemy ship passed close astern, then ahead, then directly overhead. All the time, the men in their steel coffin 165 feet below the surface cringed in anticipation of the depth charges—the creeping barrage, and then the final cataclysmic explosion that would blow them and their world apart. For some reason they could not understand, however, nothing came, and soon they heard the enemy moving quickly away.

The truth of the matter was that Commander Hibbard was caught in a cleft stick. *Skeena's* asdics had picked up a good contact, clearly identified as a submarine, and he was in a position to press home the attack. However, with the three corvettes busy clearing up the carnage of the night, he had left the convoy completely unprotected, and this troubled him. When, as *Skeena* was creeping up on U-82, the *Everleigh* reported a periscope passing ahead of the convoy, Hibbard had no hesitation in breaking off the attack to dash to the commodore's aid.

It was a wasted effort, for when *Skeena* once more reached the head of the convoy the reported submarine was long gone. By this time, MacKenzie had taken the ships into yet another emergency turn, and a certain measure of confusion reigned.

Meanwhile, 3 miles astern of SC42, the indefatigable little *Regin*, fresh from her brush with the U-boats, and with nine survivors from the *Stargard* on board, had been struggling to rejoin the convoy when the *Empire Hudson* was torpedoed. Without hesitation, the Norwegian altered course for the sinking ship, lowered a boat, and picked up 19 of the British ship's crew, including Captain Cooke.

When Cooke reached the bridge of the *Regin*, he reported that he had been unable to destroy his ship's secret code books before leaving her. Word was passed to Hibbard in *Skeena*, who ordered *Kenogami* to send a boarding party to the torpedoed CAM ship to destroy the secret books, and also the aircraft and RDF set. This was done, and Lieutenant-Commander Jackson, commanding officer of *Kenogami*, later criticised Cooke for abandoning his ship prematurely. It may be that, in retrospect, the evacuation of the ship was somewhat hasty, but it should be remembered that at the time her engine room and stokehold were flooded and her maindeck was awash. Cooke's first duty was to his men, and in this instance he served them admirably. The remaining 37 survivors were rescued by the *Baron Ramsay*, sister ship to the damaged *Baron Pentland*, and Cooke lost only four of his crew.

While, in the light of a new day, SC42 endeavoured to make good the ravages of the night, U-82 was at 20 metres reloading her tubes. At 0745, hearing propeller noises close at hand, Rollmann cautiously rose to periscope depth to investigate. He found himself astern of the convoy and in sight of two ships which, in his opinion, were acting very strangely. The smaller of the two, which appeared to be a British corvette, was zigzagging ahead of a merchantman armed with at least one heavy gun, and whose funnel had collapsed.

Rollmann had been under considerable strain during the past hours, and his imagination was working overtime. He took the merchantman to be a "Q" ship with her dummy funnel down, working with the corvette to bring about U-82's end. Without waiting to confirm his fears, he dived deep. Ironically, the German commander had, of course, been observing the ship he had so recently torpedoed, the *Empire Hudson*, with *Kenogami* in attendance. Although it may be that the *Empire Hudson*, well armed and with a strike aircraft on board, played no part in the defence of the convoy, in her dying moments she undoubtedly saved *Kenogami* from U-82's torpedoes.

Two hours later, Rollmann returned to periscope depth to find the horizon empty, except for a few plumes of smoke visible low down in the northeast. Realising that the convoy was about to slip from his grasp, he surfaced and called for all possible speed to make up the ground lost. The sky was cloudless, the visibility excellent, and with the U-boat's powerful diesels thrusting her through the calm sea at 1 7 knots this did not appear to be a difficult undertaking. Rollmann was confident he would be in a position for another attack by the time darkness came down. Fortunately for his immediate peace of mind, be was not aware that help was on the way for SC42.

Catalina H-209 of RAF Coastal Command took off from her base at Akureyri, on the north coast of Iceland, on the morning of 10 September with instructions to find and keep company with SC42. The American-built flying boat carried a crew of nine, and was armed with .5-inch Browning machine-guns and depth charge bombs. Flying at an optimum speed of 100 knots, her two 1,200-horsepower Pratt and Whitney Wasp engines gave her a maximum range of 1,000 miles when fully loaded, but she was not a comfortable aircraft to fly. Like all Catalinas, her fuselage had no soundproofing and was without heating. Her unfortunate crew, condemned to spend up to 20 hours in temperatures as low as -20°C., with the roar of the Pratt and Whitneys hammering at their ears, suffered agonies of exposure and fatigue, and might be excused if their efficiency was not always 100 percent.

On this occasion, however, H-209's lookouts were not found lacking. At 1052, the flying boat was 450 miles west of Iceland and nearing the end of her outward endurance, and had still not located the convoy. She was about to return to base when a U-boat was sighted on the surface, heading northeast at speed.

When H-209 came swooping out of the sky like a giant bird of prey, U-82 was 60 miles southwest of SC42 and closing rapidly. Luckily, the German submarine's lookouts were on their toes, and she went into her now familiar crash-dive routine without a hitch; but she was not quick enough. Her conning tower was only just beneath the surface of the water when the depth charges came plummeting down all around her. However, by the greatest of good fortune, the charges failed to explode, and the Catalina, her fuel gauges already on the danger mark, was unable to make another run.

Although H-209 was then forced to return to Iceland, she had achieved her objective in locating SC42, and other aircraft were on the way. During the next two hours, having brought U-82 warily back to the surface and resumed his pursuit of the convoy, Rollmann sighted a patrolling Catalina no less than four times. Having found SC42, Coastal Command did not intend to leave it without air cover. This involved flying a continuous system of reliefs, with each aircraft spending a maximum of two hours over the convoy before making a dash for home. It was not much in the way of protection but, as had been shown in the case of U-82, it was effective, if only in daylight. Word of the unwelcome development reached Admiral Dönitz, and he signalled to wolf-pack *Markgraf:* 'This convoy must not get away. Get at him, attack, sink!" The battle was about to move into a new and more urgent phase.

The men of SC42 were not privy to what passed between BdU and the U-boats, but they had no illusions that the lull that followed the sinking of the *Empire Hudson* was anything but a temporary breathing space. In the preceding 24 hours, there had been no less than seven separate attacks, indicating that a number of U-boats, possibly as many as seven, were operating against them. No one knew when or from where the next torpedoes would come, but come they surely would. Rear-Admiral MacKenzie, who perhaps appreciated better than most the threat facing them, took full advantage of the lull to reorganise the remaining 57 ships into a tighter formation of 11 columns. As the corvette *Orillia* had long dropped below the horizon with her two charges, leaving only three escorts, this was a largely cosmetic gesture, but it served to keep idle minds from speculating. A deterioration in the weather, the wind rising to Force 4 from the south-southeast and visibility falling to less than 5 miles, was of some advantage to the convoy, although it might favour the U-boats more.

Eberhard Greger in U-85 was one who certainly welcomed the choppy sea. Since his abortive attack on the *Jedmoor* on the morning of the 9th, Greger had been stalking SC42, and had now reached a position ahead and slightly to port of the convoy at 0959, he took U-85 down to periscope depth and waited for the opportunity to attack. With the white horses concealing her periscope, and the columns of unwieldy merchant ships slowly advancing towards her, it was inconceivable that U-85 would fail to at last open her score.

Greger was unaware that his former intended victim, the 4,392-ton *Jedmoor*, her engines functioning flawlessly, had taken over at the head of column 3. The Newcastle tramp's lookouts were as alert as ever; they sighted U-85's periscope, and the alarm was raised. Several ships opened fire, and MacKenzie hauled the convoy away from the danger with an emergency turn to starboard. While this manoeuvre was taking place, Commander Hibbard brought *Skeena* around in a tight turn and raced down the port side of the convoy at 20 knots dropping depth charges at random to frighten off the enemy. At a more leisurely pace, Hibbard then carried out an anti-submarine sweep over a 3-mile radius, but no contact was made. The destroyer returned to her station ahead of the convoy at 1045. Greger, meanwhile, having dived briefly to avoid detection, brought U-85 back to periscope depth and moved deeper into the ranks of the convoy, seeking an easier target.

On the far side of SC42, the vice-commodore ship *Thistleglen* was leading column 9 on a course of 042° at 6 knots. When the emergency was over, her master, Captain Gordon Dobson, went down to his cabin to attend to the routine duties of his command that never varied in war or peace. At 1150, he was about to return to the bridge for noon sights, when there was a violent explosion beneath his feet and the *Thistleglen* heeled heavily to starboard. The awful nightmare Dobson had lived with during the long days and nights since leaving Sydney had become reality. His ship had been torpedoed—not in the dark hours of the night as he had feared, but in broad daylight.

Stopping only to snatch up his lifejacket and a coat, Dobson ran for the bridge ladder, acutely conscious of the 7,460 tons of steel and pig-iron in the holds which would take the ship to the bottom like a stone when she lost her reserve buoyancy.

The wheelhouse was deserted, the engine-room telegraph still registering fill speed ahead, the wheel unattended. Dobson attempted to put the telegraph to stop engines, but it was jammed. He need not have been concerned, for a rush of escaping steam from the boiler exhaust and the slowing of the engine's beat told him that the engineers were shuting down.

Dobson found his crew already assembled on the boat deck, clearing away the boats and rafts ready for launching under the direction of Chief Officer Leonard Williams. It was an unhurried, well-disciplined operation, but there was a sense of urgency in the air. Williams reported that the ship had been hit in her stokehold, and was taking in water fast. Two firemen and a greaser were missing, undoubtedly killed by the explosion.

As her engine room flooded and she sank lower in the water, the *Thistlegien* righted herself, and ten minutes later, when Dobson ordered his men to abandon ship, her watertight bulkheads were still holding. One of the lifeboats had been damaged in the bad weather off Newfoundland and was unusable, but the remaining three boats and two liferafts were launched without incident. The 46 survivors were picked up an hour and a quarter later by the *Lorient* which, much to the commodore's annoyance, had for some days been straggling at the rear of the convoy. The rescue did much to redeem the British ore-carrier's reputation. The *Thistleglen* went down as her boats reached the *Lorient's* side.

After torpedoing the *Thistleglen*, U-85 was forced to crash-dive to avoid being run down by other ships of the convoy. Half-an-hour later, Greger brought her back to periscope depth and fired a double salvo at-ships near the rear of the convoy. Both torpedoes were wasted, and U-85's periscope was sighted by lookouts on the *Gunvor Maersk*, a small steamer lying at fifth position in column 10. The Danish ship raised the alarm, and shells and bullets rained down on the submerged U-boat from all sides. Greger was again obliged to dive deep to escape from the hornet's nest he had disturbed.

It was Eberhard Greger's intention to withdraw at silent speed, but he was not given the opportunity. Alerted by the merchant ships' guns, *Skeena*, accompanied by *Kenogami* and *Alberni*, came racing back through the lines of the convoy in time to get a brief sighting of U-85's periscope before she went deep. Commander Hibbard took *Skeena* in at 24 knots, firing ten depth charges set to 100 and 125 feet. The sea boiled and it was some time before the destroyer's asdics obtained a hard contact. This was identified as a possible submarine proceeding on a northerly course at about 3 knots.

ATTACK & SINK

Feeling that, for the first time, he was face to face with SC42's enemy, Hibbard decided on a planned, deliberate attack. He instructed *Kenogami* to act as directing ship, standing well off, but maintaining asdic contact with the target and guiding *Skeena* in to the target. At 1305, Hibbard dropped a further ten charges, this time set to 150 and 385 feet—a lethal sandwich in which he hoped to catch the U-boat.

Hibbard's plan appeared to bear fruit. Shortly after the second pattern of charges exploded, a large air bubble came to the surface, followed by a small patch of oil. For the next 15 minutes, the three escorts slowly circled the area, watching and listening, but no further contact was made. The corvettes then returned to the convoy, while *Skeena* remained in the vicinity carrying out an all-round sweep. No further echoes were picked up, and Hibbard felt confident that the U-boat had been destroyed. At 1427, he set course to rejoin the convoy, which was about to disappear over the horizon.

In retrospect, it was fortunate for SC42 that only one U-boat was in contact with the convoy at that time, for all three escorts were absent for over an hour while dealing with U-85, leaving the merchant ships totally undefended. Hibbard's action was a calculated risk that might have ended in disaster.

As it was, *Skeena's* depth charges did not sink U-85, but the U-boat received serious damage. Her periscope was bent, both diesel couplings knocked out of line and her exhaust valves damaged, thereby impairing her diving ability. To exacerbate her predicament, patrolling aircraft kept her under water until after midnight. At 0100 on the 11th, Greger decided enough was enough and withdrew from the conflict.

Soon after *Skeena* resumed station ahead of the convoy, Hibbard received news that help was on the way. Five destroyers of the 2nd Escort Group, HMS *Douglas*, *Veteran*, *Saladin*, *Leamington* and *Skate*, had been withdrawn from the westbound convoy ON13, refuelled at Reykjavik, and were proceeding at all speed to join SC42. The convoy also now had continuous air cover provided by one, and sometimes two, Catalinas of Coastal Command. Very soon, the odds would be heavily in favour of the Allied ships, but meanwhile, the air-waves hummed with coded W/T traffic emanating from the wolf-pack gathering on the periphery of SC42.

12

U-501 and Armageddon

Help was much closer at hand than Commander
Hibbard realised. The two Royal Canadian Navy
corvettes *Chambly* and *Moosejaw* were, at noon on the
10th, only 120 miles south of SC42, and moving in at full
speed. During the training exercise they were engaged in, the
senior officer, Commander J. S. D. Prentice, in *Chambly*, had
intentionally never strayed far from the convoy's intended
route. When, on the morning of the 9th, he received orders
from the Commodore Commanding Newfoundland Escort
Force to join SC42, he had only to increase speed to catch up.
Ironically, it seems that no one had thought fit to inform
Hibbard of his changing luck.

The newly commissioned Canadian corvettes were into their
fifth day at sea when they were ordered to SC42. During this
time, Prentice and Lieutenant Frederick Grubb, commanding
Moosejaw, had worked feverishly to turn their unblooded ships
into a credible fighting force. It was an uphill task, for both
ships' companies were woefully short of experienced men. In
two years of war, the Royal Canadian Navy had increased 20-
fold in size, and trained seamen were as hard to come by as
clergymen in hell. *Moosejaw* was typical of an RCN corvette of
the day, having only two professionals on board, her commander, Frederick Grubb, and Leading Seaman Nanteau. Grubb
was just 26 years old, and the average age of his crew was 20
years, all (except Nanteau) wartime volunteers ("hostilities-
only"), fresh from the prairies and the city streets.

Although Grubb was a patient man, and prepared to go to extraordinary lengths to guide and teach those under his command, the odds were against him. Owing to the sheer impossibility of finding replacements, he had sailed from St. John's, a severe handicap in a corvette on a wartime footing. To make matters worse, *Moosejaw* was also short of food. The fresh provisions ordered had not arrived before sailing, with the result that she was on a hard tack of tinned beef and vegetables and ship's biscuits before she was three days out of St. John's. Not that food rated very highly on board, as most of the ship's company went down with seasickness soon after leaving harbour. So stricken were they that most men were completely incapable of carrying out their duties. Food was their last concern. Certainly, serious training was out of the question, and for much of the time Grubb had difficulty in keeping the ship functioning. However, when the call came to go to the aid of SC42, the men knew they were going to war, and mood on board ship altered from one of abject hopelessness to determination.

When night fell on the 10th, *Chambly* and *Moosejaw* were steaming in line abreast, 4 cables apart and on a northerly course, which Prentice calculated would bring them into contact with the convoy. It was very dark, the sky being heavily overcast, and a fresh northwesterly wind was kicking up a rough sea which, combined with the ever-present swell, made the going heavy. The visibility was excellent, however, and Prentice anticipated no difficulty in finding the convoy. Nevertheless, he was not prepared for the dramatic suddenness with which the curtain went up on SC42. A few minutes before 2100, the horizon ahead of the corvettes turned night into day, rockets climbed into the sky and the thump of exploding depth charges carried across the water. *Chambly* and *Moosejaw* were on hand for the opening battle of the night.

Although the two corvettes were unaware of it, they were not alone in witnessing the spectacle. Hidden in the darkness 6 miles off *Chambly's* port bow, and equally unaware that she was running into danger, U-501 was on the surface and steering a reciprocal course to that of the RCN ships. Since his chance meeting with the *Einvik* in the early hours of the 5th–the sinking of which unarmed ship had cost him six torpedoes and 40 rounds of 105-mm–Hugo Förster had searched in vain for SC42. Raving concluded that he had reached too far to the north, he was then retracing his steps to the south, convinced he would soon have to abandon the search.

When SC42 unexpectedly revealed its position, Förster immediately altered course to close the convoy. As he did so, the clouds parted, a bright moon broke through, and U-501 was suddenly visible and very vulnerable. Uncannily on cue, a patrolling Catalina came swooping out of the night sky and Förster went into a hasty crash dive. The aircraft dropped no depth charges–it may well be that she did not sight the U-boat–but Förster was reluctant to surface too soon. This proved to be his undoing, for half-an-hour later U-501, still at periscope depth, and with her motors running full speed, came within range of *Chambly's* asdics.

At 2130, *Chambly's* asdic operator reported a contact identified as submarine right ahead at 700 yards, and closing. Prentice sent his men to action-stations and reduced speed to 14.5 knots, this being the minimum speed at which depth charges could be dropped without damage to his own ship. It was also, in his experience, the best speed at which to handle a corvette.

The distance between hunter and hunted closed rapidly, and at 2138 Prentice ordered a five-charge pattern to be dropped. *Chambly's* port thrower misfired owing to an inexperienced rating failing to pull the firing lever–a fault quickly rectified by the officer in charge. As a result, the first and second depth charges fell close together, creating a thunderous double explosion that all but blew the corvette out of the water.

As luck would have it, the inept fumblings of *Chambly's* port thrower party proved to be a blessing in disguise. The simultaneous explosion of the two charges caused havoc in U-501, damaging her after hydroplanes, smashing most of the instruments in the control room and extinguishing all lights. Her crew were very near to panic.

Lieutenant Hal Lawrence, a hostilities-only officer, had the watch on *Moosejaw's* bridge when the mayhem broke out. With commendable foresight, Lawrence hauled *Moosejaw* round in a wide sweep to port, in order to leave the field open for *Chambly*–at the same time being in a position to weigh in with depth charges if necessary. Lieutenant Grubb joined Lawrence on the bridge at the first peal of the alarm bells and took over command. A few minutes later, the two men were astonished to see a U-boat shoot to the surface 400 yards off *Moosejaw's* port bow.

When the U-boat was fully surfaced, she appeared to stop, and a white light blinked out from her conning tower directed at *Moosejaw*. Grubb hesitated, the thought crossing his mind that this might be a friendly submarine flashing the identification signal for the day. He called for his yeoman of signals, but before the man reached his side, black smoke issued from the U-boat's exhausts and she made off at speed, at the same time presenting her stern to *Moosejaw*. It may have been that she was just making a run for it, but, on the other hand, she might have been about to fire a salvo at *Moosejaw* from her stern tubes. Grubb was not prepared to debate the odds, and threw the corvette hard over to clear the danger and gave the order to open fire with the 4-inch.

Moosejaw's gunners needed no urging. The 4-inch barked and a shell whistled over the U-boat's conning tower. Quickly, urgently, the gun was swabbed and reloaded, but then, just when it seemed that the 4-inch was about to make its first kill, inexperience again interceded–this time in favour of the enemy. It was dark, the moment was tense, and in his haste to insert the firing tube into the lock, no. 2 in the crew jammed the lock, and *Monsejaw's* only heavy gun was out of action.

Grubb was determined not to let the U-boat get away, and ordered the 10-inch signal projector to be trained on it. This revealed a scene of chaos on board the submarine. Her conning tower and casings were crowded with men, all in an obvious state of panic. The possibility of capturing the boat occurred to Grubb, and he gave chase.

The U-boat was moving at about 13 knots and attempting to remain stern-on to *Moosejaw*. Ever-conscious of the threat posed by the submarine's stern tubes, Grubb manoeuvred to stay on her quarter, and out of the line of fire. At one point, a semblance of order appeared to be restored on the U-boat, and four men manned her forward gun. As *Moosejaw's* 4-inch was still jammed and could not retaliate, Grubb increased speed and altered course to ram. At the same time, he ordered the corvette's 0.5-inch machine-guns to open fire. Even this went wrong. In the excitement of the moment, the gun's crew omitted to cock the guns, thus completing, through sheer inexperience, the temporary suspension of all *Moosejaw's* deck armament.

At that point, fortunately for *Moosejaw*, the Germans abandoned their gun, seemingly on orders from an officer—probably Förster—who was seen making frantic signals to them from the conning tower. The U-boat then stopped, and the corvette found herself closing rapidly. Instinctively, Lieutenant Grubb stopped his engines and went full astern, but *Moosejaw* still struck the U-boat a glancing blow on her port side.

For a few brief moments, the two craft were alongside each other, hull to hull, and Grubb snatched up a megaphone and called on the Germans to surrender. There was no answer from the U-boat, but one man detached himself from the crowd milling around on the casings, and, with a leap that would have done credit to a Hollywood buccaneer, landed in the waist of the corvette. Others looked set to follow, and Grubb, fearful that his ship was about to be boarded in force, put the helm hard to port and sheered away. The U-boat followed *Moosejaw* round, laying herself across the corvette's bows, and so giving Grubb an opportunity too good to be missed. He called for maximum revolutions, and rammed the forward hydroplanes of the submarine in order to prevent her diving again.

Moosejaw, having been lying stopped before going in to ram, was not moving at a great speed when she hit U-501, and she did little damage. The submarine heeled over, but continued across the corvette's bows. She was 300 yards clear when *Moosejaw's* 4-inch gun's crew reported they were at last ready to open fire. Grubb gave the order and the long gun barrel spat flame and smoke, the shell narrowly missing the U-boat's conning tower to explode in the sea beyond. This was too much for the demoralised Germans, most of whom then threw themselves into the water.

Grubb considered sending away a boarding parry, but there

were so many Germans in the sea around the corvette that he feared a boat might be overwhelmed as soon as it hit the water. His dilemma was solved when *Chambly* came racing up astern. Prentice signalled that he would board the U-boat and ordered *Moosejaw* to carry out an anti-submarine sweep while he did so.

While *Moosejaw* moved away to cover her, Prentice manoeuvred *Chambly* to within 50 yards of U-501 and held her there. Launching a boat was difficult in the heavy swell, but a boarding party led by *Chambly's* first lieutenant, Ted Simmons, was soon on the way.

The U-boat was still under way, making about 3 knots, but Simmons took his boat in under her stern, noticing as he did so that the port hydroplane had been ripped off and there was a hole about 4 feet across in the stern. *Chambly's* party boarded without difficulty, the 11 Germans still on board offering no resistance. Simmons found one officer who spoke a little English and told him that he intended to go below. The Germans became very excited and blurted out that the seacocks had been opened and scuttling charges set. Nevertheless, having come this far, Simmons was determined to make an attempt to save the U-boat. After some heated argument, he drew his pistol, and under the threat of being shot out of hand two German ratings then agreed to accompany him below. Leaving his signalman covering the other prisoners with a Lewis gun, Simmons made for the conning tower, pushing his reluctant guides before him at gunpoint. When they reached the conning tower and heard the sea rushing into the boat, however, the Germans refused to go any further. Simmons threatened to shoot, but they would not budge.

Short of killing the two men, which would achieve nothing, Simmons could do no more, so he decided to investigate on his own. He was halfway down the conning-tower ladder when the emergency lights failed. In complete darkness, and with the swish of water in the control room below him sounding like breaking surf Ted Simmons decided that discretion was the better part of valour and returned to the deck. He did so not a moment too soon, for with a sudden lurch the U-boat went down with a rush, leaving Germans and Canadians struggling in the water side by side. Fortunately, *Chambly's* boat was standing by and moved in to pick up the boarding party. Only one man, Stoker William Brown, was missing, and it was assumed he had been drawn under when the U-boat went down. A German officer and seven ratings were also picked up and taken to *Chambly*.

While *Chambly* was dealing with U-501, *Moosejaw* circled the area watchfully, but Frederick Grubb was enough of a humanitarian to be moved by the plight of the Germans in the water. He dropped both his skiffs, which between them rescued 29 survivors–three officers, two midshipmen and 24 ratings. As the last of these men were being helped over the corvette's rail, there was a flurry of rockets from the direction of the convoy, indicating that another ship had been torpedoed. Having been informed by *Chumbly* that U-501 had sunk, Grubb decided it was time to take *Moosejaw* to the aid of SC42, which was then less than 8 miles off.

The sinking of U-501 by the two corvettes was a remarkable operation: a comedy of errors in which lack of experience and incompetence played a large part on both sides. There can be no doubt that U-501's lookouts were not as alert as they should have been, otherwise she would not have been caught on the surface by the patrolling Catalina. Also, had Förster, following the subsequent crash dive, gone to silent routine instead of attempting to make off at full speed, then *Chambly's* asdics might not have detected the U-boat. As to *Chambly's* attack, this was carried out with commendable precision, and all credit must go to Commander Prentice for the way in which he had trained his raw recruits in a short space of time and under the most difficult circumstances. However, the damage inflicted on U-501 by the two depth charges exploding as one was a pure fluke–the result of fumbling, inexperienced men doing the wrong thing when under pressure. This was also substantially true *of Moosejaw's* surface attack, when all her guns failed to fire when they were most needed. On the other hand, this was a blessing indeed for the U-boat's crew, many of whom would have been killed or injured if the guns had fired. Even the ramming of U-501 by *Moosejaw* was something of an accident, the submarine having presented herself beam-on to the corvette by running across her bows. In his report written later, Prentice said: "Although the success of this attack can only be attributed to extreme luck or the blessing of Providence, it could not have been achieved without the excellent co-operation of my officers and men."

It must also be said that U-501 was not a very enthusiastic participant in the action. When the man who had leapt aboard the *Moosejaw* with such alacrity, while the two ships were momentarily alongside each other, was brought to the corvette's bridge, Lieutenant Grubb was astonished to find himself face to face with U-501's commanding officer, Korvettenkapitän Hugo Förster. The German officer, who was extremely agitated, explained to Grubb that he had boarded *Moosejaw* in order to assist in the rescue of his own crew. Now it may be that the time-honoured practice of the captain going down with his ship is born of mythology, but for he who commands to be the first off in a case of emergency is stretching maritime protocol to its absolute limits. Förster's action certainly did not impress the Canadians, and his own crew, fresh from immersion in the icy waters of the Atlantic, were said to be furious. Later, when Grubb questioned the other German officers, he formed the firm impression that they were all glad to be out of the war. Even Förster's senior watchofficer, the politically motivated Werner Albring, had lost much of his enthusiasm for the fight.

Perhaps the most remarkable aspect to this operation was the incredible lengths *Chambly* and *Moosejaw* went to in rescuing the crew of U-501. In view of the fact that Prentice was well aware of the presence of other U-boats in the area—they were then gathering around SC42 like flies around a jampot—he would have been fully justified in withdrawing at speed after the dispatch of U-501. To have remained in the area to pick up 37 enemy survivors was an act either of great humanity or crass naïvety—probably a combination of both.

By 13 September, nothing having been heard from U-501, not even her routine weather broadcast, BdU became suspicious and repeatedly called her, requesting her position. There was no answer. U-84 reported she had spoken with U-501 several days earlier, when Förster claimed to have sunk an unidentified steamer by gunfire—this was the *Einvik*—on 5 September. That was the last any of the *Markgraf* group saw or heard of U-501. Reluctantly, Dönitz then declared her as "possibly missing." On 18 December, Förster's boat was posted "probably missing." It would be some time before her real fate became known at BdU.

13

A Thousand Miles to Go

Following her successful encounter with U-85 *Skeena* rejoined the convoy, and at 1500 resumed station ahead of the lead ships. Sunset was still nearly four hours away. Meanwhile the weather continued fine and clear, with an unusually calm sea, disturbed only by the long, undulating Atlantic swell. This was a very mixed blessing for, although the calm weather made life infinitely more comfortable in the ships, it left them cruelly exposed to hostile eyes. As a result of Rear-Admiral MacKenzie's frequent reprimands, there had been some reduction in the pall of smoke hanging overhead, but a hard core of persistent offenders continued to lay a marker in the skies. Prominent among them were two of the oldest ships in the ranks of the convoy, the 43-year-old Norwegian whale-oil tanker *Lancing* and the Swedish turret-decker *Atland*, in her 32nd year and groaning under a full toad of phosphates. In the case of the *Lancing*, poor-quality coal and her great age were excuse. enough for her transgression, but the *Atland*, although also of advanced years, was a Doxford motor-vessel. A little more care in the adjustment of her fuel valves might have cured her smoking funnel. As it was, these two ships, well supported by the Dutch steamer *Zypenberg* and the two Newcastle tramps *Waziristan* and *Caduceus*, continued to advertise the presence of SC42 far and wide.

With the *Skeena* back on station, Commander Hibbard eased his tired bones from the pilot chair and went into the tiny chart-house at the after end of the destroyer's bridge. The navigator's plot on the chart showed the convoy to be 420 miles west of Iceland, with just over 1,000 miles to go to the North Channel. Assuming that the weather remained fair—a most unlikely possibility—and that the present speed of 6 knots was maintained, another seven days' hard steaming lay ahead before safer waters were reached. This, Hibbard decided, was not a pleasant prospect to contemplate. He was, as yet, still not aware of the proximity of *Chambly* and *Moosejaw*, much less of their brilliant action resulting in the sinking of U-501. As to the ships of the 20th Escort Group, said by Iceland to be coming to his aid, at least another 18 hours would elapse before they joined. Meanwhile, the wolves were all around him.

Returning to his vigil at the compass platform, Hibbard once again counted the few arrows remaining in his quiver. *Kenogami* was covering the port side of the convoy, *Alberni* was to starboard, while two Catalinas, operating independently, were circling astern. *Orillia* was still absent, and all attempts to raise her by R/T and W/T had failed. Continuing to watch over the two damaged ships *Baron Pentland* and *Tachee*, the third corvette must by now be far astern—too far astern. It was time to call her in to help defend the main flock. Hibbard ordered his yeoman of signals to contact the Catalinas by lamp, requesting them to find *Orillia* and bring her back.

The remainder of the afternoon passed peacefully, with the convoy, having worked up to 7 knots, steering an uninterrupted course of 043°. Of the corvette *Orillia* there was no sign, neither was any communication received from her. Hibbard began to fear for her safety, and as the sun continued to sink towards the western horizon, so the tension mounted. The enemy had not shown himself again, but there was not a man in the convoy foolish enough to doubt that he was only biding his time.

The assumption was correct. U-82, U-207, U-432 and U-652 were in fact all following close in the wake of the convoy, while others were hurrying in. Had it not been for the Catalinas circling overhead, the U-boats would have long ago been tempted to make a concerted attack at periscope depth. At 1500, Rollmann, in U-82, emboldened by his success in torpedoing the *Empire Hudson* 10 hours earlier, could wait no longer and brought his boat to the surface. Trimmed down, he hauled off to the eastward and worked up to full speed with the object of pulling ahead of the convoy in preparation for an attack as soon as darkness closed in. His plan almost came to grief a few moments later, when a Catalina came roaring in at wave-top height. U-82 went into her now all-too-familiar crash-dive routine.

Either the Catalina had run out of depth charges or, more likely, her crew, cold and tired, were not at their best, for there was no attack on the U-boat. Half-an-hour later, Rollmann was able to surface and set off again at full speed with confidence. The Catalinas still circled, sometimes coming so close to the U-boat that their markings were easily discernible with the naked eye, but they seemed to be completely oblivious to the presence of the surfaced submarine. One aircraft crossed U-82's bows flying so low and so close that Rollmann instinctively reduced speed to avoid a collision. By 1800, U-82 was abreast the leading ships and to starboard of the convoy, still on the surface and undetected.

U-207, similarly engaged in overhauling the convoy some 5 miles to port, was not so fortunate. She was spotted on the surface by one of the Coastal Command aircraft, which immediately dropped two brilliant white flares. Although the sun was still above the horizon, the flares were so blinding in their intensity that they brought the uneasy peace of the late afternoon to an abrupt end. The reaction on all sides was startling. With klaxons screeching, Fritz Meyer took U-207 down in a crash dive that broke all records, the merchant ships made a hurried emergency turn to starboard, and the corvette *Kenogami* hurled herself towards the area indicated at maximum revolutions. Ten minutes later, the same Catalina dropped more flares further to port, and *Kenogami* followed, dropping speculative depth charges as she went. By then, however, U-207 was lying deep and silent. Lieutenant-Commander Jackson took *Kenogami* on in a wide, sweeping search, but no contact was made. Twenty minutes later, the convoy resumed course, and the ships settled down to await the coming of darkness with some trepidation.

At 2000, Third Officer Adrian Millar took over the watch

on the bridge of the *Gypsum Queen.* The 3,915-ton bulk carrier, loaded with 5,500 tons of sulphur for Glasgow, was lead ship in column 8, having the commodore's ship *Everleigh* on her port side. Despite her Middlesbrough registry, the *Gypsum Queen* carried a predominantly Merseyside crew, with a sprinkling of Scots and Irish. Millar, 23 years old, being American-born of Welsh ancestry, was the odd man out, but he was no stranger to the North Atlantic. He had crossed the turbulent ocean many times, in tramps, and before the outbreak of war in the Cunard liner *Carpathia*, famous for her role in rescuing survivors of the *Titanic* disaster.

Whereas Adrian Millar may have found crossing the North Atlantic in the 13,000-ton, twin-screw *Carpathia* in the days of peace an agreeable experience, the same passage in wartime aboard the *Gypsum Queen* was turning out to be a totally different matter. The small bulker, owned by Douglas Ramsay of Glasgow, and built at Haverton-on-Tees in 1927, had never had any pretensions of grace or speed, nor would she ever. She was essentially an ugly ship, with her funnel right aft and her bridge perched incongruously right forward at the break of the forecastle head. This may have been a convenient arrangement for working her bulk cargoes, allowing the grabs easy access to the holds, but in an Atlantic gale it made life hell for those on watch on her bridge. Being a mere 40 feet from the stem, the bridge took the full force of the seas each time the ship buried her bows. At times, to keep watch on the bridge of the *Gypsum Queen* was akin to being stranded on a half-tide rock, with the added discomfort of riding a roller-coaster. Such had been Adrian Millar's experience in the gales of the week just past. Every muscle in his body still ached from the constant struggle against the violent motion of this forward extremity of the ship. There were bruises too, evidence of the times when, failing to anticipate the rise or fall of the deck, he had gone crashing into some unyielding piece of bridge equipment.

With the weather now once more fine and calm, although the wind seemed to be freshening from the southeast, the *Gypsum Queen's* salt-caked bridge rode the long swells with dignified majesty. The long awaited cloak of darkness had at last arrived, but it was far from complete. A bright yellow moon, only five days past the full, hung in a cloudless sky, laying a glittering path on the sea, down which the lines of deep-laden ships plodded steadily northeastwards. Eight of their number had already paid the price of the vulnerability, and none of them knew what the night would bring.

On board the tanker *Bulysses*, occupying a reasonably sheltered position in the middle of column 10, Second Officer Robert Walker was debating the wisdom of turning in. Walker, a 28-year-old Aberdonian, kept the middle watch, and was due on the bridge again at midnight. Prudence would indicate that to sleep on top of several thousand tons of highly inflammable gas oil while creeping through U-boat-infested waters at a snail's pace was the height of stupidity, but Walker was desperately tired. He decided to compromise, and using his lifejacket as a pillow stretched out on his day bed fully clothed, determined to stave off sleep with a good book.

Two miles to starboard of the *Bulysses*, and hidden in the darkness beyond the outer perimeter of the convoy, U-82 kept pace with SC42, steering a parallel course. From his vantage point in the conning tower of the U-boat, Siegfried Rollmann judged the distance to the nearest ships to be approximately 2,000 metres—too far for an accurate shot. He made a small alteration of course to port to edge closer in and sent his crew to their attack stations.

Captain Alban Chapman joined Adrian Millar on the bridge of the *Gypsum Queen* at around 2030. The 50-year-old Nova Scotian captain was uneasy, and had good cause to be so. The *Gypsum Queen's* cargo of bulk sulphur was as volatile as the oil-rich lands of Texas whence it came. A flame, or even a spark, was enough to staff an unstoppable conflagration, the like of which had consumed many a similarly loaded ship and her crew in the past. What an enemy torpedo exploding in a hold packed with sulphur could do did not bear contemplation. As a sop to his overstretched nerves and in the absence of any other possible precaution to take, Chapman ordered Third Officer Millar to double up the lookouts.

In *Skeena's* cramped W/T office below her bridge, the duty operator, irritated by the continuous crackle of static in his earphones, switched over to the distress frequency, 500 kcs. There

Adrian E. Millar, Third Officer,
SS Gypsum Queen, *Convoy SC42,*
September 1941.
(Photo: Ian A. Millar)

the static was just as loud and persistent, and he was about to try another frequency when he heard the now-familiar grating of the spark-gap transmitter. It was the mysterious operator again, breaking the cloak of radio silence surrounding the convoy. The transmission was brief this time, just three three-letter code groups, XKI, XMI and XMK, followed by the break sign BT, the two-letter group XF, and then a prolonged, steady note, as given by a radio beacon. Once again, the ugly possibility was raised that someone in the convoy was in league with the enemy. Unfortunately, by the time the *Skeena's* direction-finder was tuned in, the transmission had ceased and was not repeated.

U-82's stealthy approach had by this time brought her to within easy range of ships of the starboard column of SC42. Rollmann, crouched over the open sight in the U-boat's conning tower, gave the order to fire tubes 1, 2, and 3 in quick succession. The boat shuddered three times and three 21-inch torpedoes, spaced at one-second intervals, sped towards the massed targets.

Rollmann straightened up from the sight and began count-

SS Gypsum Queen
(Photo: George H. Evans)

ing off the seconds elapsed. He reached 240–four minutes from firing–and, with his stomach churning in bitter disappointment, began reluctantly to accept failure. By some incredible fluke all three torpedoes had missed. Then there came a dull, almost inaudible thump, and night was suddenly turned into day.

The book had fallen from Second Officer Walker's hand, and he was drifting into a light sleep when one of Rollmann's torpedoes, having passed through two columns of ships, slammed into the starboard side of the *Bulysses*. A great red fireball erupted from the tanker, shot 400 feet into the night sky, and then flared out bathing the convoy in a garish yellow light. There was a stench of burning oil, and a searing heat swept through the ship, blistering the paint on steel bulkheads, shattering inch-thick port glasses and spontaneously igniting woodwork in the accommodation.

Walker came awake with his cabin collapsing around him, and with one instinctive movement scooped up his lifejacket and launched himself through the open doorway into the alleyway. Shaking off any remaining vestiges of sleep, he made for the bridge, only to find his way blocked by wreckage, behind which was a wall of advancing flames. He retreated aft and reached the open deck through the door at the other end of the alleyway. Here he found the *Bulysses'* third officer, John Francis, slumped against a bulkhead in a dazed condition. Francis, who was on watch on the bridge when the torpedo struck, had been blown over the rail, but by some miracle was not seriously injured. He told Walker that Captain Lamb was still on the bridge, but when the second officer went forward to investigate he saw that the bridge and the accommodation below were a mass of leaping flames. There was no way up, and Captain Bert Lamb, and anyone else up there with him, if not already dead soon would be.

Taking the half-conscious Francis by the arm, Walker hustled him aft along the open catwalk with the heat of the flames on their backs urging them on. They reached the boatdeck to find a panicking crowd of Chinese ratings attempting to launch the starboard lifeboat. Walker took charge, and the boat was successfully lowered to the water. The two British officers and 15 Chinese seamen then boarded.

Walker's first thought when the boat cleared the ship's side was for men who might be trapped in the forward end of the ship. He therefore took the boat back alongside in the region of the bridge. This was an action he regretted, for as soon as the boat touched the ship's side it was almost overwhelmed by a mob of frightened Chinese, all kicking and fighting to get on board. By the time Walker managed to restore order, the boat was crammed with a total of 47 people, far in excess of its capacity.

The lifeboat was so crowded that it was impossible even to ship the oars, let alone row. The sea was lapping over the gunwales, and it was clear that any false move would end in capsize and disaster. Luckily, as they drifted, a Catalina flew over, dropping flares, by the light of which Walker saw the small Polish ship *Wisla* bearing down on them.

The 3,000-ton *Wisla*, the rear-marker of column 10, again in direct contravention of convoy orders, had slowed down and was preparing to pick up survivors. It was a simple, though highly dangerous manoeuvre, Walker allowing his boat to drift down on the Polish ship as soon as she stopped. A ladder was thrown over the side, and was immediately rushed by the terrified Chinese. It required all of Walker's physical strength and authority to restore some semblance of order and see all safely over the rail of the rescue ship.

As soon as Walker, last man up the ladder, boarded the *Wisla*, he went to the bridge and requested the master that he be allowed to take the lifeboat away again to look for other survivors. The Polish captain refused, for Walker was by then completely exhausted and none of his crew were in a fit state to help him. The *Wisla's* motor lifeboat was sent away, and some time later returned with ten more survivors who had been found clinging to wreckage. Among them was Captain Lamb, who was injured, fortunately not seriously. Chief Officer Birdsall and three Chinese ratings could not be found, and it was assumed that they had perished.

The sudden and dramatic end of the *Bulysses* threw the rest of the convoy into confusion. Rear-Admiral MacKenzie ordered an emergency turn 45 degrees to starboard, thereby taking the ships closer to, rather than away from the danger. At the same time, *Skeena* fired starshells at random, a Catalina dropped flares, and several merchant ships opened fire at imagined enemies with 4-inch and machine-guns.

Dan Hortop, taking his trick at the wheel high on the *Jedmoor's* open monkey island, had an interrupted all-round view of the action. The young Welshman suddenly felt very alone and vulnerable. He fingered the silver whistle at his neck, wondering if this was the time when his father's foresight would be called upon to pay dividends. Then the officers' steward appeared out of the darkness, a jug in his hand and a row of enamel mugs hanging from his belt. The steaming coffee, heavily laced with rum, which he offered to Hortop was a gift from the gods. The bitter night air lost some of its deadly chill, and now, when the deck beneath his feet shook to the thunder of the *Jedmoor's* 4-inch, thoughts of revenge replaced naked fear. Dan Hortop was coming to terms with the realities of war.

The *Jedmoor's* gunners were shooting at shadows, however. Delighted, if somewhat overawed, by the havoc he had caused, Rollmann had taken U-82 at full speed into the protective darkness on the starboard side of the convoy. As she went, her W/T operator, in his tiny cabin abaft the U-boat's control room, listened in to a frantic burst of plain language Morse reporting the torpedoing of the *Bulysses*. The report, from an unidentified merchantman, served no other purpose than to inform Siegfried Rollmann of the name of his victim.

On the bridge of the *Gypsum Queen*, leading column 8 and less than a mile off the *Bulysses*, Captain Chapman and Third Officer Millar were joined by Chief Officer Henry Barnfather. The three men watched in horror as the flames consumed the stricken tanker and, presumably, all her crew. Barnfather, a 46-year-old Tynesider who had seen service at sea in the First World War, was the ship's gunnery officer. With a silent nod from Chapman, he left the bridge to roundup his 4-inch gun's crew. It was time for the *Gypsum Queen* to look to her defences. Only a few minutes after Barnfather and his men, two RN ratings and two gunners of the Maritime Regiment, reached the poop-gun platform, a surfaced U-boat glided into view only 300 yards off the *Gypsum Queen's* starboard beam. She was on a parallel course and appeared to be keeping pace with the ship. There was a mad scramble for the 4-inch, but when the gun was trained round the U-boat disappeared out of sight behind the starboard lifeboat, demonstrating the inadequacy of a stern-mounted gun. Barnfather snatched up the bridge telephone and called for a change of course.

Rollmann was as startled as Henry Barnfather when he saw the big, deep-laden steamer appear out of the shadows. She was a long ship, with her funnel aft, and Rollmann's immediate impression was that, by an incredible stroke of luck, he had stumbled on another tanker. Then he saw the goat-post masts and the tarpaulin-covered hatches, and he knew she was a dry cargo ship, but a big one—10,000 tons at the very least.

Rollmann now also became aware of the figures gathering around the gun at the ship's stern, and when he saw the long barrel swinging round he acted quickly. Calling for full speed ahead on the port diesel and half astern on the starboard, he spun the U-boat on her axis, presented her stern to the enemy ship, and fired a torpedo from the after tube.

The *Gypsum Queen* was not the 10,000-tonner Rollmann had supposed, but she was a big enough target not to miss at such short range. With her stern swinging to starboard as she canted under the full port helm called for by Chief Officer Barnfather, she caught Rollmann's torpedo squarely in her engine room. By some great good fortune, her cargo of sulphur did not ignite, but with her engines still going ahead she began to sink at once, driving under bow-first like a crash-diving submarine.

The maindeck was awash within two minutes, and those unfortunate enough to be forward on the bridge were cut off from the two lifeboats, which were carried aft. On the afterdeck, Henry Barnfather, aware that the ship was going quickly, called for men to launch the boats. It was found that the starboard boat had been smashed by the explosion, leaving only the port boat to take the survivors. There was no need to lower the boat for, as the last man scrambled in, its keel touched the water, and it floated clear of the davits. Those unlucky enough to be left on board hurled themselves over the side as the *Gypsum Queen* went down, and found themselves surrounded by patches of burning oil spreading out from the torpedoed *Bulysses*.

Close on the heels of the *Gypsum Queen* in column 8 was the small Norwegian timber-carrier *Vestland*, commanded by Captain Leonard Terjesen. When the British ship was hit, Terjesen was forced to make a hurried alteration of course to avoid colliding with her. He should then have steamed on past the sinking ship. The commodore's orders were quite explicit—no stopping to pick up survivors—but Terjesen was a seaman, and those men in the water were of his own kind. He could not, and would not, leave them to die in this alien sea.

Several U-boats were on the surface within the lanes of the convoy, provoking a spirited, if largely ineffectual, defence by the merchantmen and their escort. Starshells flared overhead, ancient 4-inch guns barked and spat long tongues of flame, fiery tracer scythed across the moonlit water and depth charges thundered under the sea. In the midst of this deadly free-for-

The U-82, which sank the SS Gypsum Queen *during the battle of convoy SC42. Later in the war she was lost in action with all hands.*
(Photo: Johannes Vahlbruch)

all, Leonard Terjesen stopped his ship and allowed her to drift astern, to where the oil burned and the cries of drowning men could be heard. Boarding nets were rigged and a boat lowered.

The time was 2130, and in wheelhouses and engine rooms throughout the convoy, in accordance with the commodore's previously signalled instructions, clocks were advanced to two hours slow on GMT. SC42 had reached the mid-point of the North Atlantic, and despite the chaos reigning all around ship's routine must be observed.

The *Vestland's* clocks remained unaltered, for her crew were far too busy snatching the *Gypsum Queen's* men from the water. Henry Barnfather brought his boat alongside the Norwegian, unloaded most of its occupants, and then went back to look for others. Within half-an-hour he found Third Officer Adrian Millar and nine men clinging to a raft. Millar, who had been on the *Gypsum Queen's* bridge when she was hit, reported that Captain Alban Chapman and First Radio Officer Adam

Williamson had gone down with the ship while dumping the secret code books.

The *Vestland* was many miles astern of the convoy when the last survivor was brought aboard. In all, she had saved 26 men from the *Gypsum Queen.* Ten others were either missing or known to be dead, some, in the opinion of Captain Terjesen, killed by depth charges dropped by the escorts who were trying to protect them. Meanwhile, the *Vestland* herself faced terrible danger. It would take her 10 hours of hard steaming to rejoin SC42.

As for U-82, the cause of much of the mayhem, her torpedo tubes were empty, and Siegfried Rollmann decided it was time to steal away into the night. This was just as well, for at that point HMCS *Skeena* arrived on the scene firing starshells.

Rollmann took U-82 away at full speed, steering a northerly course and crossing ahead of the convoy. Once clear of the ships, it was his intention to submerge, reload tubes, and then surface again to mount an attack on the port side of SC42.

The Vestland *picks up survivors of a torpedoed ship.*
(Photo: Ian A. Millar)

Unfortunately, when U-82 was halfway across the path of the convoy she was spotted by the British ship *Sarthe*, leading column 6. The *Sarthe*, a 5,271-ton Royal Mail steamer, did not mount a 4-inch, but her 20-mm Oerlikons and Hotchkiss machine-guns let fly with a broadside that came uncomfortably close to the U-boat. The tracer served to pinpoint the target for the *Jedmoor's* gunners, who quickly began to bracket U-82 with 4-inch shells. *Skeena*, still hunting to starboard of the convoy, joined in with starshells and Rollmann prudently cleared the conning tower and crash-dived.

U-432, U-433 and U-652 were still on the surface and inside the convoy, and between them they now fired a total of seven torpedoes, all of which fortunately missed their targets. At least two of the U-boats were then sighted by the merchantmen, and once again the night was rent by the crash of big guns and the wild chatter of machine-guns. The *Jedmoor* had a misfire on her 4-inch, resulting in a round jammed in the breech, and Captain Collins decided it was time to break away. He rang for emergency full speed, turned his ship on full port helm and headed south out of the holocaust.

14

Help at Hand

As the *Jedmoor* put the other ships astern of her and sought the dubious safety of the open sea, there was a lull in the battle for SC42. In the space of 24 hours ten ships had fallen to the enemy, and 150 men had gone to a watery grave. Now an uneasy peace settled over the convoy, but only a fool would have thought it was all over. The U-boats were still out there, watching, waiting, ready to pounce when the opportunity presented itself. Nevertheless, humans cannot survive without hope, and there were those who, encouraged by a freshening wind and falling visibility, felt that an uncharacteristically benign North Atlantic might be about to revert to its normal violent self, thus drawing a protective cloak around them. Then there were also the promised reinforcements from Iceland–due at first light on the 11th, or so it was said.

Help from any source, if it was to come, had to come soon, or it would be too late. It is difficult to estimate exactly how many U-boats were in contact with SC42 that night, but with the arrival of U-659 during the evening at least 18 were in the vicinity. Against this formidable attacking force was arrayed a defence of one small destroyer and two even smaller corvettes, plus the obsolescent and mainly ineffectual guns of the merchantmen. SC42's greatest weakness, however, now lay in the men who manned the ships, both naval and merchant. For almost ten days they had faced continuous harassment, first by the weather and then by the enemy, and that night they were mentally and physically exhausted.

At this point neither Commander Hibbard nor Rear-Admiral MacKenzie were aware that the corvettes *Chambly* and *Moosejaw*, having dispatched U-501, were racing in to join SC42's defences. *Moosejaw* was in the lead, with 29 German prisoners on board, a state of affairs with which her commander, Lieutenant Grubb, was distinctly unhappy. So far, the prisoners were well behaved, the majority in fact appearing to be glad that the war was over for them, which, in view of the traumatic experience they had been through, was not surprising. However, mindful that his crew numbered only 47 and might easily be taken unawares and overpowered by these fit, young Germans, Grubb had taken the precaution of separating officers and ratings. U-501's commander, Hugo Förster, his first watchofficer, Werner Albring, and second watchofficer, Hans Sittenfeld, were housed in Grubb's cabin, while the 24 ratings and two midshipmen occupied the corvette's after cabin flat. This being done, it seemed likely that Förster himself might be the only cause of unrest. His men made no attempt to conceal their intense disgust at his behaviour in the action that led to the sinking of their submarine.

Hibbard's cup overflowed when, at 2117, *Chambly* broke radio silence to report that she was closing the convoy with *Moosejaw*. Such was the nervous mood of the convoy that night, however, that when, half-an-hour later, *Moosejaw* appeared out of the shadows, ahead and to starboard of SC42, there was momentary panic. *Skeena* immediately illuminated the sky with starshells, and MacKenzie took the merchant ships into an emergency turn to port. Fortunately, Grubb had the presence of mind to switch on *Moosejaw's* navigation lights, otherwise she might have been the target of a substantial battery of shells as the heavy guns of the merchantmen came to bear.

The immediate furore died down and Hibbard ordered *Moosejaw* to take up station on the convoy's starboard quarter. Then *Chambly* hove in sight and panic broke out again, with one unidentified merchantman opening fire on the corvette with bursts of tracer. Fortunately, the shooting was inaccurate, but the final burst passed close enough to *Chambly* to cause her to use her signal lamp in self-defence. When the shooting died down, *Chambly* was ordered to take up station on the port quarter of the convoy. With *Skeena* scouting ahead and *Kenogami* and *Alberni* on the bows, for the first time since leaving Sydney SC42 was guarded on all sides. Even so, there was too much ocean for five escorts to cover effectively.

Given the opportunity, a significant contribution to the convoy's defence might be made by the ship leading column 11. She was Ropner's 4,815-ton *Stonepool*, a ship with a reputation for fighting her corner. Two years previously, on Friday 13 October 1939, while off the Cape Verde Islands, U-42 had been foolish enough to challenge this shabby West Hartlepool tramp on the surface. Commanded by Captain Albert White, the *Stonepool*, one of the first British merchant ships to be armed with a 4-inch, fought back. White put his stern to the U-boat, and with a scratch crew of sailors and firemen manning the 4-inch, engaged the enemy. A fierce gun battle followed, the *Stonepool's* 4-inch matching shot for shot with U-42's 88-mm deck gun. The U-boat was so severely damaged that she was scuttled by her crew when two British destroyers arrived on the scene in answer to White's calls for help. The *Stonepool*, herself badly knocked about, and with all her lifeboats smashed, staggered into the British Channel three days later, and lived to fight another day.

Two years on, the *Stonepool's* armament had been increased by the addition of a 12-pounder and six machine-guns, all her guns being manned by trained DEMS gunners. Her current master, Captain Nicholson, had a great deal of confidence in his ship's ability to defend herself. When the excitement had died down, and with two extra escorts in place, the convoy having returned to its original course, Nicholson passed the word for all lookouts and gun's crews to be on the alert, and steeled himself to wait out the remaining hours of darkness. It was then a little after 2200 and SC42, restrained by the speed of the slowest ships in its ranks, was making no more than 5 knots, equivalent to a fast walking pace. It promised to be a long and dangerous wait.

A quarter of a mile astern of the *Stonepool* was one of the ships responsible for the snail's pace progress of SC42. The 4,924-

SS Stonepool, *4,803 gross tons.*
(Photo: A. Duncan)

ton *Berury*, her 22-year-old engine wheezing and clattering, was hard-pressed to maintain even 5 knots. The aging steamer, built at Tacoma, Washington, in 1919 and handed over to Britain on "lease-lend," was managed for the Ministry of War Transport by Moss Hutchinson of Liverpool and was commanded by Captain Francis Morgan. She carried, in her holds and piled up on deck, constructional material for a new US Navy base to be built at Londonderry.

In view of the strategic importance of his cargo, before sailing from Sydney, Nicholson had requested that the *Berury* be given a position of relative safety in the middle of the convoy. In accordance with the operation of Murphy's Law, he had consequently found himself bringing up the rear of column 11, a particularly exposed spot on the starboard quarter of SC42. However, Morgan was a man of resource, and when on the night of the 9th the Greek ship *Mount Taygetus*, occupying a sheltered position behind the *Stonepool*, fell astern, he moved his ship up to take the Greek's place. Hemmed in on all sides by other ships, Morgan at last experienced a degree of security.

Another hour passed without incident, and the tension in the ships eased a notch. Then, without warning, the enemy lunged at the far side of the convoy. During the quiet time, Hans Ey, in U-433, had been creeping up unseen on the port quarter, and at 2312 launched two torpedoes. Ey's target was the 2,215-ton Norwegian-flag *Bestum*, last ship in column 2. Loaded with a cargo of wood-pulp, the ex-Wabana ship would not earn Hans Ey much in the way of accolades but, with U-433 as yet without a single enemy ship to her credit, any accessible target was worth trying for.

Ey's eagerness to make his mark led to careless aiming, saved the *Bestum*, and almost spelled disaster for U-433. Both torpedoes missed the target, but they were seen by those on the bridge of the *Bestum*, who lost no time in firing distress rockets. *Skeena* weighed in with starshells, and ships all around the *Bestum* broke radio silence to report that she had been torpedoed.

Commander Hibbard, believing the *Bestum* to be sinking, ordered *Kenogami* to drop astern to pick up survivors. As the corvette was about to do so, a submarine was reported on the surface to port of the convoy. A few minutes later, the submarine was seen crossing *Kenogami's* bows at a distance of about 500 yards. It was U-433 making good her escape. The U-boat crash-dived before the corvette's 4-inch could be brought to bear, but as she plunged a pattern of depth charges, set to explode at 150 and 300 feet, followed her down.

When the boiling water subsided again, *Kenogami's* asdics gained a hard contact, and Lieutenant-Commander Jackson began a more deliberate attack. Three minutes later, the contact was suddenly lost, and it was assumed that the U-boat had either sunk or was severely damaged. No search could be made for wreckage, for Hibbard was growing anxious and recalled *Kenogami* to her original station.

U-433 was, in fact, no more than badly shaken, and would remain in touch with SC42. Her intended victim, the *Bestum*, on the other hand, had received such a shock that, like the *Jedmoor*, she decided to leave the convoy and take her chances sailing alone. She eventually reached Iceland unharmed.

As U-433 retired to lick her wounds, so U-207, after a long chase, at last came within striking distance of the convoy. Built at the Germania yard in Kiel, and only three months into her first patrol, she was commanded by 25-year-old Oberleutnant-zur-See Fritz Meyer, and carried a total crew of 41, all of whom, like their commander, were in their twenties and without any real experience of war. U-207 had yet to prove herself as an effective member of the *Markgraf* group, but with 14 torpedoes ready for use Meyer and his men looked forward to a night filled with glory. Before them stretched line upon line of slow-moving merchant ships, all bathed in the light of a brilliant moon.

At 0010, Able Seaman H. Matthews stood outside the door of the *Stonepool's* galley and eyed that same yellow moon with deep suspicion. Since the *Bulysses* had erupted into flames three hours earlier, Matthews, along with those of the *Stonepool's* crew not on watch, had been on deck, fully clothed and wearing his lifejacket. These men may not have been privy to the real gravity of the situation, but they knew well enough that the fortunes of SC42 had reached a critical point. This was not the time to be below decks, cold though the night air might be.

Matthews's precautions soon proved to be fully justified. At 0015, Fritz Meyer fired his first salvo with real intent. A few minutes later, one of his torpedoes blew open the engine room on the starboard side of the *Stonepool's* hull. To Matthews, the long-expected event seemed almost like an anticlimax. There was no spectacular explosion, no searing flame and choking smoke, just a dull thud, followed by a large column of water shooting skywards, accompanied by the hiss of escaping steam. What followed was far more dramatic.

The *Stonepool* was loaded with a full cargo of grain in bulk, a simple, everyday cargo ships have carried across the Atlantic for hundreds of years. The layman might be forgiven for believing the loading and carriage of grain in bulk is a simple matter of putting the ship under an elevator and closing the hatches when the holds are full. This is far from the truth. Bulk grain is like shifting sand, and the regulations concerning its carriage are very stringent and rigidly enforced by port authorities. Amongst other things, a ship's hold filled with bulk grain must be divided centrally by temporary fore and aft bulkheads made of 3-inch-thick timbers to reduce the movement of the grain when the ship rolls heavily, and so prevent capsize.

With the sea pouring into her engine room, the largest open space in her hull, the *Stonepool* listed so heavily to starboard that the thousands of tons of grain leaning against her temporary fore and aft bulkheads was too much for the heavy timbers. They collapsed throughout the ship, allowing the grain to shift from port to starboard, so increasing the list. She wallowed in the swell, sagging further and further to starboard with each roll. She was going over.

No order to abandon ship was necessary. There was a rush for the boats, but this proved futile. The starboard-side lifeboat had been blown away by the explosion, and owing to the list it was impossible to launch the port boat. Matthews and four other seamen who had been on deck with him ran to the forward liferafts. The port-side raft was cut away and launched, the four men following it over the side. In a brave effort to get more rafts into the water, Matthews rushed aft, but before he reached the afterdeck he was thrown into the sea as the *Stonepool* capsized. Only three minutes had elapsed since the torpedo struck.

Three cables astern, on the bridge of the *Berury*, Captain Morgan witnessed the sudden end of the *Stonepool* and acted swiftly. His first priority was to avoid a collision with the sinking ship, and, with anger bubbling up in him, he was determined to ram the U-boat responsible, given the opportunity. He rang for emergency full speed and ordered the helm hard to starboard.

Even as the *Berury* heeled under helm and engines, Morgan realised that his way to starboard was blocked by the lead ship of column 12, the 5,043-ton Norwegian timber-carrier *Arosa*. Neither could he go to port without running into the big whale-oil tanker *Lancing* in column 10. Morgan's quandary was solved seconds later when a torpedo from U-207's second salvo ploughed into the *Berury's* starboard side.

Morgan was conscious of a brilliant flash, followed by a violent explosion that left him temporarily deaf and blind. The *Berury*, hit in her forward cargo hold, took a heavy list to starboard. At first, Morgan feared that the weight of her deck cargo would cause her to capsize, but the old ship straightened up and began to settle slowly by the head.

Standard convoy procedure when a ship was torpedoed called for distress rockets to be fired, and Morgan was about to do this when he thought of the *Stonepool's* men struggling in the water. Rockets might bring one of the escorts, and the depth charges would fly, with disastrous consequences for those men. Morgan compromised by blowing several blasts on the *Berury's* steam whistle, in order to alert ships close by to the attack. It was perhaps an unnecessary gesture, but it satisfied a need for action.

That the *Berury* was going down fast soon became obvious, and Morgan lost no further time in ordering his crew to abandon ship. By now a choppy sea was running, but all four lifeboats were lowered without difficulty and cleared the ship's side. By this time the *Berury's* foredeck was awash and her stern high out of the water.

Soon after midnight, *Moosejaw* was on the inward leg of her zigzag on the starboard quarter of the convoy when she sighted the sinking ship. Lieutenant Grubb closed the *Berury* and found three of her lifeboats filled with survivors. A cluster of tiny red lights bobbing on the waves indicated more men in the water. They were, in fact, survivors of the *Stonepool* who, as Captain Morgan feared, had drifted down on the *Berury* after their ship went down.

As he boarded the corvette from his lifeboat, Morgan heard the faint cries of the men in the water and called for volunteers to go back for them. Unfortunately, all the *Berury's* boats had been cast adrift, but Morgan prevailed upon Lieutenant Grubb to loan him *Moosejaw's* skiff. Ten minutes later, Morgan, accompanied by the corvette's number one, Sub-Lieutenant Hal Lawrence, and four of her ratings, was pulling the boat towards the men in the water.

The skiff was tiny and the seas appeared mountainous, but with a superhuman effort Morgan and his volunteer crew eventually reached the *Stonepool's* men. They had by then been in the icy water for almost two hours, and many of them were dead. Of the living, 12 were hauled aboard the skiff, which was all the small boat could safely take, leaving three unfortunate men still in the water.

Looking around him, Morgan now found *Moosejaw* was no longer visible, and the squat silhouettes of the merchant ships were fast disappearing into the darkness. SC42 was leaving them behind. *Moosejaw's* boat, grossly overloaded with 18 men, had no more than a few inches of freeboard, and as the sea continued to rise was in danger of being swamped. The fear of being abandoned was turning to panic, when out of the darkness like a knight-errant on a white charger came HMCS *Kenogami*. Under orders to refuel at Reykjavik and return to the convoy without delay, *Kenogami* was crowding on all steam, but when Lawrence flashed his torch at her, Lieutenant-Commander Jackson threw her engines into reverse, and with the water boiling at her stern she skidded to a halt within a few yards of the skiff.

The *Stonepool's* survivors, so far gone that they had to be hauled up the ship's side with ropes, were put on board *Kenogami*. The skiff then cast off again to look for the three men left behind. This was a commendable but futile gesture, for although they searched for two hours no sign could be found of the men.

By this time the skiff was completely alone on a large expanse of empty and increasingly hostile ocean. There was no compass in the boat and, even if it were possible to catch up with the convoy, Morgan and Lawrence were unsure of which direction to take. The awful significance of their predicament had just begun to dawn on the skiff's crew when, for the second time that night, the rescuers were themselves rescued, this time by HMCS *Chambly*. They remained alongside *Chambly* until *Moosejaw* came to reclaim them.

Back on board *Moosejaw*, Morgan at last had the opportunity to muster his own crew. He found 36 men with him, leaving six unaccounted for. The *Berury's* second officer and four others were eventually found to be safe on board *Kenogami*, but one man, Sydney Gardner, an African fireman, was never seen again.

Following her spectacular sinking of the tanker *Bulysses*, U-82 went deep and stopped to load her three remaining torpedoes into the bow tubes. With the push of the swell being felt far below the surface, this was not an easy job, and it was after midnight before she set off to overhaul the convoy. At 0110 on the 11th, she sighted a lone merchant ship, which appeared to be stopped and drifting.

To Siegfried Rollmann this looked like manna from heaven. He stopped his engines and prepared to make an unhurried attack on the surface. However, this was not to be. Three corvettes suddenly appeared and there was an exchange of lamp signals with the merchantman.

Rollmann was not one to take unnecessary risks, and assumed that the ship was a decoy, possibly fitted with asdic and working in conjunction with the corvettes to trap unsuspecting U-boats. He left the area as fast as U-82's throbbing diesels would take him.

The "decoy" was none other than the *Jedmoor*, heading south in search of quieter waters, and the warships were *Alberni*, *Kenogami* and *Moosejaw*, all engaged in searching for survivors, but Rollmann was not to know this.

An hour later, Hans-Heinz Linder, in U-202, all but came to grief through underestimating the threat posed by a seemingly helpless merchantman. The 1,386-ton *Regin*, although armed only with three .303 machine-guns and having an absolute maximum speed of 7.5 knots, had already clashed with two U-boats, forcing them to dive. When, at about 0200 on the 11th, she sighted U-202 on the surface between columns 2 and 3, she at once opened fire with her machine-guns and altered course to ram. The *Regin* was, of course, too slow to catch the U-boat before she dived, but she thoroughly peppered her conning tower with the .303. Linder, who only 10 minutes earlier had watched a full salvo of his torpedoes miss their target, was not amused.

U-82 had by this time gained a position ahead of and to port of the convoy, only to find two enemy aircraft circling overhead, while two corvettes and a destroyer were also in sight. This was certainly not the opportune time for an attack, but Rollmann was in a hurry. He had just three torpedoes remaining, and when they were gone it would be time to run for home.

As the boat's attack computer had been damaged by the depth charging received after sinking the *Gypsum Queen*, a close approach, although highly dangerous, was necessary. Reducing speed so that U-82's bow-wave would not be visible from the air, Rollmann moved in. It was his intention to target the second, third and fourth ships of the outer column.

U-82 was sighted neither from the air nor from the sea, and her torpedoes, although they missed the ships of the outer columns, eventually found targets in column 4. The 1,980-ton Swedish steamer *Scania*, also ex-SC41, and bound for Hull with a cargo of timber, came to a sudden halt when her 34-year-old plates were torn apart by high explosives. The built-in buoyancy of her timber cargo kept her afloat while her crew took to the boats, but her long career was finished.

Rollmann's second victim of the small hours of that morning did not have a buoyancy advantage. The 5,463-ton *Empire Crossbill*, loaded with a cargo of steel, to which some mindless shore-planner had added a parcel of explosives, disappeared in a cloud of smoke, flame and debris. She took with her Captain Eric Townend, his crew of 46 and one passenger. For the latter, Reginald Heraghty, a homeward-bound survivor from another North Atlantic sinking, luck had finally run out.

At this time, SC42's escort was more thinly spread than Rollmann had estimated. Only *Skeena* and *Chambly* were screening ahead, while *Alberni*, *Kenogami* and *Moosejaw* were all astern still searching for survivors in the water. The flanks of the convoy were completely unprotected.

Anticipating that a similar attack might be mounted on the other side of the convoy, Commander Hibbard hauled *Skeena* across to starboard and began a high-speed search. At the same time, *Chambly* reversed course to carry out a sweep on the port side. Neither ship made contact with the enemy, for the wolves had withdrawn again into the shadows, At 0239, however, soon after *Chambly* had resumed her station ahead of the convoy, U-207 crept up on the port quarter and torpedoed the 1,231-ton Swedish timber-carrier *Garm*, the backmarker of column 2. This was Fritz Meyer's third kill of the night.

With all his torpedoes expended, accounting for, in his estimation, more than 30,000 tons of Allied shipping, Siegfried Rollmann considered U-82's part in the attack of SC42 well played. He signalled BdU of his intentions and set course southeast for Biscay and home. In less than five days, God and the enemy willing, they would find a safe haven in a bombproof submarine pen in Lorient, where the customary hero's welcome awaited them.

It was not yet to be. In just as long as it took BdU to encode the message came back the order: "No sub to break off pursuit of convoy only because torpedoes have been expended. It has to remain in position and continue to pursue convoy. Keep in touch. Make use of radio signals. Co-operate near convoy. Depending on conditions do everything possible to assist others in closing convoy." Dönitz had no intention of breaking the ring of steel he had thrown around SC42.

15

More Reinforcements

As the first hesitant brush strokes of the approaching dawn on the morning of 11 September painted the eastern sky pale grey, the battle for convoy SC42 continued unabated. It was as though both hunter and hunted realised that the last hour or so before full daylight would see the final curtain come down on this macabre charade.

Commander James Hibbard, red-eyed and drained by his long vigil on *Skeena's* open bridge, sustained himself with the knowledge that the promised reinforcements would arrive from Iceland that morning. If by some awful mischance his confidence was misplaced, then the benzedrine supplied to him and his officers by the destroyer's surgeon, Lieutenant Chesley Oakes, would be needed for longer than anticipated. That too much of the drug produced the "mother and father" of a hangover was a consequence to be lived with.

The U-boat commanders of the *Markgraf* group, many of them no less weary than their enemy, were not in the Admiralty's confidence, but with British and American-occupied Iceland less than 20 hours' fast steaming away they realised that their virtually unopposed orgy of destruction was nearing its end. Had any of them been witness to the predicament of U-85, they might have seen it as an omen of a change of fortune.

Eberhard Greger's U-85, first to sight SC42 on the morning of the 9th, was badly savaged at the hands of the escorts after torpedoing the *Thistleglen*, but, on the orders of Dönitz, she was still hanging on to the coat-tails of the convoy. In the first light, the Catalinas spotted her on the surface and swooped. Greger dived, only to endure three frightening hours of depth charging. When she finally made her escape, U-85's diesels were running rough, her port exhaust valves jamming and her periscope rendered useless. She would take no further part in the harassment of SC42.

The fight continued, however, with a dozen or more other U-boats in contact with the convoy, operating on the surface at high speed, snarling and snapping at the heels of the bewildered merchantmen. Distress rockets hissed and crackled, flares hung motionless and starshells exploded, filling the sky with harsh incandescence. Beneath this transient canopy of man-made daylight, torpedoes streaked in all directions, and the tortured merchant ships twisted and turned frantically to avoid sudden death. Around them, *Skeena* and her attendant corvettes chased their tails scattering thundering depth charges. Despite all this frenetic activity, no Allied ship was harmed, no U-boat unduly threatened, A patent lack of experience on both sides evened out the odds.

The only real beneficiaries of the illuminations were the men in the water–and there were still many. Some miles astern of the convoy, the small Norwegian steamer *Vestland* and the even smaller corvette *Moosejaw* were clearing up the human debris of the night. The corvette's messdecks and upper decks were crammed with wet, shivering merchant seamen, rubbing shoulders and sharing blankets with the equally demoralised survivors of U-501. She would very soon have room for no more. As for the *Vestland*, in the words of Captain Hudson of the Ropner's steamer *Yearby*, observing from nearby, she "was alive with men on her decks, and was towing a dozen lifeboats full of men. She was a small ship, and during the night had been weaving through the convoy, lifeboats in tow. When the commodore made the signal 'Indicate number of survivors you have on board,' the master of the Vestland replied '185.' Those, with about 400 in the boats, made a good night's rescue effort." There may have been some understandable exaggeration of numbers here, but the *Vestland*, commanded by the tenacious

Norwegian ship Vestland, *unofficial rescue ship of SC42.*
(Photo: Ian A. Millar)

Captain Terjesen, was undoubtedly performing heroic work.

At long last, around 0530, the sun heaved itself over the eastern horizon and, with warm, healing fingers, brushed away the dreadful spectres of the night. The U-boats, banished like Dracula's handmaidens at the coming of the day, turned away and glided below into the cold underwater darkness of the sea to await another opportunity to indulge their blood-lust.

The bright sunlight also revealed to Commander James Hibbard the full extent of the convoy's losses. He counted 19 ships missing, almost one third of SC42's original complement. He had done his best with the meagre resources at his disposal, but the convoy had received a savage mauling. Had *Orillia* stayed with them, it might have been different, but Hibbard had heard nothing of the corvette since she dropped back to assist the torpedoed tanker *Tachee* 30 hours earlier. Could it be that *Orillia* had also fallen to the U-boats? What of the fresh escorts from Iceland? When would they arrive?

As Hibbard pondered on the gloomy prospects of the coming day, so the capricious North Atlantic decided to intervene. It began with a blurring of the horizon, became a swirling mist, and finally they entered the white, silent world of dense fog. This was a mixed blessing because, although it might hold off the U-boats, who would be wary of closing the convoy for fear of damaging their thin hulls in collision, for the already hard-pressed merchantmen blind station-keeping was one hazard too many. As for the additional escorts on their way from Iceland, there was a possibility that they might never find the convoy.

Nowhere was the added strain more evident than on the bridge of the *Everleigh*, where dawn had brought another unwelcome development. Worn down by the awesome burden he had carried for so long, 68-year-old Rear-Admiral MacKenzie collapsed and was taken below. It therefore fell to the *Everleigh's* master, Captain W. H. Gould, to take over as acting convoy commodore. As master of a British tramp, Gould was by necessity a tough, resourceful man, a first-class seaman and rule-of-thumb navigator capable of shaping an accurate course on the flimsiest of evidence. Yet, for all that, he was not a naval man experienced in fleet manoeuvres. The direction of this large number of ships sailing in concert would require all his talents and the willing co-operation of MacKenzie's signals team. Gould was himself 58 years old, and already suffering from fatigue. With this added weight on his shoulders, it remained to be seen how long he would stand up to the strain of this ultimate command.

One of the first acts of this new day was the sighting of a floating mine by HMCS *Kenogami*, a grim reminder to those who saw it of the increasing dangers threatening the convoy as it moved closer to the epicentre of the war.

Moosejaw was lifting the last of the *Berury's* survivors out of the water and endeavouring to sink the crippled merchantman with her 4-inch when the fog closed in. The task proved far more difficult than Lieutenant Frederick Grubb had imagined. Even after he had poured 66 rounds of 4-inch into the ship, she was still afloat—on fire and down by the head, perhaps, but stubbornly refusing to sink. Mindful of the need to conserve ammunition for another day, Grubb was forced to break off and steam away from the wreck.

This was a fitting end to a thoroughly wretched 24 hours for Frederick Grubb. In addition to the stresses of war, he had discovered that he was burdened with an executive officer unable to measure up to his job under pressure, and his chief

ERA was of a similar bent. During the night, two engine-room ratings had been found the worse for drink and, more serious, the watches had omitted to run the distillation plant. As a consequence of this last inaction, *Moosejaw's* boilers ran out of water soon after she pulled away from the *Berury*, and the corvette lay drifting helplessly for some time, saved from attack, perhaps, only by the thick fog hiding her from the enemy. Little wonder Lieutenant Grubb was by then suffering from severe chest and stomach pains, and was unable to keep any food down. He was a fit man, but the immense pressure put on him by the pace of events was more than his body could stand.

The fog had also put a protective blanket around the *Jedmoor*, lying stopped some miles astern of *Moosejaw*. Captain Collins had decided to rejoin the convoy at the rendezvous for the day, but was first taking advantage of the cover of the fog to clear the stoppage in his 4-inch. It was while the *Jedmoor* drifted that the armed trawler HMS *Buttermere* stumbled upon her. *Buttermere*, in company with her sister trawler HMS *Windermere* and the corvettes *Gladiolus*, *Mimosa* and *Westaskiwin*, British, Free French and Canadian respectively, had sailed from Reykjavik 36 hours earlier under orders to join SC42 with all dispatch. They made good time, but when *Buttermere* met up with the *Jedmoor* they were casting about in the fog, hopelessly lost. So, the *Jedmoor*, originally partly responsible for attracting the first U-boats to SC42, redeemed herself by guiding in the escort reinforcements so urgently needed for the convoy's survival.

While the five new arrivals, with the *Jedmoor* following in their wake, hurried to join SC42, another chance meeting occurred in the fog. U-202 was attempting to re-establish contact with the convoy, when she came upon the *Scania*, abandoned by her crew after being torpedoed by U-82 in the early hours of the morning. The little Swedish steamer, listing heavily and down by the head, was quite alone, and Hans-Heinz Linder took his time putting another two torpedoes into her. She sank shortly afterwards, her going unseen except by her executioner. Being 34 years old, less than 2,000 tons gross and loaded with nothing more vital than pieces of timber, it is debatable whether she was worth the three expensive torpedoes used to bring about her demise.

The fog was short-lived, lifting soon after 0930, by which time *Moosejaw* had rejoined the convoy. Hard on her heels came *Gladiolus*, *Mimosa*, *Westaskiwin*, *Windermere* and *Buttermere*. The sun broke through and, for the first time since he accepted responsibility for the defence of the convoy nine days earlier off Newfoundland, Commander James Hibbard felt the odds shifting in his favour. Nor was that the end of Hibbard's good fortune. Two hours later, over the horizon came the destroyers of the 2nd Escort Group, led by Commander W. E. Banks in HMS *Douglas*. With *Douglas* were HMS *Veteran*, *Saladin*, *Skate* and *Leamington*, bringing SC42's escort up to a formidable six destroyers, seven corvettes and two armed trawlers. Veteran, *Saladin* arid *Skate* were First World War vintage, *Leamington* was an ex-US Navy four-stacker, and the trawlers were armed only with 12-pounders, but the increased numbers alone were significant. Commander Banks, being the senior officer on the scene, now took over command of the escort from Commander Hibbard and deployed his ships around the convoy. *Veteran* and *Leamington*, both equipped with RDF, were detached to scout ahead.

While Banks tightened his defensive ring around SC42, just over the horizon to the south a lone merchant ship steaming eastwards was unwittingly converging on the convoy's course. The 1,549-ton *Montana*, US-owned but sailing under the flag of Panama, was an early example of a "flag-of-convenience" ship, although her foreign registry was more a matter of political than commercial necessity. The former Danish ship sailed from Wilmington, North Carolina, on 29 August, bound for Reykjavik and carrying a cargo of 1.5 million board feet of timber for the US Maritime Commission. Her crew of 26 was made up of 18 Danes, five Norwegians, one Greek, one Belgian and one Spaniard. Although the *Montana* was officially a neutral, her cargo was consigned to the US Marines in Iceland, and she could be construed as a legitimate target for the U-boats. In any case, the wisdom of her sailing alone in this area had to be questioned.

It was also quite by coincidence that U-105, having lost

contact with SC42, was patiently trawling the seas directly in the path of the *Montana*. Commanded by Kapitänleutnant Georg Schewe, U-105 was a Type IXB, built at Bremen in 1940. Armed with 22 torpedoes, a 105-mm deck gun and four 20-mm AA cannon, she had a top speed on the surface of 18.3 knots and a maximum range of 13,450 miles. She was a long-range boat with a proven record, having sunk on her first patrol 14 Allied ships of 81,809 tons. This earned Schewe the Knight's Cross.

U-105's second voyage was proving less fruitful. Having sailed from Lorient on 2 July, she joined the *Markgraf* group almost two months later without so much as a single ship added to her score, and so it had remained. Schewe was therefore delighted when the unescorted *Montana* hove in sight. Taking U-105 down to periscope depth, he sank the steamer with one well-placed torpedo.

That the *Montana* was US-owned and a neutral, Schewe neither knew nor cared; but he did the German cause no good by sinking this ship. Fortunately, her crew took to the boats and reached Iceland safely, but her destruction was yet another tug at the strings drawing the United States into the war.

Following the torpedoing of the *Garm* at 0230, Fritz Meyer had spent the rest of the day patiently overhauling the convoy. At 1430, U-207, trimmed right down with only her conning tower above the surface, was lying about 15 miles ahead of the leading ships. It was Meyer's intention to hold this position until dark, when he hoped to drop back unseen into the convoy and resume the attack.

Lockheed Hudsons of Coastal Command had now taken over the air defence of SC42, and were flying continuous patrols. Inevitably, one of these aircraft, taking a long sweep ahead of the convoy, spotted U-207 and roared in at her. It was the work of just a few seconds for Meyer to take his trimmed-down boat to periscope depth, a move that proved unnecessary. The Hudson was nearing the end of its patrol and had no depth charges left. As soon as the aircraft moved away, Meyer surfaced again and resumed his course. He was not aware that SC42's escort had been heavily reinforced.

The Hudson reported the U-boat sighting to *Douglas*, and

Commander Banks at once ordered *Veteran* and *Leamington* to investigate. The two destroyers were at that time some 7 miles ahead of the convoy and carrying out a sweep of the starboard bow. They both altered course immediately, and working up to 22 knots headed for the position given. At 1515, they sighted U-207 at about 7 miles off and raced in to attack. At this point, Meyer became aware of their approach, and for the second time within an hour was obliged to make an undignified escape below the waves.

Unlike the Hudsons, *Veteran* and *Leamington* were armed. Furthermore, their commanders were experienced submarine-hunters, Both ships went into a well-practised drill, stalking as a team. Within 20 minutes, *Leamington* gained a contact at 2,000 yards, classified as "submarine with doppler and distinctive hydrophone effect." She immediately carried out a deliberate attack with six depth charges set to 100 and 250 feet. By this time, *Veteran* was also in asdic contact, and she weighed in with another nine charges set to 150 and 300 feet, *Leamington* then raced back in and dropped a further six charges set at 100 and 150 feet. It was a brutal attack, carried out with clinical efficiency, but its result was inconclusive. About 20 seconds after the last depth charge exploded, *Leamington's* asdic operator heard noises he identified as tanks being blown, indicating that the U-boat had gone deep. Then all contact was lost.

Leamington signalled *Douglas* for more help, and Banks dispatched *Skate* and *Saladin* to join the hunt. The four destroyers, acting in concert, then carried out a careful search of the area, and whenever a contact was made the spot was thoroughly saturated with depth charges, raining down from all sides. The last "probable sub" contact was made at 1702 by *Veteran*, and from then on, although the search continued until 1930, the scent was lost. No wreckage or oil came to the surface after the final depth charging, but the destroyers were confident they had destroyed the U-boat. Their confidence was not misplaced, for U-207 was never seen or heard from again. It was later assumed that Fritz Meyer and his crew of 40 perished deep in the North Atlantic following an unprecedented ordeal by depth charging on that late afternoon in September.

Coincident with the hunt for U-207 in the van of the convoy, 20 miles astern, Hudson K-269 sighted another U-boat on the surface steering east. K-629 was fully bombed-up and carried out an accurate attack on the submarine as she dived. There was no evidence to suggest that the unidentified U-boat had been damaged, but the attack most certainly foiled her plan to overhaul the convoy, for she was not sighted again.

More Catalinas arrived from Iceland that evening, providing extensive and continuous air cover for the convoy. At 0145, Catalina N-209 sighted a U-boat surfaced 8 miles off the port quarter, and attacked with depth charges. Unfortunately, the first charge, which would have dropped very close to the U-boat, failed to release, and those charges that did fall were well wide of **thee** mark. However, N-209 dropped flame floats, which were seen by *Douglas*. Commander Banks ordered *Skate* to investigate, but the destroyer found nothing.

The watch from the skies, combined with the large number of surface escorts, kept the U-boats at bay throughout the rest of the night. SC42 was now only 390 miles west of Iceland, and drawing nearer by the hour.

Skeena was running short of fuel, and Banks ordered Hibbard to detach and make for Reykjavik. The Canadian destroyer, which had borne the brunt of the sustained onslaught on SC42 by the powerful *Markgraf* group, reached Iceland 26 hours later with just 20 tons of oil remaining in her bunker tanks. No more could be expected of any ship, and for James Hibbard and his men, although they had lost so many of the merchantmen in their charge, the battle had been hard-fought and full of honour.

As *Skeena* peeled away from the convoy in the grey light of dawn on the 12th, four more U-boats arrived to sniff at the heels of SC42. U-522, commanded by the experienced Korvettenkapitän Erich Topp, had been at large in the North Atlantic since March, accounting for 10 Allied ships of 55,249 tons. She was soon due to return to base, but before she did so Topp intended to use his last remaining torpedoes against SC42. The three other boats, U-373 (Oberleutnantzur-See Paul-Karl Loeser), U-572 (Kapitänleutnant Heinz Hirsacker) and U-575 (Kapitänleutnant Günther Heydemann) were all on their first patrol, and eager to show their mettle.

Daylight came in quietly on the morning of the 12th with the visibility down to half a mile in a thin sea mist. The horizon of each ship in the convoy was limited to her immediate neighbours, keeping station around her like grey ghosts in the swirling mist. At 0926, unidentifiable wireless transmissions were again heard within the convoy, on this occasion only two long dashes of approximately eight seconds each. No ship was able to obtain a directional bearing, but the signal was strength 9 and, as before, a spark-gap transmitter was being used.

U-82 was by this time some 270 miles to the south of the convoy and making for Lorient on the surface at an economical speed. In accordance with orders from BdU, Rollmann had remained in contact with SC42 for as long as possible, but a dwindling fuel supply with no possibility of replenishment at sea had obliged him to set course for home. Six days later, a minesweeper escorted the battle-scarred U-boat into Lorient with both her diesels firing erratically as she sucked up the last sludge-thickened dregs of oil from her tanks.

At 0930, SC42's escort was further reinforced by the arrival of the destroyers HMS *Belmont*, HMCS *Columbia* and HMCS *St. Croix*. Overhead, no fewer than eight Hudsons kept unceasing watch, and to add to the convoy's already considerable defences nature obliged with the return of dense fog.

Although the defences were tight, the fog brought back the nightmare of blind steaming with all the horrendous possibilities of collision between the ships sailing in close formation. With the sun shut out, there was no opportunity for sights, and position-fixing was a matter of dead reckoning based on experience and intuition. The great assembly of ships sailed on in silence, while on every bridge and lookout station, keen ears listened and redrimmed eyes kept watch for the approach of danger.

The destroyers of the 2nd Escort Group had used up a great deal of their fuel in the high-speed dash to come to SC42's aid, and were now in urgent need of fresh bunkers, as were some of the corvettes. The C-in-C Western Approaches now decided to take advantage of the lull, and signalled Commander Banks to detach ships with the most urgent need in pairs, as from daylight on the 13th. They were to make all possible speed to Iceland, refuel, and return to the convoy, again at maximum speed. Sir Percy Noble advised that the absence of the refuelling ships would be covered by three US Navy destroyers, then already on their way from their base at Havalfjord. HMCS *Skeena*, due to arrive at Reykjavik at 0600 on the 13th, would sail to rejoin as soon as she had completed refuelling.

Wrapped in its protective cocoon of fog, SC42 weathered the night with only one upset, when the Polish steamer *Wigry*, fourth ship in the starboard outer column, unwittingly romped ahead and cut across in front of the lead ships of the convoy. A collision with the *Everleigh* was only averted by violent helm and engine movements in both ships.

At 0600 on the 13th, in accordance with the orders of C-in-C Western Approaches, *Kenogami* and *Alberni* left the convoy and proceeded towards Iceland for refuelling. The coming of daylight had thickened the fog even further, and the departure of the Canadian corvettes went almost unnoticed. When she was well clear of the convoy, *Kenogami* hove-to, and while she lay rolling gently in the swell, hidden from all prying eyes by the fog, the bodies of Captain Nicholson of the *Stonepool* and seven of his men were committed to the deep.

Meanwhile, as a barely perceptible lightening of the gloom heralded the start of another day, SC42 reached longitude 28° west and altered course to the southeast for the Minches. The naval and air bases of Iceland lay only 125 miles to the east, and the shelter of the North Channel was a mere four days' steaming away. As the day progressed, so the fortunes of the convoy seemed to improve. The fog cleared during the forenoon, and in the early afternoon three US Navy destroyers joined the escort.

USS *Charles F. Hughes*, USS *Russell* and USS *Sims*, in contrast to the tired, rust-streaked ships of the British and Canadian Navies, were smart, bright-painted, and moved with the confident air of warships fresh and eager to take on all corners. Officially, they were still neutrals, authorised to defend themselves if attacked, but no more. However, in the event of an assault on the convoy, it would be well nigh impossible for the Americans not to become involved.

ATTACK & SINK

They did not have long to wait for their first taste of action, for soon after the three US destroyers arrived the enemy once more began to probe the defences of SC42. *Chambly*, stationed on the port bow, obtained a firm asdic contact and went into the attack at once. The corvette dropped two patterns of five depth charges with medium settings, but although double echoes were picked up during a stern sweep of the area, these soon died out and the target was lost. A heavy underwater explosion was heard about two minutes after the second attack, but no evidence of a sinking emerged. *Moosejaw* was detailed to assist *Chambly*, but although the two corvettes searched patiently for another three hours, no further contact was obtained. Both Prentice and Grubb were of the opinion that the U-boat had escaped. By this time, *Chambly's* oil was running dangerously low, and she was ordered to Iceland to refuel.

That the U-boats were still in attendance on SC42 was plainly evident, but they were being kept at bay by increased air activity over the convoy. Hudsons, Whitleys and Northrops of Coastal Command kept an unceasing watch, flying over and around the ships in broad, low-level sweeps. On two occasions, U-boats were surprised and attacked on the surface, one of these being 20 miles to the south of SC42. Both attacks did no more than force the submarines to beat an undignified retreat below the waves, but the presence of so many hostile aircraft was playing havoc with the aspirations of the *Markgraf* group.

16

To Iceland

L
egend has it that Iceland was first settled in the year
AD 750 by a band of Celtic monks seeking to escape
the incessant raids on their British homeland by vora-
cious Norsemen. The monks, their numbers maintained by
periodic infusions of fresh blood from North Britain, lived in
peaceful isolation for 120 years before the Vikings followed
them to this barren, icebound land.

The monks were driven out, their monasteries destroyed and
thereafter, Gardarholm—as the Vikings named Iceland—became a
temporary home to Nordic sea rovers, fugitives and fortune-
hunters, few of whom were tempted by its inhospitable shores to
remain long. In the year 862, Leif Arnarson, wanted for murder
in his native Norway, found sanctuary in Iceland, bringing with
him a number of his fellow country men and women and 12 Irish
slaves captured on the voyage. It was Leif Arnarson's intention to
establish a permanent colony, but, ironically, those he had
enslaved brought about his downfall. The Irish mutinied, killed
Arnarson, seized his women and his boat, and fled to a small
island off the southern coast of Iceland. Here they were soon
besieged by other Vikings seeking revenge for the death of
Arnarson. For several months the Irish held out against their
attackers, but eventually faced certain defeat. Rather than surrender, the proud Celts threw themselves off the high cliffs of
their island into the raging sea below. Thereafter, the island was
known as Vestmannaeyjar, or Irishman's Island.

On 13 September 1941, 1,079 years after the Irish slaves chose death rather than dishonour, a local fishing-boat entered the main fjord of Vestmann Island with a ship's lifeboat in tow. The lifeboat, battered and salt-caked, was manned by a band of twentieth-century Vikings. Captain Wetteland and 11 of the *Einvik's* crew were all in remarkably good shape, despite an ordeal lasting more than eight days.

When the *Einvik* became U-501's first, and only, victim, Captain Wetteland was confronted with the same awesome decision faced by so many of his cloth in the course of this bitter war. He and his crew of 22 were adrift in two small boats on an ocean notorious for its malevolence, and over 300 miles from the nearest land. Should he wait for rescue or make a bid for the land?

At the time the *Einvik* disappeared beneath the grey Atlantic waves, the weather was reasonable, in that the visibility was good and no storm appeared to be in the offing. The temptation was, therefore, to remain in the area in the hope that the SOS sent by the ship's courageous wireless operator had been picked up. The other, less attractive, alternative was to make sail for Iceland. It was not impossible to reach the island, but the *Einvik's* 23-year-old wooden boats, like most ship's lifeboats, were so ungainly as to be incapable of sailing closer to the wind than eight points. At best, the boats would average around 2 knots, and the voyage would take at least a week, given that the weather held good. Furthermore, the area was plagued by fog and poor visibility, and navigation was likely to be largely guesswork. If they missed Iceland, then they would sail on for another 700 miles or so, before fetching up on the west coast of Norway. How many of them would survive? After some consideration, taking into account the prevailing shortage of British warships and the unlikelihood of any vessel being spared to search for two boatloads of survivors when so many lives were at risk, Wetteland decided to make for Iceland.

Fortunately, the *Einvik's* two lifeboats were each built to carry 30 men, so neither was overcrowded. Captain Wetteland's boat held 12 men, including himself, and the other boat, under the command of the *Einvik's* chief officer, had only 11. Both boats were also well provisioned, a state of affairs largely due to the far-sighted Wetteland. At that time, regulations required a ship's lifeboat to carry only 2 pints of drinking water, 2 lbs. of biscuits and 1 lb of condensed milk for each man on board, sufficient to sustain life for a few days, and no more.

The convenient assumption made by those safe ashore was that the unfortunate men would have died from exposure long before their food and water gave out. Wetteland was of a contrary opinion, and each of the *Einvik's* boats had on board an extra 10 gallons of water, a large bottle of sugar syrup, 18 cartons of tinned meatballs and a primus stove on which to heat them, 500 cigarettes and a few tins of pipe tobacco. In an age when nine out of ten men smoked, the latter was an essential morale-booster. Again on Wetteland's initiative, the boats' lockers were stocked with woollen sweaters and oilskins, sufficient for all on board, and each of the survivors had brought with him extra woollen underwear and stockings. Some also had one-piece rubber exposure suits, supplied while the ship was in the United States. By and large, Wetteland and his men were as well prepared for the ordeal facing them as they could ever expect to be.

As soon as it was light enough, Wetteland passed a line to the other boat, and they hoisted sail and set a course for Reykjavik, which lay some 330 miles to the east-northeast. Progress was painfully slow, for the wind was only a light breeze from the east, and the heavy boats could make little use of it. Eventually, in order to make any headway at all, they were forced to steer due north with the wind on the beam.

The wind stayed stubbornly in the east for the next 48 hours, rarely exceeding Force 3, and the two boats edged slowly northwards, deeper into the Denmark Strait. Wetteland divided his crew into two watches, he and his second officer taking turns at the helm while the others tended the sails or bailed. In this way, a necessary semblance of ship's routine was maintained, with half the crew working while the remainder rested.

There was little hope of making land for at least seven days, and Wetteland was honest enough to spell out the true situation to his men; but, in spite of the increasing cold as they moved northwards, they were all in good spirits. The only exception was the Canadian fireman, Thomas Dwyer, who, having been partly responsible for the predicament they were in, now refused to take any part in crewing the boat. In different circumstances, the troublesome Dwyer might have found himself being taken to one side and severely dealt with by his own kind. As it was, he was left to his own devices, completely ignored by the others–perhaps a fitting punishment for his contemptible behaviour.

The prudent Wetteland issued no food on the first day, and water only to those who asked for it. Thereafter, he rationed the water to half a pint per man per day, and this, along with three biscuits and a few meatballs heated on the primus, plus a spoonful of the energy-rich sugar syrup, provided adequate nourishment. Warmly clothed, protected from wind and spray by oilskins, and with two or three cigarettes a day, the men were well satisfied with their lot–except, of course, Thomas Dwyer, who continued to grumble.

There was a moment of elation when, on the night of the 6th, the sound of engines was heard close by in the darkness. Men began to shout and scrambled for flares, but Wetteland recognised the distinctive throb of a U-boat's diesels and quietened the men. The U-boat, one of the *Markgraf* group speeding southwest to join in the attack on SC42 either did not see the *Einvik's* boats, or chose to ignore them.

On the morning of the 7th, the wind dropped altogether, then in the afternoon it came away strongly from the north. By this time, Wetteland estimated they must be to the northwest of Reykjavik, and was therefore able to put the wind on the quarter and run to the southeast. The two boats, still roped together, came about and were soon making good speed. As the afternoon wore on, however, the wind reached gale force, and with a heavy quarterly sea running it became very difficult to hold a course. The coming of darkness aggravated the situation, and before long both boats were yawing wildly as their helmsmen fought to control them. It was too much for the 3-inch manilla rope joining them, which snapped taut once too often and parted with a crack heard above the howl of the wind. They quickly drifted apart and lost sight of each other.

Having the wind in his favour, Wetteland was reluctant to shorten sail, and sped on into the night with heavy canvas sails booming, and angry white-topped rollers racing in astern, every one threatening to swamp the boat. The rain lashed down and spray lopped over the gunwales, so that, although they bailed continuously, the occupants of the boat were soon up to their thighs in icy water. They spent a thoroughly miserable night, made all the more wretched when around midnight the boat's overburdened mast snapped, bringing a tangle of sails and rigging down on them.

When the confusion subsided, Wetteland streamed the sea anchor and rode bow to wind and sea while a makeshift repair was made to the mast, using two oars as a splint. In the darkness, and in the weather prevailing, the work was difficult enough, but when the sea anchor carried away and the boat broached-to, this was almost the end. Yet again Wetteland rallied his men. The remaining oars were shipped and a desperate fight began to prevent the boat capsizing and bring her blunt bows back into the wind. The men were tired, cold and thoroughly demoralised, but urged on by a tenacious will to survive they put their backs to it, and the battle was won.

Next morning brought blessed relief, for the gale had blown itself out, and the wind was backing to the northwest. The repaired mast was stepped, the sails hoisted, and with a gentle breeze on the quarter Wetteland was able to steer an east-northeasterly course for Iceland. The sea had gone down considerably, so that the boat was steady and no longer shipping water. They looked around for the other boat, but there was no sign of it, and Wetteland feared that it may have been overwhelmed by the storm of the night.

During the course of the morning, the grey, forbidding clouds cleared away, and with the sun shining down out of a sky washed blue by the rain a new air of optimism settled over the boat. A hot meal of meatballs and biscuits, prepared on the primus stove, gave a further boost to morale, and even the reluctant Dwyer declared himself ready to take a watch. Shortly before noon, the periscope of a submerged submarine passed close by, but the sighting created only a momentary panic.

The day passed comfortably, with the boat making good progress to the east, but, as it so often does, the wind went down with the sun and by dark the sails were hanging slack. Conscious that every mile gained was vital for their ultimate survival, Wetteland ordered the oars to be shipped. Working in two watches, the men, Dwyer included, put their backs into it, and the boat continued to creep eastwards, albeit at a snail's pace. The wind got up again during the night, much to the relief of the rowers, but the blow was short-lived. This was to be the pattern over the next four days—a few hours running before the wind, then back to the drudgery of the oars, hands a mass of broken blisters and muscles screaming in agony. The cold and the cramped conditions also began to take their toll, lack of circulation causing a painful swelling of the feet and legs in many of the survivors. Wetteland could do nothing to help, other than to encourage the sufferers to stand up and move around in the boat, not an easy feat under the circumstances.

On the morning of 12 September, seven days after taking to the boats, food and water were running short, and still no land was in sight. Wetteland began to suspect that the persistent northerly winds had swept them far to the south of Iceland. If this was so, then they were condemned to struggle on for another 700 miles, before reaching the west coast of Norway. Few of them, if any, would survive to see that land.

Nevertheless, Wetteland held his course, and at noon that day his perseverance was rewarded when the tall, snow-capped peaks of the Vestmann Islands hove in sight. They spent another cold and miserable night at sea, then soon after daybreak on the 13th, with the rising sun striking the steep cliffs of the Vestmanns, the boat was seen by the Icelandic fisherman and taken in tow. Four hours later, eight and a half days after abandoning their ship, the *Einvik's* survivors were on dry land.

Tired though he was, for he had shouldered a heavy responsibility during the long passage, Wetteland's first concern after he had seen his men in good hands was for the safety of the *Einvik's* other lifeboat, lost sight of during the night of the 7th. He was relieved to learn that the boat, containing his chief officer and ten men, had landed at Herdisarvik, on the south coast of Iceland, that same morning. They also were well, although the chief officer later reported that he had on one occasion found it necessary to restore order at the point of a gun when fighting broke out over the rations.

Despite spending more than eight days in open boats, enduring extreme cold and exposed to severe weather, the *Einvik's* entire crew of 23 had survived with only a few men requiring minor medical treatment when landing. It was a happy ending to a voyage cursed by bad fortune and malevolence.

While the *Einvik* survivors counted their blessings in Iceland, 300 miles to the west, aboard the damaged Socony Vacuum tanker *Tachee*, Captain Bannan and his crew of volunteers were nearing the end of another harrowing day. During the morning, her tug, the Canadian corvette *Orillia*, had signalled that she was running short of fuel, and requested a top-up from the *Tachee's* cargo tanks, which still contained several thousand tons of oil. The wind was light, and with only a slight sea running it was anticipated that the operation would be a relatively easy one. It was not to be.

At 1015, both ships stopped and *Orillia* slipped her tow. Unfortunately, when the *Tachee* came to heave in her starboard anchor cable, to which the tow wire was attached, the tanker's windlass ran away, and the whole length of the cable and the wire were lost overboard. As neither ship had a replacement wire on board–and, in any case, the *Tachee's* windlass was no longer of any use–there could be no further talk of towing.

At 1245, *Orillia* came alongside the *Tachee*, and using a 2 1/2-inch canvas fire hose and a coupling made by the tanker's engineers, the transfer of fuel was begun. That is to say, the *Tachee's* pumps were started, but one and a half hours later only just over a ton of oil had flowed through the hose. It was pointless to continue with the operation, for the tanker's steam-heating coils were not working, and in the temperatures prevailing the oil in her cargo tanks was little more than thick sludge. *Orillia* cast off again, and the *Tachee* proceeded under her own steam, while her engineers worked into the night to repair the heating coils.

Prior to heaving-to with the intention of refuelling the corvette, the *Tachee* had been under way for 63 hours, using her engine and with *Orillia* towing. During this time, with the exception of some drizzle and fog, the weather had been favourable, and the two ships covered some 295 miles. Although this worked out at an average speed of only 4.5 knots, under the circumstances it was a considerable achievement.

The hazardous undertaking began some 19 hours after the *Tachee* was torpedoed. Captain Bannan, having established that with *Orillia's* co-operation it might be possible to save his ship, called for volunteers to reboard the tanker. As he had anticipated, his officers were with him to a man, as were the majority of his deck and catering ratings, and the four DEMS gunners. Only the engine-room crew let him down, eight out of the 11 ratings being unwilling to return to the ship. This was unfortunate, as a full complement was needed below to handle the *Tachee's* boilers, main engine and auxiliaries, none of which had been updated since she was built in 1914. However, in the light of the frightening experience they had already been through, Bannan was reluctant to coerce his firemen. When three of *Orillia's* engine-room hands offered to go with him, he readily agreed.

Anxious to get under way before dark, Bannan returned to the *Tachee* at once with his crew of volunteers, whose first task was to hoist on board two lifeboats retrieved and brought alongside by the corvette. The boats were an essential precaution, for the odds on the ship being torpedoed again were very high, a thought that must have been in the mind of every man as he boarded the tanker.

It took some ten hours for the *Tachee's* engineers, led by Chief Engineer Charles Probert, to raise steam on one boiler. While this was being done, Chief Officer Archie Canner and his men cleared the tangle of debris from the decks and rigged the emergency steering gear. In consultation with Lieutenant-Commander Briggs, Captain Bannan had decided that, for the coming night at least, the *Tachee* would proceed as best she could under her own steam, with *Orillia* screening her. If circumstances and the weather allowed, the corvette would attempt to tow next morning.

At 1930, with sufficient steam raised on the starboard boiler to turn the main engine, the *Tachee* set off in the general direction of Iceland, making about 2 knots. This was barely steerage way, but the very fact that the ship was once again on the move was a great comfort to those on board, who had spent an uncomfortable 12 hours drifting at the mercy of the U-boats. Bannan and his deck officers went onto double watches, six hours on and six off, with one officer on the bridge and one on the poop, from where the emergency steering gear was being operated. At the best, only a very approximate course could be steered, for, although there was a magnetic compass on the poop, this was wildly inaccurate. No stars were visible as a guide, and steering was accomplished by holding the ship's head at roughly the same angle to the wind, as indicated by the wave-tops. Any major deviation from the course was signalled from the bridge by whistle blasts.

It was a long and gruelling night, particularly for Chief Officer Canner, who in addition to his watches had to supervise the breaking of the anchor cable in preparation for the tow. At 1000, the ship was stopped and *Orillia* came alongside. The tanker's 6-inch circumference towing wire was brought out and shackled on to her starboard anchor cable. The free end of the heavy wire was then passed to the corvette's stern, where it was made fast with five parts of a 3 1/2-inch manilla rope, which could be cut with a sharp axe in case of emergency. As *Orillia* eased away from and moved slowly ahead of the *Tachee*, the tanker's starboard cable was paid out to five shackles, giving a total length of the tow between the two ships of about 900 feet, the weight of the cable serving to take any direct strain off the wire.

The weather remained fair, and with *Orillia* towing and the *Tachee* making her best speed, tug and tow gradually worked up to 6-7 knots. A fine, misty drizzle set in after noon, and at times it became impossible to see the corvette from the *Tachee's* poop. *Orillia* streamed a fog buoy and showed a light at her stern but, even so, steering the tanker once again became extremely difficult.

Later in the afternoon, the *Tachee's* engineers succeeded in raising steam on the port boiler, and speed was increased slightly. The poor visibility persisted until the afternoon of the 12th, when a freshening wind cleared the mist, easing some of the burden on those on watch on the decks of both ships. With one difficulty removed, however, another soon took its place. The wind brought with it a heavy swell, and the *Tachee* began to labour awkwardly in the seaway, her damaged bulkheads giving out ominous groans and creaks. Bannan was obliged to reduce speed to avoid breaking the ship up.

After the abortive attempt to supply *Orillia* with fuel on the 13th, the *Tachee's* engineers worked throughout the rest of the day repairing the steam heating lines for the oil tanks. This was a long, painstaking job, for the deck piping was holed in many places. However, although steam was still escaping all along the afterdeck, at 1800 the heat was applied to the forward bunker tank, and continued throughout the night.

At 0900 on the 14th, with the oil flowing freely in the tanker's pipes, *Orillia* was called back alongside, and within three hours had taken on 40 tons of oil, sufficient for her to reach Reykjavik. The corvette then cast off again, and both ships proceeded in company. The wind and sea were slight, and with both her boilers under all possible pressure, the *Tachee* was able to maintain a speed of 7.5 knots. She sighted Iceland on the afternoon of the 15th, and running ahead of deteriorating weather, anchored off Reykjavik that night. Although she was severely damaged by U-652's torpedo and the fire that followed, the *Tachee* had steamed a distance of 592 miles, and arrived in port with most of her precious oil cargo still intact.

17

The Last Victim

On the afternoon of the 13th, the fog which had so considerately wrapped its protective cloak around the battered SC42 finally thinned and cleared away. The weak sun that broke through to shine down on the convoy revealed a brave sight. This great armada of ships which, through the discipline and fortitude of its people, had challenged the might of the North Atlantic and the massed ranks of Admiral Dönitz's U-boats, still retained its order and dignity. The payment extracted, however, had been high. Of the 68 merchant ships that set out on the long passage from Canadian waters, 16 had fallen to the U-boats and four others were missing. Fortunately, the odds in favour of the convoy reaching its final destination without further loss were lengthening. Reykjavik lay only 95 miles to the northeast, and the sanctuary of the Minches was within 600 miles.

The hungry wolves of the *Markgraf* group, which had for four days and nights mounted an all-out assault on the convoy, now skulked nervously on the horizon. Their hour was gone, for SC42's escort—sadly too late for so many—was now an impenetrable fence surrounding the slow-moving merchantmen. Under the command of the Senior Officer Escort, Commander W. E. Flanks, in HMS *Douglas*, were the destroyers *Veteran*, *Saladin*, *Skate*, *Leamingon*, *Columbia*, *St. Croix* and *Belmont*, the corvettes *Moosejaw*, *Mimosa*, *Gladiolus* and *Westaskiwin*, and the armed trawler *Buttermere*. In addition, although they were officially only neutral observers, the three American destroyers *Charles F. Hughes*, *Russell* and *Sims* were keeping station 10 miles south of the convoy, their guns and depth-charge throwers manned with men eager to demonstrate their ability to fight. Overhead, aircraft of Coastal Command, flying in relays from Iceland, maintained a constant vigil.

The morning of the 14th dawned fine and clear, with the sea benignly smooth and the swell a gentle rise and fall like the breathing of a sleeping giant. With a confident air, but with lookouts on the alert and guns manned, the ships of SC42 steamed determinedly eastwards towards the beleaguered islands of Britain, to which their cargoes would bring new hope. With the U-boats held at bay, a successful conclusion of the voyage was more likely, but there were still fearful dangers to be faced. The convoy was now within range of the great four-engined Focke-Wulf Kondors operating out of bases in Norway. Bristling with heavy machine-guns, and carrying a 2-ton bomb load, "the scourge of the Atlantic," as they had been christened by Winston Churchill, might yet cause dreadful havoc in the ranks of SC42.

As the sun climbed higher and the chill of the night just past became a fading memory, the Newcastle tramp *Jedmoor*, shepherded by the trawler HMS *Windermere*, finally overhauled the convoy and resumed her original station at the head of column 3. Since she had broken ranks in the terrible mayhem of the night of the 10th and fled to the south, the *Jedmoor* had never been far away, willing to rejoin the others but hopelessly lost in the fog. It soon became apparent that she had returned to the fold only just in time, for during the morning two Hudsons of 269 Squadron Coastal Command sighted and attacked a U-boat motoring on the surface in the area so recently vacated by the *Jedmoor*. The depth charges dropped by the Hudsons put the U-boat down, but there was no evidence of damage.

Around noon, the three US destroyers, *Charles F. Hughes*, *Russell* and *Sims*, wheeled away and made off to the west at speed. The American ships had served their purpose, for although they had taken great pains not to be associated with SC42's official escort, the mere presence of these modern, powerful men-of-war had contributed to the withdrawal of the U-boats.

The numbers of the convoy were swelled again when, that evening, the merchant ships *Eildron, Kull, Ronan, Emberly* and *Toward* joined from Iceland. The 1,500-ton *Toward*, owned by the Clyde Shipping Company of Glasgow, and chartered to the Ministry of War Transport, was the first of the specially equipped rescue vessels, with berths for several hundred survivors and carrying the latest rescue equipment, a surgeon and full medical staff. Her role would be to bring up the rear of the convoy and rescue men from the water as their ships went down. There was nothing new in this arrangement, for ships like the *Toward* had been used extensively in convoys at the latter end of the First World War. Unfortunately, for so many men of SC42, the rescue ship came too late.

The fog came back again soon after nightfall, once more drawing its damp curtain around the ships and shrouding the comings and goings of the escorts as they slipped away, singly or in pairs, to make a quick dash to Reykjavik to refuel. As the night progressed, however, so the fog thickened, until the visibility was down to 500 yards. For the merchant ships, now 53 strong and steaming in nine columns abreast, the darkness became full of unseen dangers. Fog buoys were streamed and shaded blue lights shown from the stern of each ship, but station-keeping soon developed into an endless nightmare of nervous anticipation, of urgent helm orders and constant adjustments of engine revolutions.. That there were no collisions, only near misses, was a tribute to the vigilance and expertise of the men who manned the bridges and engine rooms of this motley collection of ocean-going tramps.

Only a subtle lightening of the fog at around 0500 on the 15th announced the dawning of a new day. It would not be a day to lift hearts or set pulses racing, but merely a continuation of the night before, marked only by the monotonous ticking of the clock and the arrival of hot food and drink. The hours passed slowly and with increasing tension. Noon came and went, and there was no improvement In the visibility. If anything, the fog thickened as the hidden sun began its descent to the western horizon. Darkness returned, and the twisting ordeal continued as the invisible fleet, spread out over some 10 square miles of the ocean, groped its way through the murk. Somewhere outside the perimeter of the convoy, *Kenogami*, having landed her survivors in Reykjavik and taken on fuel and depth charges, had returned and was attempting to make contact. With her were her stable-mate *Alberni*, the destroyer HMS *Salisbury* and the corvette HMS *Narcissus*, both new on the scene. All four ships were in touch with *Douglas* by R/T but prevented by the fog from joining the escort.

The dense fog persisted throughout that night, but at sunrise on the 16th the visibility lifted to about 1 mile. This was far from ideal under the circumstances, but the improvement was a godsend to those involved in station-keeping. It also enabled *Kenogami* and her consorts to close with the convoy. When the new arrivals were in position, Commander Banks judged that it was safe to detach *St. Croix* and *Moosejaw* to proceed to the Scottish base of Loch Ewe to refuel. This was to be the end of *Moosejaw's* involvement in the defence of SC42, and not before time. The Canadian corvette had been at sea for 12 days, waging continuous war against the elements and the enemy, and she was in need of a respite. The tremendous strain imposed on her commanding officer, Lieutenant Frederick Grubb, in bringing this untried ship, with her inexperienced hostilities-only crew through her brutal introduction to war had proved too much. Grubb was a very sick man, having for some days been suffering from acute chest pains and unable to keep food down. Finally, during the course of that morning, he had no alternative but to report his condition to Commander Banks and request medical advice. Banks immediately sent *Douglas's* surgeon across to the corvette, who advised that Grubb be hospitalised as soon as possible. As *Moosejaw* was by now running dangerously short of fuel, and had on board 29 German prisoners and 38 survivors, the obvious solution was to send her to Loch Ewe, 12 hours' steaming away.

Moosejaw left the convoy for Loch Ewe in company with the destroyer St. *Croix*, also in need of refueling. The two ships had not gone many miles when they sighted what appeared to be a small craft, possibly a ship's lifeboat. They at once altered course and closed the target which, as they drew near, was recognised as the conning tower of a U-boat running partially submerged. As the destroyer and corvette went into action, the

U-boat dived and, although four determined depth-charge attacks were made, the enemy slipped away. Destroyers from the convoy escort joined in the search, but no further contact was made.

Records show that on that morning, despite the poor visibility, at least five units of the *Markgraf* group remained in the vicinity of SC42. One of these was U-98, commanded by Kapitänleutnant Robert Gysae. U-98, a Type VIIC, had begun her first operational patrol at the end of March 1941, scouring the North Atlantic sea lanes in company with seven other boats. It was an immensely successful maiden voyage for Gysae, during which he sank six Allied ships totalling over 31,000 tons, including the 10,549-ton armed merchant cruiser HMS *Salopian*.

When, on that misty morning in September, U-98 was surprised on the surface by *Moosejaw* and St. *Croix*, she was two months into her second patrol, and had another 10,842 tons of Allied shipping to her credit. However, the time was fast approaching when a shortage of fuel would oblige her to return to Biscay. First, Robert Gysae, who like all of Dönitz's young lions had his eye on the 100,000 tons needed to gain the coveted Knight's Cross, badly needed another victory. It was this need that led him to take the risk of penetrating SC42 in daylight and on the surface.

Had it not been for Grubb's indisposition, Gysae might have got away with it. Instead, he ended up being hunted by a total of nine destroyers and corvettes. The chase lasted for a terrifying 45 minutes, during which time a continuous hail of depth charges rained down on U-98. Using all his experience and instinctive guile, Gysae threw his boat around the ocean, twisting and turning like an eel, going deep, then shallow, running away at full speed, or lying stopped and silent while the propellers of his pursuers threshed overhead. fly her commander's tactics, and the stoical courage of her crew, U-98 survived. The chase was abandoned, the escorts returned to the convoy, and St. *Croix* and *Moosejaw* went on their way.

Sights taken at noon put SC42 in position 59°37' north 11° 58' west, about 100 miles northeast of the lonely island of Rockall and 190 miles from the Outer Hebrides. There was just a breath of wind from the southwest, the sea was calm and the visibility varying between half a mile and 2 miles. At the convoy's current speed of 5.5 knots, another 46 hours would see the ships rounding the Butt of Lewis and entering the heavily guarded Minches. The escort was now down to six destroyers and four corvettes, but only 60 miles to the north-east, other naval ships, including several destroyers, were accompanying the westbound convoy ON16. For the U-boats, these waters had now become extremely hazardous, but to the men of SC42 it seemed that the end of their long struggle was drawing near.

The sun dipped at 1820, and by 1900 it was fully dark. In the midst of a terrible war this was a night filled with peace, the wind no more than a zephyr, the sea an oily calm. There was no moon, but the sky was cloudless, and the visibility increasing by the hour. There were experienced seamen in the convoy who sniffed at the cold air and forecast a return of the fog as inevitable. Many of them were in fact willing the fog to come back, for, although the defences of SC42 appeared sound, the night was too calm and they felt cruelly exposed.

The first hint of impending trouble came an hour or so later, when C-in-C Western Approaches signalled a warning that several U-boats were known to be shadowing the convoy. At 2100, asdic operators aboard HMS *Douglas*, sweeping ahead of SC42, heard hydrophone effect on the starboard bow. The echoes appeared to be a long way off and the bearing remained steady for nearly 20 minutes. This led Commander Banks to conclude that the hydrophone effect, which had been categorised by his operators as "high speed engines–definitely not diesel," originated from the special destroyer force known to be covering ON16. The commander's conclusion was wrong.

Following his narrow escape in the afternoon, Robert Gysae took U-98 well to the south before resurfacing. He then spent the next few hours working his way around and ahead of the convoy, taking great care not to be seen. When darkness fell, he trimmed the boat so that only her conning tower was above water, and then dropped back on the approaching lines of ships. It was Gysae's intention to allow the convoy to overtake him and attack as suitable targets presented themselves. With the visibility well over 2 miles, he was taking a fearful risk of being seen and swiftly dealt with by SC42's escorts, but time was running out. When this night was gone, there was unlikely to be another opportunity to strike at the merchantmen.

The *Jedmoor* was by this time comfortably settled in her old position at the head of SC42's third column. On her bridge, Captain Robert Collins was one of those more concerned with the weather than the threat posed by the U-boats. The day had been relatively warm, but with the coming of the night and clear skies the air temperature was falling rapidly. Further to the west this would have been of little consequence, other than the need for an extra layer of clothes. Now, however, the convoy was coming under the influence of a new climatic phenomenon, originating many thousands of miles to the south.

The Gulf Stream has its roots in the North Equatorial Current, which flows anticlockwise around the Azores High, sweeps past the southern shores of the islands of the West Indies, and enters the Gulf of Mexico. Trapped in this vast, warm-water bay, the current slows down and heats up as it follows the curve of the Mexican coast and the southern shores of the United States. When it finally escapes again through the Straits of Florida, the water has reached a temperature of 84°F. (29°C.), and during the enforced passage of this 50-mile wide channel between Florida and the Bahamas its speed increases to around 5 knots. The Gulf Stream, as it is now called, flows up the east coast of the United States as far as New York, losing speed as it goes. It then turns east-northeast into the Atlantic, spreading out to form a river of warm water, 250 miles wide, flowing through a comparatively cold ocean. In mid-Atlantic the stream divides, one arm curving east and south to brush the Portuguese coast and form the Canaries Current; this, having come full circle, merges back into the North Equatorial Current whence it came. The other arm of the Gulf Stream swings northeast and meanders past the west coasts of the British Isles, bringing to these shores an average sea temperature of 60°F. (15°C.). In winter, without the warm kiss of the Gulf Stream, much of the Atlantic coast of Britain and Ireland would be icebound. So far as the seaman is concerned, however, this apparent bounty has one great disadvantage. The air flowing over the Gulf Stream in this area can often be at a temperature as much as 20 degrees lower than that of the sea. The cold air chills the warm vapour rising from the surface of the water, causing the moisture it contains to condense out and form fog. The fog is dense and long-lasting.

On that night of 16 September 1941, convoy SC42 was in the Gulf Stream with conditions ideal for the formation of a thick fog, and Captain Collins, like many others, could smell it in the air. There was no mistaking the damp, salt-laden message. Collins ran his hand over the varnishwork of the bridge tailrail, and it came away wet. There would be fog within the hour and, although it would undoubtedly cause many navigational headaches, he welcomed it. They were now only a little over 24 hours from British coastal waters, and a night and a day spent steaming blind was a small price to pay for a safe arrival in port.

Coincidentally, as Robert Collins contemplated a successful end to his voyage, so another Robert, Kapitänleutnant Robert Gysae, laid his plans to prevent this happening. U-98 had penetrated SC42's ring of escorts and then lay submerged between columns 3 and 4, on a parallel course, and keeping pace with the unsuspecting merchant ships on either side of her.

Gysae ran his periscope over the ships on the U-boat's port side. They were all heavily laden, and steaming so slowly that they had the appearance of being hove-to on the flat, calm sea. In the lead was the 4,392-ton *Jedmoor*, down to her marks with a full cargo of iron ore for Glasgow. Following in her wake came Leighton Seager's *Campus*, 3,667 tons, loaded with steel and timber for Immingham, the 4,556-ton *Maplewood* with a similar cargo for London, the 4,499-ton Greek tramp *Nicolas Piancos*, again with steel and timber for London, and, finally, the 3,645-ton *Hampton Lodge*, bound for Middlesbrough with iron ore.

It was a sight to set any U-boat commander's pulses racing, and Gysae was no exception. As he swung U-98's bows around to port, his mouth was dry and his knuckles white on the handles of the periscope. The range was 2,000 metres. Gysae took careful aim and called for the four bow torpedoes to be fired in quick succession, one for each of the first four ships in SC42's column 3, or so he hoped.

As Gysae fired, so the already cold night air fell another

degree or so to reach its dew point, and became saturated. The moisture in the air began to condense out in the form of mist, and the outlines of the targeted ships, which had been in clear silhouette, suddenly blurred, and then disappeared altogether. Before they were halfway across the intervening stretch of water, U-98's carefully aimed torpedoes were swallowed up in the fog. Gysae could only wait and count the seconds. At 2115 precisely, one muffled thud was heard, and that was all.

On the *Jedmoor's* 4-inch gun platform, at her stern, three men kept watch: Able Seaman Dan Hortop, Boatswain Charles McQueen and DEMS Gunlayer Andrews. It was a fine, crisp night, and, reassured by the presence of SC42's powerful escort, the men of the gun watch were in good spirits. The voyage would soon be over, and the memories of the horrors they had endured were already fading. McQueen, a boisterous Irish-Australian, keeping his voice low so as not to be heard by the bridge, sang a cheerful song, and the others joined in. Then, suddenly, the fog rolled in, shutting out the world around them, and their voices died away. For a few seconds there was absolute silence, then a loud bang. The *Jedmoor* shuddered and stopped dead in her tracks. The only one of U-98's torpedoes to find its mark had caught the Runciman's ship in her no. 1 cargo hold.

The pyramid of iron ore in the *Jedmoor's* forward hold, stowing at only 12 cubic feet to the ton, occupied less than a third of the space, leaving two thirds to be filled by the sea pouring in through the jagged hole blasted in the ship's side. She began to go down by the head.

As the *Jedmoor's* stern rose in the air, her propeller still threshing, there was a loud and ominous rumble as thousands of tons of iron ore in the holds shifted and ran towards the bows. One by one, the steel watertight bulkheads of the holds collapsed under the weight, and the *Jedmoor* stood on her head as the whole of her cargo ended up in the forward part of the ship. Wrapped in a damp shroud of grey fog, she began her long descent to the bottom of the Atlantic.

Taken completely unawares, Dan Hortop and his watchmates found themselves sliding downhill as the ship tilted sharply. They were confused, but they realised they must act quickly to

Dan Hortop (left) and Boatswain Charles McQueen, two of the six survivors of the Jedmoor. *When the photo was taken, Dan Hortop was recovering from injuries sustained when his ship, the SS* Maclaren, *was mined on 3 December 1941. (Photo: F. C. Hortop)*

save their lives. Andrews was first to recover. Shouting to the others to follow, he jumped from the gun platform onto the deck below and cut away one of the after liferafts. The heavy wooden craft slid over the side and, without hesitation, Andrews went over after it. Hortop climbed over the crazily tilting ship's rail and followed him down into the darkness.

The drop was long, and the shock as he hit the icy water enough to stop the strongest heart in mid-beat; but it was the long slide down into the cold, green depths that frightened Hortop. It seemed to go on and on for ever. Then, when his lungs were at bursting point and the silent world into which he was falling had gone black, the buoyancy of his lifejacket took charge, and he began to rise again. He shot back to the surface, only to find himself in a dark, empty world whose boundaries stretched only as far as the swirling fog that surrounded him. The *Jedmoor* was gone, and so were the men who had shared his optimism only a few moments before. As the ice-cold water seeped through his thick clothing and gripped his body, he suddenly felt very alone and frightened.

Once again fate was kind to Dan Hortop, for within a few moments he bumped against an obstacle, which turned out to be the liferaft released by Andrews. Hortop hauled himself aboard the raft, and was soon joined by Andrews and two others, Wardle, the

Jedmoor's senior apprentice, and also her first radio officer.

Eyewitnesses to the sinking of the *Jedmoor*–and there were some–gave the time she took to sink as anything from nine seconds to two minutes. She certainly went down with a rush, but not before someone on her bridge fired two distress rockets. These were seen by the corvette HMS *Narcissus*, commanded by Lieutenant W. Bolton, which was screening the convoy's port quarter. Bolton immediately increased speed to 14 knots, and ordered his asdic operator to sweep broadly either side of the corvette's mean course. No contact was made. *Douglas*, *Skate* and *Alberni* also joined in the hunt, firing starshells and snowflake rockets. A number of depth charges were dropped, these more to give vent to frustration than with serious intent, for U-98 had already fled the scene. In the poor visibility prevailing, the danger of collision between escorts was so great that any organised anti-submarine operation was out of the question. Commander Banks called off the hunt, but ordered *Narcissus* to make an RDF search for the *Jedmoor*, which he believed to be still afloat.

Hidden in the fog, and invisible to *Narcissus's* radar sweep, the small liferaft supporting Dan Hortop and his three companions drifted slowly astern. All around them they could hear the beat of ship's engines, the crack of guns and the thump of exploding depth charges, but they might just as well have been in another ocean. They tried shouting, but their voices echoed back from the surrounding fog, mocking them. Then Hortop recalled his father's words and felt for the whistle hanging at his neck. He put the whistle to his lips and began to blow long, urgent blasts.

The miracle worked for Dan Hortop. Half-an-hour later, when his breath was all but gone, and he was about to give up blowing the whistle, the creak of oars was heard, and a small boat appeared out of the fog.

When the *Jedmoor* was torpedoed, the master of the *Campus*, next ship astern, was quite understandably reluctant to risk his ship by stopping to look for survivors; the other ship had gone down so fast that there seemed little point anyway. It was only in response to the pleading of his chief officer that he eventually agreed to drop the ship's jolly boat for a quick search, and he would not have done this had the sea not been calm. The risk taken proved justified when the four survivors were hauled up the side of the *Campus.*

The *Jedmoor's* boatswain, Charles McQueen, had an even more miraculous deliverance. He had missed the liferaft in the fog, and was drifting aimlessly and without hope, when he was rescued by the rear ship of column 7, the Norwegian steamer *Knoll.*

Throughout the remaining hours of darkness, *Narcissus* and *Alberni* searched in vain for the *Jedmoor.* After sunrise on the 17th, the visibility improved, giving way to a fine, sunny day. It was only then that the two corvettes came upon a large patch of oil, in the middle of which floated scraps of wreckage, all that remained of the *Jedmoor.*

In her 13 years of life, the *Jedmoor* had crossed many oceans and faced many perils. It was unfortunate that, when straggling astern on the morning of the 9th, she had been largely responsible for giving away the position of SC42 to the enemy. Ironic, then, that she should be the last of the ships to pay the ultimate price. She found her final resting place 120 miles northwest of the tiny island of St. Kilda, furthest outrider of the Hebrides and home only to the basking seal and the wheeling gull. She took with her Captain Robert Collins and 31 of his crew.

18

Journey's End

At 1040 that morning, 17 September, the convoy was met by Coastal Command Ansons from Stornoway. These cumbersome, lightly armed aircraft were a poor substitute for the American-built Catalinas and Hudsons, but their presence overhead was significant, signaling the entry of SC42 into British home waters. A few hours later, land was sighted to starboard, and the sense of relief that swept through the ships was undisguised. Just 18 days after sailing from Nova Scotia, and having come through the gates of hell itself, the men of SC42, those who still lived, were nearing journey's end.

Glimpsed from the heaving decks of the ships, the tall mountains of the Outer Hebrides offered a sombre welcome. Dark and forbidding, they were the first glimpse of one of the lonelier outposts of the northern hemisphere. Running north-eastwards for 120 miles, from Barra Head in the south to the Butt of Lewis, the islands form a natural breakwater, shielding northwestern Scotland from the worst excesses of the Atlantic Ocean. In small, whitewashed cottages scattered across the mountain slopes lived the Macleods, the Macdonalds, the Maclennans and the Macleans, the oldest of Scotland's clans, from whose ranks came some of Britain's finest seamen.

Yet, even at this late hour, with the land in sight, and the protective arms of the Royal Navy and Coastal Command reaching out for it, SC42 was still in danger. The recently joined Free French corvette *Renoncule*, scouting ahead of the convoy, picked up two simultaneous asdic contacts classified as "submarine," and a short, fierce engagement followed. *Renoncule*, supported by a number of other escorts, saturated the area with depth charges, but there was no definite outcome to the fight. The U-boat appeared to have escaped, but at the very least it must have been subjected to a very severe shaking.

At around 1800, with the sun going down behind it, SC42 neared the Butt of Lewis, and on the commodore's orders, closed up into two lines abreast. With the escorting warships screening to seawards, and the white flash of the lighthouse on the headland marking the turning point, the long crocodile of merchantmen wheeled to starboard and entered the Minches.

In these high latitudes, the twilight was long and unhurried, the change from day to night being so gradual as to almost pass unnoticed. A gentle easterly wind came off the mainland, bringing with it the smell of green fields, cattle and wood smoke. As the ships steamed through an untroubled sea with friendly land on both sides, the memories of life-and-death battles with the elements and a ruthless enemy faded as easily as did the day. On bridges and in engine rooms, on deck and below, men's thoughts were turning to the other world they were about to enter; a world where the touch of a woman's hand and the laughter of children would soon banish all nightmares.

At 2130, off Tiumpan Head, the easternmost point of the island of Lewis, SC42 split into two sections, those ships bound for the northeast coast and the Thames peeling off for Loch Ewe, where they would re-form before heading north-about. The remainder, ships for Glasgow, Liverpool and the Bristol Channel, continued on south. As a convoy, SC42 had ceased to exist.

Viewed in retrospect, the battle for SC42 was a magnificent victory for the ships of the Royal Canadian Navy led by Commander James Hibbard. That *Skeena* and her corvettes, untried ships with hastily cobbled-together crews of untrained men, ventured out onto a violent ocean capable of destroying them with a casual twitch of its powerful muscles, was challenge enough. To be additionally charged with the protection of a huge fleet of merchantmen, often moving at little more than a slow walking pace, was a truly impossible task. When, in those terrible 48 hours, from 9 to 11 September, the *Markgraf* group, totalling 21 of Admiral Karl Dönitz's finest U-boats, made its bid to smash the convoy, only the raw courage and determination of Hibbard—and the officers and men of his tiny flotilla saved the day. The U-boats, although most were also untried in battle, had the advantage at all times. Even before Lieutenant Ted Briggs, on his own initiative, took *Orillia* out of the fight to escort the tanker *Tachee* to Iceland, there were never enough escorts to guard successfully the 25 square miles of ocean covered by the ships of SC42. In brilliant moonlight, with good visibility and just the right amount of chop on the sea to confuse the convoy's lookouts, the U-boats had little difficulty in penetrating the lines of merchantmen. Having fired their torpedoes, the U-boats' speed on the surface was such that, for much of the time, the escorts were left chasing their own tails. All the escorts were equipped with powerful searchlights, which could have been used to illuminate U-boats on the surface. Unfortunately, perhaps in the heat of the moment, these appear to have been forgotten. Instead, there was indiscriminate firing of starshells and flares, especially by the corvettes. In most cases, this served also to blind the escorts' gun crews and spoil their aim. There was also an indiscreet use of the radio telephone. Orders and reports were passed in plain language, which often must have given the U-boats fair warning of the moves being made against them.

In the interval between *Orillia* leaving and *Chambly* and *Moosejaw* joining, SC42's escorts were outnumbered three or four to one by the attacking U-boats. Also, there appears to have been a loose agreement that the small Norwegian timber-carriers *Regin* and *Vestland* would act as rescue ships, but whether out of necessity or through misunderstanding (it is not clear which) the corvettes invariably joined in. There were, therefore, times when *Kenogami* and *Alberni* were astern picking up survivors, that the defence of the convoy was in the hands of *Skeena* alone. She could not be everywhere at once, and the result was a massacre.

Captain (D) Newfoundland commented: "I consider that he

ATTACK & SINK

[Commander Hibbard] handled what must have appeared to be a hopeless situation with energy and initiative throughout, probably therefore averting disaster." The Commodore Commanding Newfoundland added: "Not only did Hibbard never lose hope which, with the meagre force at his disposal, a lesser man might have done, but his mental and physical stamina was sufficient to keep him alert and active from the time of the first report of attack at 1004, 9th September, until he left for Hvalfjord at 0400, 12th September, a period of 66 hours, much of which was a continuous battle." Both senior officers were passing judgement from afar, and were not then aware of the full story. Prior to the U-boat attack, SC42 had gone through five days and five nights of fierce northerly gales, with visibility sometimes so poor that only adjacent ships were in sight of each other. The fine-lined destroyer *Skeena*, built for speed rather than durability, was out of touch with the convoy for 29 hours, from 0700 on the 6th to 1200 on the 7th, hove-to in mountainous seas and unable to alter course for fear of being swamped. When the battle with the U-boats started, Hibbard must already have been a very tired man. His subsequent achievements, in what amounted to defending the convoy with his ship alone, were superb.

Equally remarkable was the action in which the corvettes HMCS *Chambly* and *Moosejaw* sank U-501. Both ships were on their first training cruise, scheduled to last ten days, and really designed only to introduce their crews to the rigours of the North Atlantic, most of them having had no previous experience of deep waters. It was no coincidence that the corvettes were close at hand when the main assault was mounted on SC42, for their experienced senior officer, Commander Prentice, had arranged it so. However, that they should stumble upon U-501 as she was attempting to penetrate the convoy was pure chance. The subsequent sinking of the U-boat was probably due more to the faint heart of her commander and the incompetence of his crew rather than the expertise of the Canadians; but the unshakable resolution of the latter when they came face to face with the enemy was something of which Horatio Nelson would have approved. They came very near to capturing U-501 intact.

Dönitz later claimed that the dense fog which set in on the 11th brought with it such a serious danger of collision that he was forced to withdraw his U-boats. As this coincided with the arrival of the destroyers of the 2nd Escort Group, this claim seems to have little substance. It is more likely that, having thus far failed to wreak the havoc in the convoy they should have done, the U-boats simply lost heart and withdrew on their own initiative when the British reinforcements arrived.

Although for the naval ships escorting SC42 those early autumn days in 1941 may have been filled with danger and mind-numbing fatigue, they were also made heady by the thrill of the chase, the thunder of the gun and the depth charge. For the merchant ships, the majority of them old and worn out by years of tramping in the service of skinflint owners loath to pay for maintenance and repairs, it was a different matter. For them, day and night merged into an unending fight merely to stay afloat and make way through the water in approximately the right direction. By necessity, the speed of the convoy was governed by the slowest ship, and over a period of four days, when the weather was at its worst, the average speed made good was only 3 knots. In heavy seas, the deep-laden, bluff-bowed ships had great difficulty in steering, and with visibility often reduced to a few hundred yards station-keeping was a torment that aged watchkeepers overnight.

When it came to the fight for survival against a cunning and powerful enemy, the merchantmen, although classed as non-combatants, were legitimate targets, and yet they were virtually powerless to hit back. Under International Law, a merchant ship may be armed in time of war, but only in such a way that she is able to fight a defensive action. She is permitted to have a heavy gun mounted aft of the bridge, so that when attacked she is able to run away, at the same time firing on a pursuing enemy. In recognition of the merchantman's limited fighting capability, her attacker is bound by the same law to show mercy to her crew. The minute a merchant ship mounts a heavy gun forward, however, she becomes a warship, and her enemy is entitled to treat her as such, offering no quarter.

Right from the start, the U-boats had shown their contempt for International Law, the unarmed British passenger ship *Athenia* being torpedoed and sunk without warning only a few hours after the outbreak of war on 3 September 1939. Incredible though it may seem, two years later, Britain was still attempting to fight the war at sea by the Queensberry Rules. Although up to 100 ships a month were being lost, most of them sunk without warning by the U-boats, the Admiralty steadfastly refused to mount a heavy gun on the foredeck of a merchant ship, on the grounds that this contravened International Law, and might render the ship liable to unprovoked attack. This was plainly a ludicrous attitude to adopt, and one which was soon to change. Meanwhile, the ships of SC42 laboured under a crippling disadvantage.

At the time, there was a great shortage of heavy weapons for merchant ships, the stock of 4-inch guns left over from the First World War being exhausted, and new guns coming off the production-lines were urgently needed elsewhere. Consequently, the majority of the ships in SC42 were armed only with .303 machine-guns, effective perhaps against low-flying aircraft, but of little use against U-boats. There were some exceptions in the ranks, but even these were paper tigers. The *Jedmoor*, for example, carried a 4-inch and a 12-pounder–she was, in fact, more heavily armed than the corvettes charged with her defence. However, in accordance with the law the Admiralty held sacrosanct, both the big guns were mounted on her poop, and were so restricted in their arc of fire as to be practically useless. If she, and others like her, had been equipped with a heavy gun forward, then the outcome of the battle might have been very different. In a few sentences, Captain William Bannan, of the *Tachee*, said it all: "Germany has already broken the international laws...why shouldn't we? The submarine on the surface that night was a sitter and a gun forward would have been the very thing...If there had been room for turning between the columns that night I would have taken the chance and turned through 180 degrees, steamed in the opposite direction and opened fire with the 4-inch."

As it was, the merchant seamen of SC42 seldom had chance to defend themselves, and it was most unfair that, when it was all over, the bravery of some of them was questioned. Lieutenant-Commander Jackson, in command of the corvette

HMCS *Kenogami*, wrote in his report: "There was evidence in many cases of crews abandoning their ships when there was no need to do so. The *Stonepool* was still well afloat when we closed her, but all the crew had left...In the case of the CAM ship *(Empire Hudson)*, a good many secret books were left on the bridge and no attempt had been made to destroy the aircraft or RDF equipment...The ship could certainly have been salvaged, as the torpedo had only flooded the engine room, the bulkheads either end not being damaged."

The stories told by the men sailing in the ships were somewhat different. Able Seaman H. Matthews, one of the few men to survive the sinking of the *Stonepool*, said: "...I then went towards the after welldeck, but before I reached there I was thrown into the water as the ship capsized. From the water I saw her turn over to starboard and capsize, sinking in about 2 to 3 minutes." As a simple able seaman, Matthews had no axe to grind, and, having been catapulted into the sea as the *Stonepool* went over, he was certainly in a better position than Lieutenant-Commander Jackson to judge how long his ship took to go down on that night.

As for the *Empire Hudson*, said by Lieutenant-Commander Jackson to be capable of being salvaged, her master, Captain John Cooke, reported: "The mainmast was buckled. The accommodation bulkhead over the engine room was blown out and the plates were opened out on the port side of the ship. There was also a small hole, about 2 feet square, on the starboard side. The funnel carried away as all rivets were blown out. The ship sank in the water to the maindeck and then held this position and we stepped from this deck into the lifeboats." It may be that, by some stretch of the imagination, Cooke might have been able to save his ship, but it must be remembered that, in the eight hours preceding the torpedoing of the *Empire Hudson*, six other ships had suffered a similar fate. Also, at the time, three of the four escorts were astern picking up survivors, the convoy being virtually undefended, with U-boats running unchallenged on the surface between the lines of merchant ships like slavering wolves in amongst a frightened flock of sheep. The general atmosphere was one of nervous apprehension, and it may be that this led to Captain Cooke omitting to destroy valuable equipment and secret books. As master of the ship, however, his first priority was to save the lives of his crew, and this he did, with the exception of four men killed when the torpedo struck. There is a great difference between being part of a fighting ship with the adrenalin running high, and sweating it out on a defenceless merchantman waiting to be killed. That takes a very special kind of bravery, which the naval men found difficult to comprehend.

With regard to the mysterious radio signals heard from time to time, which raised the possibility of there being a traitor in the convoy, this is one question that may forever go unanswered. The first signals, a series of long dashes, were heard on the morning of 5 September, when SC42 was hove-to and riding out the storm nearly 400 miles southwest of Cape Farewell. The most likely explanation is that the convoy was then being shadowed by a U-boat, which was sending out radio signals to guide others in. However, so far as is now known, the nearest U-boat was more than 600 miles away at the time. The subsequent transmissions, on the 8th, 9th, 10th and 12th, were all made with the U-boats in close attendance, but on all the occasions the transmitter used was positively identified as of the spark-gap type, which gives off a distinctive grating note. Only an old tramp—and there were plenty in the ranks of SC42—would carry such obsolete equipment. German U-boats invariably had the best of modern, high-powered radio gear.

Only one conclusion can be drawn, and that is that all the signals heard, whether made with malicious intent or not, must have emanated from one of the merchantmen in the convoy. It is highly unlikely that a British ship was responsible, but there were many others in SC42 who flew the flags of German-occupied countries—ships from Norway, Holland, Denmark, Poland and Greece, and even a few neutral Swedes. Who can say what compelling reason there may have been for someone in one of those ships to commit such an act of betrayal? Whoever he was, and wherever he was, his motive for attempting to contact the enemy must indeed have been pressing for him to engage in a week-long game of Russian roulette—for that is exactly what he did. Under the conditions prevailing, the U-boats could not pick and choose their targets, and were just as likely to condemn their collaborator to a watery grave as anyone.

EPILOGUE

If and it has never been proven, the resolution of some of the merchant ships' crews was in question, then this might not be surprising. The conditions they served under, and the treatment they received at the hands of those concerned with their welfare, was often appalling. James Corcoran, a 16-year-old steward in the *Berury*, had this to say 50 years later: "The thing that remains very bitter in my mind was the fact that the day we were torpedoed our leave started and our money stopped...when I arrived home, I had no money due to me." It is now almost impossible to accept that a British seaman, having had his ship summarily blown from under him in the dead of night was considered to be on leave from the moment he scrambled into a lifeboat, and that his leave expired while he was in a survivor's camp in Iceland. When he reached home, James Corcoran was penniless and out of work. This was in direct contravention of Section 158 of the Merchant Shipping Act of 1894, but, to their everlasting shame, it was an attitude adopted by many British shipowners.

The treatment of the survivors landed in Iceland again spoke volumes for the contempt in which the merchant seaman was held by those who failed to understand the dreadful suffering he had endured. Chief Officer van der Moolen, of the *Winterswijk*, wrote: "The treatment we received in Iceland was very bad. When we landed we were put in a car and were taken to a transit camp three miles from Reykjavik. We were there put in a military hut which contained no proper sleeping facilities, only benches without mattresses or pillow, and we were supplied with four blankets each. The food was extremely bad; it was served to us in nearby huts and most meals consisted of hash stew. The officers were in one hut and the men in another. We were looked after by two soldiers and if we were five minutes late for a meal they would not serve us and we had to go without. When we went to get a bath or a wash, the water was usually turned off in the midst of our wash and we would be left without water."

Captain J. K. Lindberg, of the *Sally Maersk*, confirmed van der Moolen's observations: "We were put in huts and were given straw palliasses...the food was not at all good. This camp was run by the Army and if we were five minutes late we did not get any food at all. There was a great shortage of clothing..." Captain Campbell, of the *Baron Pentland*, added: "The sanitary arrangements were not at all good, and we had to use a small washplace belonging to the troops; this washplace was meant for about 50 men and there were about 200-300 of us using it. The food was very bad indeed and we had to walk to the other end of the camp to get what there was of it...It was not so much the food of which I complained but the manner in which it was served, it was almost thrown at us. After a time the conditions of messing so appalled me that I went into town to the hotel for my food."

It was Captain Campbell who finally took it upon himself to speak for all the survivors, and went to the Naval Authorities in Reykjavik to complain. He was received civilly enough, but was told that, as the officer in charge was away for the week, nothing could be done. Campbell then went to the British Consul, who disdainfully informed the British captain that he considered conditions for the survivors were quite satisfactory, and brought the interview abruptly to a close.

The plain fact was that the merchantship survivors under the care of the British authorities in Iceland were treated more like enemy prisoners of war than men who had been to hell and back in the service of the British people; and it did not end there. On landing in the UK, survivors were again given short shrift. There were no welcoming crowds, no Champagne flowed. Men mentally and physically exhausted by the traumatic ordeal they had been through were given a rail travel warrant and told to find their own way home, often half-clothed and hungry for a decent meal. It was as though they were an embarrassment, a nuisance to be swept out of sight as soon as possible. Very few people in the country realised that without such men the ships would not get through, and without the ships Britain would starve, and the war would be lost.

How different was the welcome accorded to the men of the

Markgraf group when they returned home. They, too, although as short on active service experience as Hibbard's Canadians, had achieved a considerable victory. For the loss of only two boats, they had sunk a total of 18 Allied ships of 71,792 tons, destroying in the process more than 100,000 tons of cargo desperately needed by a Britain under siege.

Siegfried Rollmann's U-82 was first home. On the afternoon of 18 September, having spent a harrowing six days motoring on the surface with both diesels firing erratically, she was escorted into Lorient by a minesweeper of the Kriegsmarine. Just 39 days after setting off on her first operational patrol, she was returning with a score of 23,362 tons of Allied shipping. Rollmann and his men warranted a hero's welcome, and this they were given. A military band played them alongside a quay lined with cheering crowds, their hands were shaken by immaculately uniformed senior officers, and the exquisite, hand-picked secretaries of Admiral Dönitz's staff presented them with flowers and Champagne. There followed hot baths, gargantuan meals and, at long last, sleep free of the threat of exploding depth charges and the fear of slow death by suffocation.

The respite for U-82's crew proved to be much longer than anticipated. Her damage was severe, and it was early January 1942 before she returned to sea. On 6 February, Rollmann reported that he was in touch with a convoy of 20 ships some 500 miles northeast of the Azores. That was the last ever heard from U-82, and on 12 May she was posted missing, believed lost with all hands. Later it was learned she had been sunk by the sloop HMS *Rochester* and the corvette HMS *Tamarisk* while attempting to attack the Freetown-UK convoy OS18. She was the first of the *Markgraf* group to go. For the others the day of reckoning followed as night follows day.

Eberhard Greger's U-85, credited with the initial sighting of SC42, met her end off Cape Hatteras on the night of 4 April 1942. She was caught on the surface by the US destroyer *Roper* and sunk by gunfire. Her last minutes were attended by circumstances which did no credit at all to the US Navy. Greger and most of his men abandoned the boat before she went down, and were in the water when *Roper* approached and dropped a pattern of depth charges amongst them. There were no survivors. U-85 was the first U-boat to be sunk by the US Navy, and whether the unnecessary slaughter that followed was a deliberate action, or due to the confusion of the night, has never been established. However, to this day, German submariners still regard the deaths of those men as a war atrocity of the worst kind.

U-652 moved to the Mediterranean after damaging the *Tachee* and *Baron Pentland*. There she distinguished herself by sinking the British destroyers *Heythrop* and *Jaguar*, but on 2 June 1942, she was severely damaged by aircraft off the coast of North Africa. Her crew was rescued by another participant in the SC42 battle, U-81, which was operating nearby. Georg-Werner Fraatz was accorded the honour of sinking his own boat with a torpedo fired from the stern tube of U-81.

As for the others, U-98, responsible for sinking the *Jedmoor*, disappeared with all hands on 20 November 1942, while off the Atlantic coast of Morocco. U-432 was sunk in the North Atlantic after torpedoing the British destroyer *Harvester* on 11 March 1943. Of the U-boat's crew of 46, only 20 survived. U-202 was lost on 2 June that year while operating against a North Atlantic convoy, 18 men going down with her. Five days later, U-105 sank with all hands off Freetown. The last to go was Friedrich Guggenberger's U-81, executioner of the *Empire Springbuck* and all her crew. Before she went, she distinguished herself by sending the much-hunted British aircraft-carrier *Ark Royal* to the bottom. U-81's own end was ignominious, being sunk alongside by aircraft when sheltering in the Italian port of Pola on 9 January 1944.

Coincident with the arrival in Lorient of U-82, on the afternoon of 18 September, the Canadian corvette *Moosejaw* secured alongside Princes Pier, Greenock, in the Firth of Clyde. Armed guards waited on the quayside, and as soon as the gangway was in place the 29 German prisoners were taken ashore.

Unlike an earlier occasion, when on that dark night in the North Atlantic he had been first to leave the sinking U-501, Korvettenkapitän Hugo Förster was the last man to step ashore in Greenock. He stood at the top of *Moosejaw's* gangway, a fixed smile on his face, offering his hand to the surviving members

U-82 *returns from patrol.*
(Photo: Horst Bredow)

of his crew as they went ashore, but every man brushed past him, eyes averted. Hugo Förster was spurned by the very men whose respect he should have commanded.

Förster was sent to POW Camp no.1, at Grizedall Hall, a large country mansion overlooking Lake Windermere, which held 100 German naval and airforce officers. The senior German officer was the fabled U-boat ace Otto Kretschmer, who had been captured in the Atlantic six months earlier. Word had already reached the camp of Förster's alleged desertion of his crew under fire, and Kretschmer informed him that he would have to face the Council of Honour. This amounted to no more than a court-martial convened by Förster's fellow officers in the camp, at which he was to be charged with cowardice, the penalty for which was death by execution. Fortunately, the camp authorities got wind of the plan, and Förster was quickly transferred to another camp. So Hugo Förster survived again, only to die by his own hand later. The shame of the night of 10 September 1941 had never left him.

For all those defeated U-boat men who returned to a Germany in ruins at the end of the war, the homecoming was a bitter experience. They, who had been young gods charged with starving Britain into submission–and had so nearly succeeded–came back to their native land in 1945 with no status, no jobs, and often with no homes to go to. The real tragedy was that the cause for which they had endured so much was a lost one, and doomed from the start.

The German U-boat arm suffered grievously in the war, losing 739 U-boats and 28,728 men. The names of those who died are recorded on the magnificent U-boat Memorial at Möltenort, near Kiel, and their story is kept alive for future generations at the shrine-like U-boat Archives at Altenbruch, near Cuxhaven.

Otto Kretschmer said: "The battle at sea was fought with chivalry and without hatred." That may have been his impression, but it is unlikely that the merchant seamen who died in the attack on convoy SC42 would have agreed with him. Theirs was a cruel fate, a violent and undeserved death, often in the dead of night, going down into a cold, dark ocean that had no bottom but eternity; and who remembers *them* now?

BIBLIOGRAPHY

Beaver, Paul, *U-boats in the Atlantic*, Patrick Stephens, 1979.

Bucheim, Lothar-Günther, *U-boat War*, Collins, 1978.

Churchill, Winston S., *The Second World* War, Cassell, 1949.

Graves, Philip, *The Sixth Quarter*, Hutchinson.

Hoyt, Edwin P., *U-boats*, McGraw-Hill, 1987.

Lamb, James B., *The Corvette Navy*, Macmillan.

Lawrence, Hal, *A Bloody War. One Man's Memories of the Canadian Navy 1939-45*, Macmillan, 1979.

Lenton, H. T., *Warships of World War II*, Ian Allan, 1965.

Macintyre, Donald, *The Battle of the Atlantic*, Lutterworth Press, 1970.

Mason, David, *U-boat: the Secret Menace*, Macdonald, 1968.

Middlebrook, Martin, *Convoy*, William Morrow, 1976.

Poolman, Kenneth, *Periscope Depth*, William Kimber, 1981.

Robertson, Terence, *The Golden Horseshoe*, Evans Brothers, 1955.

Robertson, Terence, *Walker R. N.*, Evans Brothers, 1956.

Rohwer, Jürgen, *Axis Submarine Successes 1939-1945*, Patrick Stephens, 1983.

Terraine, John, *Business in Great Waters*, Leo Cooper, 1989.

GLOSSARY

ABAFT: Behind in relation to something on the ship.

ABEAM: At right angles to the fore and aft line of the ship.

ABLE SEAMAN: A first-class or certificated deck rating.

AFT: Towards the stern of the ship.

AHEAD: Before the ship

ALDIS: Daylight signalling lamp.

AMIDSHIPS: The middle part of the ship.

APPRENTICE: Deck officer-in-training in a merchant ship.

ARMED MERCHANT CRUSIER (AMC): Merchant ship commandeered and armed for war service.

ASDIC: Underwater sound-ranging apparatus for determining the range and bearing of a submerged submarine.

ASTERN: Behind the ship.

BdU: (Befehlshaber-der-U-boote) Flag officer U-boats.

BEAM: Width of the ship at her widest part.

BOATSWAIN: Senior deck rating in a merchant ship.

BOFORS: Quick-firing anti-aircraft gun (Swedish).

BOW-WAVE: Water thrown aside by the ship's bows when under way.

BRIGANTINE: Two-masted sailing vessel square-rigged on the foremast and fore-and-aft rigged on the mainmast.

BULKHEAD: A partition between two compartments.

BULWARK: Steel plating around the deck of a ship to prevent persons or cargo falling or being washed overboard.

CABLE: One-tenth of a sea mile, or about 600 feet.

CAPTAIN (D): Captain, Destroyers.

CASINGS: That part of the outer shell of a submarine forming the upper deck.

CIRCULATING PUMP: Pump circulating cooling water in the engine room.

C-in-C: Commander-in Chief.

COMMODORE (convoy): Officer charged with the organisation and progress of a convoy, usually a retired naval officer.

CORVETTE: Small convoy escort vessel, based on the design of a pre-war Antarctic whale-catcher.

CROSS-TRADES: Trade between countries other than the country of origin of the ship.

DEADWEIGHT:
Maximum weight of the cargo, fuel, fresh water, and stores that can legally be carried in a ship.

DEMS: (Defensively Equipped Merchant Ships) Commonly used to refer to a merchant ship's naval gunners.

DONKEYMAN: Senior engine-room rating in a merchant ship.

ENGINE-ROOM TELE-GRAPH: Apparatus used to relay orders from the bridge to the engine room.

FIREMAN: One who tends the fires of a ship's boilers.

FLAG HOIST: A number of flags spelling out a message.

FLYING ANGEL: Seamen's club run by the Missions to Seamen.

FORECASTLE (FO'C'SLE): Space below deck in the bows of a ship, used for crew accommodation or stores.

FORECASTLE HEAD: Deck above the forecastle.

FOREDECK: That part of the maindeck forward of the bridge.

FORWARD: Towards the bows of the ship.

GALLEY: Ship's kitchen.

GAS OIL: Highly inflammable light diesel oil.

GIG: Small, open boat used mainly for contact with the shore while in harbour.

GREASER: Engine-room rating employed in oiling and greasing machinery.

GREAT CIRCLE: The shortest distance between any two points on the Earth's surface.

GUNWALE: Point where the hull plating joins the maindeck.

HA/LA (gun): High angle/Low angle.

HEAVE-TO: To stop the ship at sea.

HELM: Steering apparatus of the ship.

HF/DP: High-frequency direction-finder.

HOTWELL: Engine-room tank in which hot water from the condenser is collected.

HX: Fast North Atlantic convoy. Minimum speed, 9 knots.

HYDROPHONE: Underwater listening device.

HYDROPLANE: Movable fin on the hull used to control the up-and-down movement of a submarine.

JOLLY BOAT: Small boat, similar to a gig.

KAPITÄNLEUTNANT:
German naval rank,
equivalent to Lieutenant
in the Royal Navy.

KNIGHT'S CROSS:
Coveted German naval
decoration.

KNOT: One nautical mile
per hour (a nautical
mile being 6,080 feet).

KORVETTENKAPITÄN:
German naval rank,
equivalent to
Lieutenant-Commander
in the Royal Navy.

MAINDECK: The principal
deck in a vessel which
has more than one deck.

MAINMAST: The second
mast from forward.

MARITIME REGIMENT:
British Army regiment
formed to man guns of
merchant ships.

MIDDLE WATCH: The
periods from midnight
to 0400 and noon to
1600.

MONKEY ISLAND:
Enclosed deck directly
above the wheelhouse.

NORTH CHANNEL: The
channel between Ireland
and Scotland.

NORTHERN PATROL:
Royal Navy patrol cov-
ering waters between
Scotland and Iceland,
principally to watch for
blockade runners.

NORTHERN LIGHTS
(**Aurora Borealis**):
Display of atmospheric
lights seen in high lati-
tudes.

NOVA SCOTIAN SLACK:
Inferior-quality coal
mined in Nova Scotia.

OBERLEUTNANT-ZUR-
SEE: Rank in German
Navy, having no equiva-
lent in the Royal Navy,
but between Sub-lieu-
tenant and Lieutenant.

PANIC BAG: Small canvas
bag containing personal
papers and a few luxu-
ries, kept handy in case
of abandoning ship.

PILOT CHAIR: High
wooden chair on the
bridge, allowing the
captain to rest while
still commanding a
good view of the hori-
zon.

PORT: Left-hand side of the
ship when facing for-
ward.

PUMP ROOM:
Compartment in an oil
tanker, containing cargo
pumps.

"Q" SHIP: Merchant ship
fitted with concealed
armament.

QUARTER: That part of
The ship which is
halfway between the
beam and the stern.

RDF: Radio direction-finder.

RN: Royal Navy.

ROD AND CHAIN:
Antiquated method of steering, using a system of rods and chains driven by a steam engine.

ROMP: To run ahead of station when in convoy.

R/T: Radio telephone.

SC: Slow North Atlantic convoy. Maximum speed 9 knots.

SCOTCH BOILER: Boiler heated by smoke passing through internal tubes.

SCUPPER: Drain at ship's side to carry away excess water.

SEA ANCHOR: Cone-shaped canvas drogue used to keep the boat's head up into wind and sea in heavy weather.

SIGHTS: Celestial observations taken by sextant to calculate a ship's position.

SKIFF: Small open boat, similar to a gig and a jolly boat.

SLOOP: Small anti-submarine warship of about 1,000 tons.

STARBOARD: Right-hand side of the ship when facing forward.

STARSHELL: Shell containing a pyrotechnic flare suspended from a small parachute, fired to illuminate the attack area.

STOKEHOLD: Compartment containing boiler furnaces.

STRAGGLE: To fall behind the convoy.

SWELL: Vertical movement of the sea caused by a distant wind or storm.

TAFFRAIL: Upper part of the ship's rail.

TELEMOTOR: Hydraulic system which transmits movements of the steering wheel to the steering engine over the rudder.

TRAMP: Merchant ship not employed in any regular trade.

TUBE RUNNER: Torpedo running out of control.

WATCHOFFICER: Officer in charge of the watch in a U-boat.

WHEELHOUSE:
Deckhouse on the bridge housing the steering wheel, compass, and engine-room telegraph.

WHITE HORSES: Small waves breaking into white foam.

WINDLASS: Steam winch used to hoist the ship's anchors.

WING (bridge): Deck outside the wheelhouse on each side of the bridge.

WOLF-PACK:
Concentration of U-boats acting together against a convoy.

W/T: Wireless Telegraphy.

BEAUFORT WIND SCALE

Force	Name	Speed (Knots)	Description
0	Calm	<1	Sea like a mirror.
1	Light air	1-3	Ripples with the appearance of scales are formed but with out foam crests.
2	Light breeze	4-6	Small wavelets, still short but more pronounced; crests have a glassy appearance and do not break.
3	Gentle breeze	7-10	Large wavelets, crests begin to break; foam of glassy appearance; perhaps scattered white horses.
4	Moderate breeze	11-16	Small waves, becoming longer; fairly frequent white horses.
5	Fresh breeze	17-2	Moderate waves, taking a more pronounced long form; many white horses are formed (chance of some spray).
6	Strong breeze	22-27	Large waves begin to form; the white foam crests are more extensive everywhere (probably some spray).
7	Near gale	28-33	Sea heaps up and white foam from breaking waves begin to be blown instreaks along the direction of the wind.

8	Gale	34-40	Moderately high waves of greater length; edges of crests begin to break into spindrift; foam is blown in well-marked streaks along the direction of the wind.
9	Strong gale	41-47	High waves; dense streaks of foam along the direction of the wind; crests of waves begin to topple, tumble and roll over; spray may affect visibility.
10	Storm	48-55	Very high waves with long over hanging crests; the resulting foam, in great patches, is blown in dense white streaks along the direction of the wind; on the whole, the surface of the sea takes a white appearance; the tumbling of the sea becomes heavy and shock-like; visibility affected.
11	Violent storm	56-63	Exceptionally high waves (small and medium-sized ships might he for a time lost to view behind the waves); the sea is completely covered with long white patches of foam lying along the direction of the wind; everywhere the edges of the wave crests are blown into froth; visibility affected.
12	Hurricane	64 plus	The air is filled with foam and spray; sea completely white with driving spray; visibility very seriously affected.

INDEX

INDEX

INDEX

INDEX

For sales, editorial information, subsidiary rights information
or a catalog, please write or phone or e-mail
Brick Tower Press
1230 Park Avenue
New York, NY 10128, US
Sales: 1-800-68-BRICK
Tel: 212-427-7139 Fax: 212-860-8852
www.BrickTowerPress.com
email: bricktower@aol.com.

For sales in the UK and Europe please contact our distributor,
Gazelle
Falcon House, Queens Square
Lancaster, LA1 1RN, UK
Tel: (01524) 68765 Fax: (01524) 63232
email: gazelle4go@aol.com.

For Australian and New Zealand sales please contact
INT Press Distribution Pyt. Ltd.
386 Mt. Alexander Road
Ascot Vale, VIC 3032, Australia
Tel: 61-3-9326 2416 Fax: 61-3-9326 2413
email: sales@intpress.com.au.